# The Civil Rights Lobby

SHAMIRA GELBMAN

# The Civil Rights Lobby

*The Leadership Conference on Civil Rights and the Second Reconstruction*

TEMPLE UNIVERSITY PRESS
*Philadelphia • Rome • Tokyo*

TEMPLE UNIVERSITY PRESS
Philadelphia, Pennsylvania 19122
*tupress.temple.edu*

Copyright © 2021 by Temple University—Of The Commonwealth System of Higher Education
All rights reserved
Published 2021

Library of Congress Cataloging-in-Publication Data

Names: Gelbman, Shamira Michal, author.
Title: The civil rights lobby : the Leadership Conference on Civil Rights and the second reconstruction / Shamira Gelbman.
Description: Philadelphia : Temple University Press, 2021. | Includes bibliographical references and index. | Summary: "Explores the early years of the Leadership Conference on Civil Rights, the interest group coalition that has coordinated the efforts of more than fifty organizations to secure civil rights legislation since the 1950s. Explains the LCCR's organizational dynamics and the role its lobbyists played in the Second Reconstruction"— Provided by publisher.
Identifiers: LCCN 2021003986 (print) | LCCN 2021003987 (ebook) | ISBN 9781439920459 (cloth) | ISBN 9781439920466 (paperback) | ISBN 9781439920473 (pdf)
Subjects: LCSH: Leadership Conference on Civil Rights—History. | Public interest lobbying—United States—History—20th century. | Public interest groups—United States—History—20th century. | Civil rights—United States—History—20th century. | Civil rights movements—United States—History—20th century. | Coalitions—United States—History—20th century. | United States—Race relations—Political aspects.
Classification: LCC JK1118 .G46 2021 (print) | LCC JK1118 (ebook) | DDC 323.0973—dc23
LC record available at https://lccn.loc.gov/2021003986
LC ebook record available at https://lccn.loc.gov/2021003987

*In memory of my grandmother,*

*Shirley Gelbman (1923–2019),*

*and the unsung women whose clerical labor in*

*mid-twentieth-century lobbying and congressional offices*

*made the research for this book possible.*

# Contents

| | |
|---|---|
| Acknowledgments | ix |
| Introduction | 1 |
| 1 Trying to Mesh All of These Groups into Some Sort of a Force | 8 |
| 2 Nothing like the Present Ferment Has Been Seen for Seventy-Five Years | 21 |
| 3 We Have No Formal Structure | 41 |
| 4 The Unity among These Groups Is Truly Tremendous | 71 |
| 5 The Leadership Conference Plans to Continue | 102 |
| Conclusion: To Speak for Millions | 131 |
| Appendix: Methodological Note, Interviews, and Archival Collections | 141 |
| Notes | 145 |
| References | 185 |
| Index | 195 |

# Acknowledgments

A book about the early history of the Leadership Conference on Civil Rights (LCCR or Leadership Conference) has been a very long time coming. At least two attempts were initiated decades prior to my own protracted efforts to write *The Civil Rights Lobby*, but neither came to fruition.[1] Perhaps the third time is a charm, but I could not have pulled it off without an army of support.

I am fortunate to work at Wabash College, where I have been astonished time and again by the sheer volume of faculty, administrators, staff, students, and alumni who have filled presentation rooms, posed poignant questions, and reached out with kind words of encouragement throughout my work on this project. While so many in the Wabash community have shown interest and support, I am especially indebted to my writing group colleagues and friends, whose unyielding camaraderie helped me bring it to the finish line: Jeff Drury, Sara Drury, Colin McKinney, Heidi Walsh, and Laura Wysocki.

Wabash has also provided financial support for this project, including Byron K. Trippet funding to conduct archival research; a sabbatical leave and McLain-McTurnan-Arnold Research Scholar Award that enabled me to take a year off from service and teaching to write the manuscript; and generous funding for conference travel to present draft chapters. Additional funding for archival research came from a Visiting Scholars Program grant from the Carl Albert Congressional Research and Studies Center and a Small Research Grant from the American Political Science Association.

Many colleagues beyond Wabash have encouraged my work and offered incisive suggestions for its improvement. I am especially grateful to David Bateman, Connor Ewing, Kim Johnson, Tim Lindberg, and Greg Wawro, whose careful reading of draft chapters as conference panel discussants greatly enhanced the final product. Constructive feedback from two anonymous reviewers for Temple University Press likewise pushed me to clarify the book's theoretical and historical contributions. Several other political scientists merit special mention: Kerry Haynie has long been a reliable source of advice and encouragement. I am thankful for this support and his invitation to spend part of my sabbatical as a visiting scholar at the Center for the Study of Race, Ethnicity, and Gender in the Social Sciences. I have counted Abhishek Chatterjee as a good friend and sounding board for many years. I thank him for this and for giving me a place to stay in Missoula to kickstart my writing. Last but not least, I could not have brought this project to fruition without Julia Azari's friendship and accountability check-ins.

I am grateful to Aaron Javsicas for his editorial guidance and encouragement, and to everyone at Temple University Press who helped me through the publication process.

When a commissioned history of the Leadership Conference was contemplated in 1973, it was understood that interviewing people who had been part of the action would be essential for telling the early story of the LCCR.[2] While the passage of time has ruled out interviews with most of the participants in the developments recounted in this book, I was fortunate to have the opportunity to speak to two of the few remaining individuals who participated in the LCCR's lobbying campaign for the Civil Rights Act of 1964. I'm grateful to Ora Pescovitz and Lisa Haywood for connecting me to them and, especially, to Rabbi Richard Hirsch and Jane O'Grady for taking the time to share their recollections and dredging up memories from more than a half-century ago to help me understand the LCCR's mid-1960s operations. I would also like to thank the archivists and staff at the Library of Congress, Center for Jewish History, Carl Albert Congressional Research and Studies Center, Dirksen Congressional Center, Walter P. Reuther Library, J. Willard Marriott Library, and the George Meany Memorial AFL-CIO Archives. Finally, I am grateful to Allyn Brooks-LaSure, who invited me to meet with current Leadership Conference staff and tour its office in Washington, DC. Seeing what the Leadership Conference has become some seventy years after its creation was a humbling experience that drove home the importance of doing justice to its historical development.

*The Civil Rights Lobby* features many men and a few women who led and represented their home organizations and the LCCR in civil rights policymaking arenas during the Second Reconstruction. Supporting their efforts behind the scenes, hundreds of unnamed women took minutes and dictation, prepared correspondence, coordinated schedules, fielded calls, and otherwise kept organizational offices running. This work was easy to overlook as I waded through reams of expertly typed and formatted communiqués, but sometimes it became painfully apparent—whether in scrawled notes by organizational officials apologizing for the inscrutable handwriting or the error-laden typescript they produced on their own after "the girls" had gone home for the day, or in the occasional memorandum describing the harassment receptionists suffered at the hands of a self-important caller. While the identities of most of these women are lost to history, their unseen labor was essential to the developments described in this book and made my own efforts to reconstruct them that much easier. I dedicate the book to them and to the memory of my grandmother, Shirley Gelbman.

# The Civil Rights Lobby

# Introduction

About a month before Arnold Aronson's death in February 1998, he was awarded the Presidential Medal of Freedom. At a ceremony honoring fifteen individuals for their civil rights contributions, President Bill Clinton declared that Aronson was "a glowing symbol" of the coalitions that had united diverse constituencies in support of civil rights reform since World War II. "He . . . cofounded the Leadership Conference on Civil Rights," Clinton continued, "helping hundreds of disparate groups keep their eyes on the prize and speak with one booming voice."[1]

This citation alludes to the frequently unsung feature of the mid-twentieth-century civil rights movement that is the subject of this book—namely, the expansive lobbying coalition of civil rights, labor, religious, civic, fraternal, and professional groups that took shape under the aegis of the Leadership Conference during the early 1950s. In addition to recounting the story of the LCCR's founding, *The Civil Rights Lobby* explores Aronson's and other coalition leaders' efforts to coordinate its members' professional and grassroots lobbying resources in support of federal civil rights legislation and sheds light on the LCCR's contributions to the signature civil rights policy achievements of the 1950s and 1960s.

While this book is not the first to recognize that intergroup alliances had a hand in the enactment and implementation of civil rights policy during the postwar era, its focus on the LCCR's organizational development and legislative activities offers two distinctive contributions. The first is its emphasis on lobbying as an underrecognized and undervalued activity that mid-twentieth-century civil rights organizations undertook to advance their goals. This neglect is perhaps unsurprising. In contrast to the high-risk revolutionary protest campaigns commonly associated with the civil rights movement, lobbying is a fairly safe and conventional approach to exerting pressure on the policy-making process. It is also a behind-the-scenes activity that does not typically make for eye-catching headlines or dramatic video footage. And it is unpalatable. Often associated with corruption, ill-begotten political influence, and moneyed special interests at odds with the public good, lobbying and lobbyists are widely regarded as a blight on U.S. democracy—not a vehicle for its improvement. As Matt Grossmann's study of the public interest advocacy sector highlights, however, lobbying is carried out on behalf of a wide array of constituencies, including many "not-so-special" groups seeking basic rights and interest representation; in his words, "organizations . . . acting on behalf of such broad social movements as environmentalism and feminism have taken up permanent residence in downtown Washington," where they seek to "exercis[e] countervailing power against established interests."[2] As *The Civil Rights Lobby* shows, the mid-twentieth-century civil rights movement was no exception. The same organizations that orchestrated the civil rights movement's signature protest campaigns maintained an active lobbying presence in Washington, where they collaborated with numerous others to square off against entrenched segregationist opposition in the halls of Congress. The LCCR became the principal vehicle for this cooperation by the mid-1950s, and its efforts to bring the concerns of civil rights advocates to bear on the legislative process helped shape the policy achievements of the ensuing decade.

The second contribution—suggested by President Clinton's insinuation that the groups composing the Leadership Conference needed help to speak with one voice—is this book's focus on the mechanisms through which civil rights and allied organizations coordinated their lobbying efforts. This is not to suggest that other studies, whether of cooperation among pro–civil rights organizations specifically or of interest group coalitions generally, ignore coordination altogether. Rather, they tend to conceptualize it as a cost coalition partners assume upon entering into alliances and, in turn, to emphasize individual groups' decisions to join coalitions and the actions they take unilaterally in support of each other's goals. In contrast, *The Civil Rights Lobby* envisions coordination as a process coalition leaders enact iteratively to identify common ground among members, develop coalition positions on substantive and strategic questions, and exhort organizations to mobilize professional and grassroots lobbying resources accordingly. The emphasis, therefore, is on how coalitions operate once they are formed and on their facilitation of concerted action by member groups. Moreover, it contends that coordination is consequential. In its absence, or if managed poorly, organizations on the same side of an issue can work at cross-purposes or undermine the impression that they are in fact united in support of the same policy goals. Done well, coordination can indeed make groups "speak with one booming voice," amplifying their efforts to broadcast widespread support for reform and recasting policy makers' sense of the politically possible.

## Bringing the Lobbyists Back In

Southern politics and American political development scholars have long designated the era during which the Leadership Conference was founded and pursued its first legislative victories as the Second Reconstruction. Just as the original Reconstruction era had—however briefly—upended the South's traditional racial order in the wake of the Civil War, the mid-twentieth century witnessed a tidal wave of protest and reform against the web of disenfranchisement, segregation, and racial violence that had taken root in the First Reconstruction's aftermath.[3] Both reconstructions featured significant legislative accomplishments. In addition to three transformative constitutional amendments, the postbellum Congress enacted numerous laws to secure civil rights for newly freed slaves.[4] The federal civil rights gains of the Second Reconstruction were exclusively of judicial and executive provenance at first, as segregationist forces within the U.S. Congress doggedly obstructed successive efforts to pass civil rights legislation through the mid-1950s. But it, too, eventually produced several signature laws, including the Civil Rights Acts of 1957, 1960, and 1964; the Voting Rights Act of 1965; and the Fair Housing Act of 1968.

In accounting for these legislative developments, scholars have focused primarily on institutional actors—executive branch officials and members of Congress—who were instrumental in shaping and securing civil rights laws. To the extent that other forces—for example, international pressure or protest activity—come into play, they are depicted as exogenous stimuli to a legislative process that generates outcomes endogenously based on partisan and interbranch wheeling and dealing, presidential and legislative personalities, and the creative use of congressional procedure. Lobbyists do appear in these accounts with some frequency; sometimes they are referenced by individual name or organization, though often more vaguely as "civil rights advocates" or "civil rights groups." But their role is more that of a plot device than a character. They show up as convenient for the institutional narrative with little introduction or fanfare, their activities consist largely of sound-bite reactions to policy developments, and there is practically no effort to theorize their participation in the policy-making process.

At first blush, this is not surprising. Governmental institutions are where policy decisions are made, after all, and their incumbents hold the authority to determine which bills are introduced, how they progress through the legislative process, whether they are enacted into law, and how they are implemented and enforced. As Megan Ming Francis reminds us, however, "institutions do not act in a vacuum; meaningful political development is also a product of . . . the contestation that happens between those on the sidelines and those in power."[5] Her own work illustrates this dynamic in the early development of the modern civil rights state, when the NAACP launched a multifaceted antilynching campaign to reframe public awareness of the issue, encourage executive and legislative action, and sponsor litigation that yielded a favorable ruling by the United States Supreme Court in *Moore v. Dempsey*. This lesser-known episode in civil rights movement history, Francis maintains, "shap[ed] the path of development" that has become well-trod ground for institutionalist studies of the civil rights state.[6]

Other scholars have revealed similar dynamics in more recent contexts. For example, Vanessa Burrows and Barbara Burney show how medical civil rights activists were instrumental in leveraging the new Medicare program to facilitate hospital desegregation after 1965. "Federal civil rights policy was not created and implemented in an exclusively unidirectional, top-down manner," they conclude; rather, "the medical civil rights movement created a matrix of social resources, human capital, and will for reform that energized the Johnson administration's hospital inspection campaign."[7] And, in a sweeping study of housing market regulation, Chloe Thurston documents how various "boundary groups"—essentially, organizations that identify and challenge facially neutral regulations that contribute to their constituents' marginalization—have managed to reframe and ameliorate African Americans' and women's exclusion from homeownership. These groups, Thurston writes, have "helped to expand the scope of conflict around issues that otherwise might be regarded as individual, idiosyncratic, or private," urging their redefinition as systematic public problems and advocating for the revision of offending regulations to permit greater inclusion.[8]

*The Civil Rights Lobby* joins these authors in contemplating how non-institutional actors have shaped the trajectory of the civil rights state.[9] The Second Reconstruction–era Leadership Conference, it argues, was an important vehicle for the sort of contestation Francis highlights. Though not a grassroots membership organization per se, it aggregated and channeled the lobbying resources of numerous social movement organizations and advocacy groups to showcase broad support for civil rights legislation and bring an array of lobbying resources to bear on the legislative trajectory of promising reform proposals. Its work was multifaceted. It had a core group of experienced legislative affairs specialists who were constantly engaged in direct lobbying—that is, in making personal contact with institutional actors, both to coordinate with those who were most supportive of civil rights and to persuade those who were not to support LCCR positions. An array of outside lobbying activities—such as publication of educational materials, media outreach, letter-writing campaigns, mass gathering events that brought well-briefed delegations of citizens from around the country to meet with their representatives—complemented these professional efforts. All this work was well integrated with the legislative process and, while not always successful, it pushed institutional actors to reconsider their initial perceptions of which civil rights provisions their congressional colleagues and the mass public would tolerate and to tailor their legislative behavior accordingly.

In recounting these efforts to influence the course of civil rights policy development during the 1950s and 1960s, this book examines how the LCCR's own organizational features shaped its lobbying capacity. Above all—and unlike the unitary organizations Francis, Burrows and Burney, and Thurston highlight—the Leadership Conference was (and still is) a coalition of autonomous organizations. While all member groups were committed to legislative civil rights reform in principle, they differed in their specific policy preferences and strategic orientations. As a result, the LCCR's objectives were circumscribed by a consensus-oriented approach to determining coalition priorities. Member organizations remained free to lobby on their own for civil rights bills not in the LCCR's purview or to advocate for strengthening provisions to LCCR-supported legislation beyond those for which consensus was obtained. But, to the extent that the civil rights lobby's influence hinged on its ability to present a united front of diverse constituencies in support of controversial reforms, appreciating how the LCCR's organizational parameters helped set the coalition's lobbying agenda is crucial to understanding its role in shaping civil rights policy outcomes.

## Plan of the Book

As the foregoing suggests, making sense of the LCCR's role in the Second Reconstruction necessitates understanding how it functioned as an interest group coalition—that is, as an alliance of civil rights, labor, religious, professional, fraternal, and civic organizations that joined forces in pursuit of their shared interest in securing civil rights legislation. The book begins, therefore, by situating its study of the LCCR's early development in a burgeoning political science research literature on interest group coalitions. As Chapter 1 shows, scholars have identified diversity as a boon to coalitions' influence within the policy-making process, as it enables lobbyists to deploy an array of resources to signal broad-based support for reforms that seem risky to legislators' electoral prospects. Far less attention has been given to the tradeoffs diversity entails, however—a task the chapter tackles by considering how diversity can complicate coalition leaders' coordination efforts and sketching a framework for understanding how coalitions' organizational practices can shape their capacity to bring their members' aggregated resources to bear on the policy process.

The next four chapters trace the LCCR's organizational development from its founding in the early 1950s through the adoption of its first by-laws in January 1967. Chapter 2 locates the LCCR's origins in a wave of collaboration among pro–civil rights interest groups during the mid- to late 1940s. While World War II has generally been heralded as a bellwether for the Second Reconstruction, one particular wartime measure—President Franklin D. Roosevelt's Executive Order 8802, which established a temporary Fair Employment Practices Committee—set the stage for coordinated lobbying initiatives by a number of interest groups that would eventually become the LCCR's founding members. The chapter describes these developments and their culmination in the founding of the Leadership Conference, first as an election-year campaign to shape the civil rights planks of the Democratic and Republican Party platforms and ultimately as a permanent lobbying coalition.

Chapters 3 and 4 contrast LCCR operations during its first decade and in the year leading up to passage of the Civil Rights Act of 1964. During the 1950s and early 1960s, Chapter 3 shows, the Leadership Conference functioned as what one participant called "a permanent ad hoc body."[10] While there were some formal organizational trappings, it was a largely unstructured enterprise with limited means for engaging member organizations in coalition activity on a routine or sustained basis. This hampered the LCCR's capacity to harness the resources of its member groups and goad them to "speak with one booming voice" when legislative opportunities arose in the post-*Brown v. Board of Education* milieu. New organizational practices adopted during the summer of 1963 transformed this capacity, however. As Chapter 4 recounts, these changes enabled the Leadership Conference to coordinate professional and grassroots lobbying for the omnibus bill that would become the Civil Rights Act of 1964 with unprecedented efficacy and endurance.

Chapter 5 explores how the LCCR fared in the two years after passage of the Civil Rights Act of 1964. This momentous legislative accomplishment marked a turning point for the Leadership Conference, which emerged from the long campaign for its passage with an enhanced reputation and organizational capacity to coordinate civil rights lobbying but strained to find its footing in a changing policy-making environment. It was also a critical juncture for the civil rights movement more broadly, as activists of various stripes confronted limitations of the mid-1960s legislative achievements, struggled to pursue further gains in the face of backlash and diminishing support, and came increasingly into conflict over the movement's means and ends. The chapter describes how, in light of these developments, an increasingly expansive civil rights lobbying agenda took shape in 1965 and 1966 and, simultaneously, how internal and external pressures drove LCCR leaders to finally formalize the coalition's structure and operational procedures in January 1967.

The book's Conclusion reprises key lessons from the LCCR's organizational development and participation in civil rights policy making through the mid-1960s. To that end, the final chapter suggests new directions for research on interest group coalitions and explores how the LCCR's experience sheds light on the politics of the Second Reconstruction.

# 1

# Trying to Mesh All of These Groups into Some Sort of a Force

Some fifty-five years after she first encountered the Leadership Conference as a fresh-faced lobbyist for the Amalgamated Clothing Workers, Jane O'Grady reflected on the daunting task facing the coalition during its yearlong campaign to secure passage of the Civil Rights Act of 1964. She recalled that the Leadership Conference

> had to try to mesh all of these groups into some sort of a force . . . to give some energy to the bill that was in the Congress. Many of these groups were not in an organizational position to have much of a presence in Washington. . . . Many of these groups were just one person sitting in an office who would come to the Leadership Conference meetings in an effort to show solidarity and to do some lobbying if they could, so I must say as I look back on it, the Leadership Conference leadership had one tough time trying to mesh all of this together.[1]

The challenge O'Grady identified—the attempt "to mesh all of these groups into some sort of a force"—is at the heart of this book's inquiry into the LCCR's role in the Second Reconstruction. As others have recounted (and as Chapter 2 describes in some detail), an array of civil rights, labor, religious, civic, professional, and fraternal organizations had grown active in advocating for federal civil rights legislation by the end of World War II. But their general agreement that Congress should enact civil rights reform was not sufficient to ensure that they would collaborate in pursuit of this shared goal—or, for that matter, that they would even unite around a common vision of what federal civil rights legislation should entail. Nor was their coalescence under the aegis of the Leadership Conference by the mid-1950s enough on its own to facilitate such coordination. Rather, it took deliberate and persistent initiative by entrepreneurial interest group officials to facilitate the formation of civil rights lobbying coalitions (including the LCCR) and coordinate professional and grassroots lobbying activity by their member organizations on an ongoing basis.

While subsequent chapters trace these processes as they played out in the LCCR's organizational development through the mid-1960s, the current chapter proposes that the challenge O'Grady identified was not an idiosyncratic feature of the Second Reconstruction–era Leadership Conference but is an essential undertaking for interest group coalitions more generally. Building on the insights of prior research on interest groups' role in policy making, it problematizes interest group coalitions' capacity for coordination and contends that the very qualities that allow them to signal broad-based support for their policy positions simultaneously complicate their efforts to advance such claims effectively. The chapter further proposes that interest group coalitions' coordination capacity derives from their organizational parameters. Coalitional operating procedures can facilitate or hinder interest group coalition leaders' efforts to mobilize member groups for concerted lobbying activity, in turn shaping their ability to actualize their resource potential to influence the policy process.

## Interest Group Coalitions in U.S. Politics and Political Science

The LCCR was not quite a decade old when Donald R. Matthews, a political scientist and observer of the postwar Senate, posited that "the full potential of a lobbying coalition is seldom if ever achieved." While the pooled resources of numerous groups with common interests should in principle enhance their ability to achieve shared legislative goals, he sensed that, in practice, "a broad-based coalition is likely to be shot through with conflicts of interest and opinion." Conversely, "a homogeneous coalition of groups may suffer from fewer internal strains but will be less effective." Either way, he concluded, "the in-fighting between lobbyists is likely to be substantial."[2] Interest group coalitions have nevertheless become ubiquitous in contemporary politics. Within a decade of Matthews's assertion, fellow political scientist Donald R. Hall observed that "cooperative and intergroup lobbying . . . are becoming increasingly important as influences on group activity and on governmental decision making."[3] Fully two-thirds of the 175 organizations Kay Schlozman and John Tierney surveyed during the early 1980s reported an increase in coalition activity in the preceding decade.[4] Recent interviews and surveys of interest group officials have similarly found that participating in coalitions is an activity organizations commonly undertake in pursuit of their policy goals.[5] Michael Heaney thus writes that collaborative lobbying has become "a standard part of interest groups' strategic repertoires" in the United States and, in a new study of lobbying coalitions in Europe, Marcel Hanegraaff and Andrea Pritoni claim that coalitions are "perhaps the most widespread tactic interest groups use to channel constituent demands to the political arena."[6]

In addition to highlighting their prevalence, political scientists have identified interest group coalitions as a potential means for leveling the playing field in a pluralist system that is notoriously imbalanced.[7] Though she does acknowledge several limitations, Dara Strolovitch maintains that "coalitions hold a great deal of potential as a form of advocacy for intersectionally disadvantaged subgroups." To the extent that doubly marginalized constituencies tend to fall through the cracks of interest representation, "coalitions . . . can encourage advocacy . . . by highlighting connections among issues and constituencies; by promoting feelings of trust, solidarity, and intersectionally linked fate; and by advancing more comprehensive solutions to the complex issues that face marginalized groups."[8] Robin Phinney similarly contends that various parameters of the social policy advocacy sector in the United States encourage those advocating on behalf of low-income constituents to adopt coalition lobbying strategies. Appreciating these interest group coalitions' role in representing low-income interests and the conditions under which they are most influential, she argues, is important for understanding why disadvantaged groups sometimes secure important policy gains in a political system that is, by and large, stacked against them.[9] And, in a recent analysis of a large survey of lobbyists in five European countries, Wiebke Marie Junk demonstrates that active cooperation among less advantaged groups can yield policy results akin to those of an individual organization's resource expenditure. "Coalitions can *effectively* function as 'a weapon of the weak,'" she concludes, "allowing less advantaged interests to exert more influence on policy" than their relatively meager resource endowments would normally permit.[10]

Still, for all their ubiquity and potential significance for democratic interest representation, interest group coalitions' role in the policy-making process is not well understood. A burgeoning political science literature sheds a good deal of light on interest groups' motivations to form and join coalitions,[11] their behavior within the coalitions they join,[12] and the impact of coalition membership on individual groups' policy influence.[13] A growing number of studies have begun to investigate interest group coalitions' impact on policy outcomes.[14] But, as recent reviews suggest, the field is still far from having definitive answers as to whether interest group coalitions do in fact enhance groups' influence on policy outcomes and, to the extent that they do, the conditions that contribute to or detract from their impact.[15] While this chapter does not purport to answer these questions conclusively, it advances the conversation by synthesizing insights from prior research and drawing on the LCCR's experience to revisit an emerging consensus around the implications of diversity for coalitions' influence within the policy process.

## *Diverse Interest Group Coalitions as Robust Policy Signals*

Most efforts to theorize interest group coalitions' policy influence build on prior studies that identify signaling—essentially, indicating to public officials where key constituencies stand on important policy questions—as a key mechanism through which interest groups influence legislative outcomes.[16] Policy makers value this input from interest groups because it mitigates uncertainty about the substantive and electoral consequences of policy change. For members of Congress in particular, interest group signals can alleviate concerns about new policy proposals while easing demands on resource-strapped legislative offices.[17] Viewed from this standpoint, interest group coalitions are signal boosters that enable interest groups to convey pertinent information to policy makers more forcefully than is possible when acting on their own. In principle, such amplification might accrue for interest group coalitions across the board; as David Nelson and Susan Yackee write, "government decision makers are influenced by coalition lobbying because it sends a signal regarding the *overall* strength of support or opposition for a policy proposal."[18] But their own and others' empirical findings suggest that the mere fact of coalition and even coalition size alone tell at most part of the story.[19]

An emerging consensus identifies diversity—that is, the extent to which a coalition's member organizations represent different constituencies or bring different skill sets, expertise, and political connections to the table—as a key determinant of interest group coalitions' effectiveness.[20] Unified signaling by groups known to represent constituencies that do not always see eye to eye assures policy makers that the interest group coalition's preferred policy outcome enjoys broad support. A diverse interest group coalition's signal is thus not merely louder than that of an individual organization or even a very large alliance of similarly situated groups.[21] It is, rather, a qualitatively different signal that provides uncertainty-mitigating information that may encourage hesitant legislators to act in accordance with interest group coalition interests. Clear evidence of heterogeneous support for a particular policy change can ease concerns about its electoral ramifications. It can also facilitate legislators' efforts to gauge the substantive impacts of the policy in question. And, finally, it can assure supportive legislators that their sponsorship or other work on behalf of the interest group coalition's position early in the legislative process will not be for naught—that, as Phinney writes, the "issue is likely to progress through Congress with minimal disruptions."[22]

In addition to signposting the breadth of support for coalition positions, diversity enhances the possibility of assembling a broad array of resources that might be deployed in service of conveying a strong signal to policy makers. As Phinney explains, "diversity within coalitions matters because it gives a set of organizations access to different types of information and enables varied tactics for communicating information. This informational and tactical diversity in turn allows the coalition to reach the large number of legislators who share authority in a given policy area."[23] Frank Baumgartner and his coauthors similarly note that "the resources of an individual organization are much less important than the aggregate resources on their side of the issue."[24] Their expansive study of lobbying on ninety-eight policy issues finds that "one group's resources are only weakly correlated to the resources of the other groups sharing the same policy side." Consequently, they maintain, "aggregation of advocates into policy sides helps provide a greater range of resources for the policy fight. Teams are stronger than individuals because of the diverse resources most teams bring to the table."[25]

## *The Downside of Diversity*

I have been careful thus far to couch interest group coalitions' signaling capabilities in terms of possibility and potential. In doing so, I heed Darrin Halpin's caveat that the availability of resources does not guarantee effective resource mobilization; as he writes, "resources alone are not enough; they have to be purposefully utilized by groups to generate specific capacities. . . . Resource levels alone do not tell us about the capabilities groups possess; groups must decide how to put these to use and develop what they see as important abilities."[26] To bridge the leap from measuring organizational resource endowments to gauging the impact of their deployment in policy-making contexts, Halpin suggests scholars consider how interest groups' policy-oriented activities reflect their policy capacity—essentially, their readiness to engage in specific types of policy work, a trait that is in turn a function of their organizational design. "Groups are surely not all *equally capable*," Halpin writes; rather, "the organizational form a group manifests at one point of time shapes the range of capacities a group might reasonably generate and thus possess."[27]

In problematizing interest groups' capacity to act on their resource potential, Halpin exhorts researchers to be more attentive to organizational form when studying the policy work of individual groups acting as standalone units within the political arena. But it stands to reason that the task of transforming resource potential into effective policy work is even more critical for interest group coalitions, whose resources are diffuse and subject to disparate mobilization by the leadership and staff of each member organization. Similarly, the coherence of a coalition signal cannot be taken for granted. Nelson and Yackee find that interest group coalitions' influence depends on the extent to which the signals they convey to policy makers represent a consensus position among coalition members,[28] but this raises the question of when and how such consensus comes about—or, put differently, why some interest group coalitions succeed at presenting a united front to policy makers while others do not.

Viewed from this standpoint, diversity is a double-edged sword. Even as it creates the possibility for a coalition to signal uncommonly broad support for a policy position, it exacerbates the challenge of actually aligning and activating numerous organizations with different legislative priorities, resource endowments, governance structures, and approaches to advocacy. Member groups vary in their attentiveness and commitment to coalition affairs, moreover. While some eagerly make the coalition's cause their own and bring the full weight of their organizational capacity to bear on its work, others "tag along," lending their name to the cause but contributing little if anything at all to coalition maintenance and collaborative advocacy.[29] Capitalizing on a diverse interest group coalition's potential for signaling broad, unified support for a coalition policy position is thus no easy task. It is not simply a matter of pooling member organizations' resources nor is it even a straightforward function of their combined policy capacities. Rather, as O'Grady's recollection of the LCCR's Civil Rights Act of 1964 campaign highlights, coalition leaders have "one tough time" corralling groups with different orientations and capacities to agree on shared legislative priorities and tactics, adjust their consensus as new developments unfold, channel professional and grassroots lobbying resources accordingly, and sustain this unity over the course of lengthy lawmaking episodes.

These activities all fall under the rubric of *coordination*, the process of aligning or otherwise priming parts of a larger whole to work together effectively. That interest group coalitions entail coordination is acknowledged in prior scholarship, which counts coordination costs among the disincentives to groups' willingness to form and participate in coalitions.[30] Instead of conceptualizing coordination as a cost individual groups assess in deciding whether and how to engage in coalition work, however, I view it here as an iterative process coalition leaders enact to build, maintain, and project a united front in support of coalition policy objectives. Effective coordination hinges on member groups' willingness to commit time and resources to coalition endeavors, to be sure, and this willingness merits ample consideration.[31] But in shifting the focus to coalition leaders' management of the coordination process, I suggest that fully appreciating diverse interest group coalitions' signaling capabilities requires shining light into the black box of coordination to reveal how coalitions go about producing unified signals and why some interest group coalitions manage to do so with greater facility than others.

## *Coordination Capacity*

Just as individual organizations with similar resource levels might differ in their capacity to engage in policy work, interest group coalitions with similarly large and diverse membership rosters may vary considerably in their readiness to coordinate their member groups' lobbying activities. It is thus useful to think about interest group coalitions' ability to overcome the fundamental challenge of converting coalition resource potential into unified signaling in the policy arena in terms of their *coordination capacity*—that is, the facility with which they can identify coalition positions and mobilize the resources of their member organizations for concerted action in pursuit of shared objectives. Much like Halpin's policy capacity, moreover, coordination capacity derives from coalitions' organizational design; simply put, some interest group coalitions operate in ways that enable them to readily determine points of common ground among their members and motivate them to engage their professional lobbyists and grassroots constituencies accordingly. In contrast, some lack adequate organizational mechanisms for negotiating agreement among member groups and encouraging them to direct resources in ways that advance coalition goals.

There are no doubt myriad ways in which interest group coalitions see fit to organize themselves in light of prevailing technologies and approaches to organizational management; as Donald Hall explained his decision not to catalog the forms interorganizational cooperation take, "there simply are not one or two methods of arriving at a consensus."[32] Rather than identify a one-size-fits-all organizational chart or list of must-have operating procedures, therefore, the present discussion teases out the capabilities interest group coalitions need to coordinate effectively.

First and foremost is some mechanism for engaging member organizations in coalition decision making. To the extent that interest group coalitions' value rests with their potential for presenting a united front to policy makers, they need to be able to identify what exactly the consensus of their members is with respect to both substantive preferences, including which policy objectives to prioritize and which policy positions to advocate, and legislative strategy. Identifying the nature of member organizations' consensus is particularly important for interest group coalitions whose purview encompasses a broad policy area. As subsequent chapters show, a recurring challenge for the Leadership Conference was to find agreement on the coalition's lobbying agenda. While the prevailing understanding of what properly fell under the rubric of civil rights was relatively narrow through the mid-1960s, and while all the LCCR's member groups were firmly in favor of civil rights, there was substantial disagreement about which specific civil rights policy objectives were most vital and politically salable. Nor was identifying coalition priorities ever quite a done deal. Exogenous developments—especially unanticipated actions by presidents and legislators to propel new issues to the forefront or otherwise alter lobbyists' sense of the politically possible—periodically compelled Leadership Conference officials to revisit an established consensus and reach out to member groups to clarify the extent of their agreement, identify which organizations would join in a newly drafted statement or action on behalf of a subset of members rather than the coalition as a whole, or otherwise discern the possibility for the coalition's response to changing circumstances.

Interest group coalitions must also be able to implement the collaborative decisions they make. Implementing these decisions necessitates some means of promulgating agreed-upon positions and strategies among member organizations as a first step toward mobilizing their resources for concerted action. By definition, interest group coalitions lack the authority to deploy collective lobbying resources unilaterally; rather, they rely on member organizations to serve as faithful mouthpieces for coalition preferences and enjoin their professional and grassroots lobbying forces to act in accordance with coalition plans. It is therefore essential that these preferences and plans are well understood by member groups' officials and staff, a task that may be complicated by bureaucratic distance between those delegated by their home organizations to participate in coalition deliberations and those who direct organizational policy and rank-and-file engagement. Moreover, just as compositional diversity can be a double-edged sword for interest groups, the federated structure of many U.S. interest groups enhances the potential for showcasing nationwide support for coalition positions but also exacerbates the challenge of unified mobilization.

Implementing collaborative lobbying plans also necessitates some administrative capacity to orchestrate member groups' participation in coalition initiatives. This capacity encompasses a wide-ranging set of activities: fielding suggestions and inquiries, circulating joint statements for endorsement, event planning, printing and distributing promotional and instructional materials, compiling feedback from professional and grassroots lobbying interactions, facilitating information sharing among groups, managing publicity, and other tasks too numerous to catalog exhaustively. Though mundane, these tasks can be critical to the success of a lobbying campaign and can fall through the cracks if there is no mechanism for ensuring that they are well attended to—a possibility that is exacerbated when coalition objectives compete with member organizations' individual priorities for attention and resources.

Finally, it is important for coalitions to be able to sustain coordinated mobilization once they achieve it. While some policy-making episodes are of relatively short duration, many span long months or even years as bills progress slowly through a legislative process that is prone to delay by obstructionist veto players. A very forceful point-in-time signal might yield fruit in such cases. It is likelier, however, that persistent activity by the full range of member groups' professional lobbyists and grassroots constituents is necessary to assure sympathetic policy makers that public opinion remains broadly supportive of the coalition's view, persuade their more hesitant counterparts to come around to the coalition's position, and ensure that the policy proposal in play is not sidelined or diluted. It is especially difficult to sustain momentum within a diverse interest group coalition that includes member organizations for whom the coalition's focal issue is of secondary concern. While these groups may be amenable to committing resources to an initial or otherwise high-profile push for the coalition's legislative objectives, it is another matter to encourage them to continue devoting staff hours and mobilizing their base in support of coalition goals that, although not in conflict, still compete with other organizational priorities. While issue salience can alleviate this challenge—as it likely did during the LCCR's year-long lobbying campaign for the Civil Rights Act of 1964—it does not eliminate the challenge entirely nor is the mitigation necessarily automatic.[33] Rather, coalition leaders must be able to capitalize on these rare opportunities to keep member groups engaged and active in coalition efforts.

## *Improving Coordination Capacity*

The discussion thus far has implicitly treated coordination capacity as a static trait, which raises the questions of whether and how readily coalition leaders can introduce organizational changes to facilitate more effective coordination. While perhaps less relevant to ephemeral interest group coalitions that form on an ad hoc basis to coordinate a single lobbying campaign, for coalitions like the Leadership Conference, which exist on a relatively formal and enduring basis, the ability to rework their organizational structure and operating procedures when deficiencies become apparent could have portentous consequences for their ongoing relevance and, ultimately, their survival.[34]

Prior research on interest group coalitions offers little insight into the possibilities for improving coordination capacity for reasons alluded to earlier: the literature tends to focus on the incentives for coalition-oriented action by individual member groups rather than the maintenance of interest group coalitions as organizational entities in their own right; it tends to black-box coordination and other organizational processes; and its empirical approaches tend to home in on episodic coalition activity and discrete policy-making situations rather than delve into the mechanics of long-term intergroup relationships. Some starting points can be gleaned from research on standalone interest groups, however. Halpin, for example, emphasizes that organizational form is usually quite durable. "After taking decisions on organizational form and structural set-up," he writes, "groups are not always easy to change—even where circumstances seem to demand it."[35] This is not to suggest that organizational structures are immutable. Indeed, Halpin's own work with Carsten Daugbjerg offers an illustrative account of what they call "radical change" in one British interest group, which transformed from an amateur scientific society into an environmental campaign organization several decades after its founding.[36] But such drastic change is rare, and scholars who have explored the dynamics of organizational change have highlighted a number of factors that predispose groups to maintaining their organizational status quo. To the extent that interest groups seek out niche identities and specializations within a competitive interest group sector, introducing new ways of doing business is risky. As McGee Young observes, "all organized interests face an essential tension between the organizational desire to maintain a stable identity and changing political circumstances that threaten such efforts."[37] Young further suggests that several "path-inducing effects" militate against change. Group leaders may view continuing returns on their earlier investments in existing operating procedures as "large enough to reduce short-term incentives to experiment with alternative organizational designs," for example, and they may be disinclined to innovate in ways that render existing human resources and process knowledge obsolete.[38]

While securing a niche within a crowded organizational field may be less of a priority for interest group coalitions than it is for unitary groups, other factors that tend to promote organizational stasis are likely still at play. Moreover, it stands to reason that implementing capacity-enhancing change could be even more difficult for a coalition than for a standalone group. Coalition leaders might sense that proposing such change would be unduly disruptive, or potentially even threatening to the coalition's survival if member organizations opt to disaffiliate rather than adapt to new procedures that they perceive as compromising their autonomy or that place great demands on their resources. Coalition leaders might also lack authority to implement such change without the express consensus of member groups, which they might in turn perceive to be too arduous to obtain. Indeed, to the extent that coordination capacity is lacking, simply ascertaining member groups' appetite for reform to the coalition's structure and operating procedures may be—or may at least be perceived to be—unfeasible.

These change-inhibiting dynamics were evident in the LCCR's early development, as Chapter 3 details. For a full decade after Leadership Conference officials decided to institutionalize their alliance, they presided over a coalition with rather feeble coordinating capabilities—a state of affairs they acknowledged and justified in terms of a perceived tradeoff between coordination capacity on the one hand and, on the other, the continued participation by key member groups that fiercely guarded their autonomy. But Chapters 4 and 5, which examine the LCCR's organizational development during and after its campaign for passage of the Civil Rights Act of 1964, illustrate how changes in the policy-making context can motivate coalition leaders to overcome inertial tendencies and introduce organizational reforms that enhance coordination capacity.

The circumstances that prompted Leadership Conference officials to enact changes to the coalition's organizational structure and operating procedures in 1963 and 1967 were quite different. They were capitalizing on a momentous political opportunity in the former and reacting to a confluence of threats to both coalition solvency and the advancement of civil rights in the latter. Nevertheless, these disparate episodes of organizational development yield similar observations. In line with Young's expectations, LCCR officials were generally disinclined to revolutionize the coalition even as they implemented changes that had transformative effects; rather than invent new organizational practices out of whole cloth, they opted to refine or repurpose existing arrangements, or to borrow "familiar scripts" from within the broader advocacy group sector when innovation was necessary.[39] Both change episodes also suggest that coalition leaders do indeed understand their organizational capabilities to be at least as important as the diversity of their membership roster. While Leadership Conference officials did engage in strategic coalition expansion (and sometimes culling) to enhance the variegation of their support base and gain access to resources that were not already extant within their existing membership ranks, their focus during these critical junctures was primarily on developing organizational practices to facilitate coalition decision making and collaborative lobbying.

## Conclusion

The framework sketched out in this chapter envisions diverse interest group coalitions as potentially—but not necessarily—robust signalers and understands their capacity for presenting a united front of broad-based support for coalition positions as a function of their organizational wherewithal to coordinate member groups' lobbying activities. While not quite at odds with prior research, this approach does suggest some reorientation. Following Junk, it suggests that the value of compositional diversity for interest group coalitions is conditional.[40] However, where Junk's framework conditions the impact of diversity on issue salience—that is, a feature of the policy-making context within which interest group coalitions operate, I suggest that it is mediated by coalitions' own organizational properties, which constrain coalitions' ability to capitalize on political opportunities as well. In turn, my framework calls for delving into the organizational mechanisms interest group coalitions use to orchestrate collaborative advocacy. This approach necessitates defining interest group coalitions as deliberately cooperative enterprises,[41] and it calls for understanding interest group coalitions as having an organizational life of their own; that is, they are not merely the sum of their constituent parts or an abstract product of intergroup transaction.

I return to these considerations in the Conclusion, which further explicates the implications of this framework for research on interest group coalitions. First, however, Chapters 2 through 5 tell the story of the LCCR's founding, organizational development, and participation in federal civil rights policy making through the mid-1960s. Their narrative is analytical rather than comprehensive; rather than detail every initiative the Leadership Conference undertook during the Second Reconstruction era—a task that would exceed the scope of any book of reasonable length—it zeroes in on LCCR officials' approach to coalition management at different points in the coalition's early history and key policy-making episodes that illustrate how their organizational choices shaped their capacity to mobilize and bring the resources of LCCR members and allied organizations to bear on the legislative process.

The Second Reconstruction–era Leadership Conference was a singular coalition operating during a unique historical juncture; as such, its experience cannot purport to serve as a definitive test of the framework presented in this chapter. But it is an instructive case for several reasons. As the lobbying arm of the civil rights movement during its heyday, the LCCR is historically significant; just as the civil rights movement has served as an important touchstone for the development of social movement theory,[42] the Leadership Conference ought to be an influential case in the study of lobbying coalitions. The Leadership Conference has also enjoyed unusual longevity and resilience. Rather than a uniform snapshot of coalition dynamics, its organizational development during the 1950s and 1960s presents within-case variation that enables exploration of different organizational arrangements and their implications for coordination. The LCCR's endurance well beyond the civil rights movement's prime likewise sheds light on interest group coalitions' adaptation to changing circumstances. While this book's coverage ends in 1967, its examination of the challenges the Leadership Conference faced in the aftermath of the Civil and Voting Rights Acts' passage lends insight into the politics of coalition maintenance and collaborative lobbying as the Second Reconstruction's window of opportunity was closing.

# 2

# Nothing like the Present Ferment Has Been Seen for Seventy-Five Years

In 1951 Joseph B. Robison, a staff attorney for the Commission on Law and Social Action of the American Jewish Congress surveyed the field of advocacy groups that were active in promoting civil rights legislation in the postwar United States. He described a core set of African American and other minority-group organizations from which emanated "the direction and principal motivating force" for a burgeoning movement to eradicate racial discrimination. But, he added, "a very important part of the work and energy has been supplied" by what he called "peripheral groups," or "organizations whose general viewpoint inclines them to support the cause of equality even though that cause is not the primary reason for their existence."[1] Robison further observed a series of initiatives to coordinate pro–civil rights organizations' efforts and "set up machinery through which they can speak with a single voice, particularly with respect to legislation."[2] The first attempts at such coordination coalesced around specific policy objectives—for example, to abolish poll taxes or promote fair employment legislation. But, he wrote, they eventually came to embrace "a broader function, that of reaching and implementing joint decisions as to priorities of goals."[3]

This chapter situates the LCCR's formation within this organizational landscape. A coordinating agency that was just barely in the offing at the time of Robison's writing, the Leadership Conference grew out of and exemplified the developments he described. As a relatively late-forming coalition, moreover, the Leadership Conference took shape against the backdrop of earlier efforts to coordinate the activities of pro–civil rights organizations. Most, if not all, of its original member organizations had prior experience as partners in civil rights interest group coalitions. Even more crucially, the LCCR's founders were centrally involved in previous collaborations, which shaped their understanding of the promise and pitfalls of coalition projects and influenced their decisions about which organizations would be eligible to join, what demands would be placed on member organizations, how the Leadership Conference would be administered, and how its lobbying agenda and policy positions would be determined.

In unpacking these developments, this chapter joins Eric Schickler in highlighting the emergence of "a broad liberal coalition that upheld civil rights support as a central tenet" during the 1940s.[4] As I do here, Schickler grounds this development in wartime conditions that propelled civil rights causes to the fore, and he explains how several groups within an incipient "liberal lobby" came to view civil rights as integral to their larger project and began to speak out or act in support of civil rights.[5] But while Schickler identifies several postwar interest group coalitions and gives some sense of the breadth of their membership rosters, his account offers little insight into their cooperative dynamics.[6] In contrast, my focus is less on coalition partners' interest in promoting civil rights, or even the pro–civil rights actions they took on their own, than on the mechanisms they established to facilitate interorganizational collaboration—that is, on the machinery Robison observed interest group leaders creating to facilitate "speak[ing] with a single voice" in support of civil rights legislation.[7] This shift from a preference similarity approach to one that highlights instances of intentional cooperation among disparate pro-civil rights forces sets the tone for subsequent chapters' organizational analysis of the LCCR's development and legislative interventions during the 1950s and 1960s.[8]

The present chapter proceeds in four parts. The first two conceptualize the 1940s as a critical juncture and describe how various advocacy sectors adapted in ways that inclined them toward alliance. In addition to accounting for the emergence of a collaborative spirit among pro–civil rights groups, this discussion introduces many of the LCCR's key organizational players. The third section turns to the civil rights interest group coalitions that took shape during the 1940s. Rather than offer an exhaustive catalog of collaborations, it gives a sense of the range of such initiatives undertaken during the mid- to late 1940s and highlights the collaborative experiences that most influenced the men who presided over the LCCR coalition. The final part of the chapter zeroes in on the creation of the Leadership Conference itself. Though rooted in earlier developments, the story begins with the National Emergency Civil Rights Mobilization, an event spearheaded by the NAACP and cosponsored by many other organizations seeking congressional action on civil rights. This mobilization set the stage for a collaborative campaign to influence the Democratic and Republican Party platforms' civil rights provisions in 1952 and the subsequent decision to maintain that election-year collaboration as a permanent interest group coalition known as the Leadership Conference on Civil Rights.

## World War II and the Rise of Civil Rights Interest Group Coalitions

World War II transformed the possibility for civil rights reform in the United States. There were modest breakthroughs during the war itself—most notably, President Franklin D. Roosevelt's Executive Order 8802, which prohibited employment discrimination in defense industries and established a wartime Fair Employment Practices Committee (FEPC), but also passage of the Soldier Voting Act, which waived poll taxes for military servicemen, and the Supreme Court's invalidation of racially exclusive primary elections.[9] Even more significant were forces and conditions precipitated by the war, which recast the political landscape in ways that, while by no means guaranteeing significant policy change, made it far more feasible than it had been previously. The U.S. confrontation with Nazism laid bare, or at least created poignant opportunities to highlight, hypocrisies embedded within its own racially circumscribed democracy.[10]

Rather than dissipate at the war's end, the incipient Cold War extended and reinforced the kairotic moment. While anticommunist fervor sometimes hindered civil rights advocates, concern for the international reputation of U.S. democracy generally strengthened their case against Jim Crow.[11] Public opinion also grew more supportive of civil rights, though new research shows that the wartime liberalization of white racial attitudes was not as widespread as heretofore supposed.[12] Black veterans in particular returned with heightened motivation to challenge the status quo and drew on their military experience as inspiration for subsequent civil rights activism.[13] Meanwhile, wartime employment opportunities accelerated domestic demographic changes that had been underway since the turn of the century. As African Americans migrated to northern urban centers in rising numbers, racial issues were nationalized and black voters became an increasingly relevant component of northern politicians' electoral calculus.[14]

Within this milieu, a diverse set of civil rights, labor, religious, civic, and other organizations began forming interest group coalitions—not merely siding with each other, but actually working together in explicit partnership to promote civil rights policy reform. This was facilitated by policy feedback from the Fair Employment Practices Committee (FEPC) President Roosevelt established in June 1941. The March on Washington Movement that led to the FEPC's creation did not exemplify the variegated organizational membership that would characterize subsequent civil rights coalitions; on the contrary, the initiator of the March on Washington Movement, A. Philip Randolph, insisted on an all-black movement and selected prominent figures from African American organizations to join him in negotiations with President Roosevelt.[15] Once the FEPC was created, however, it yielded a diverse support base vested in its maintenance and enhancement. The FEPC's intrinsic limitations—it had no enforcement powers, and it was established as a temporary wartime measure rather than a permanent agency—meant that groups were mobilized on its behalf practically from the start.

As Anthony Chen describes, moreover, the FEPC was an early-career way station for a number of individuals who subsequently held key positions within the postwar civil rights lobbying community.[16] Among them were Clarence Mitchell, who would go on to direct the NAACP's Washington Bureau; Elmer Henderson, who would found the American Council on Human Rights to coordinate lobbying by black fraternities and sororities; Will Maslow, who would become Director of the American Jewish Congress's Commission on Law and Social Action; and Boris Shishkin, who would direct the AFL-CIO's Civil Rights Department. For Chen, the significance of the FEPC as "a kind of training ground" for these men lay in the "valuable experience in navigating the world of Washington politics" they obtained.[17] But it also incubated a fledgling network of pro–civil rights professionals who came to know each other and grew accustomed to working together—a network that extended not just to FEPC personnel but also those who interacted with them as organizational representatives of communities seeking relief from employment discrimination. Arnold Aronson, for example, got to know Elmer Henderson, director of the FEPC's Chicago field office during the war and subsequently an early director of the National Council for a Permanent FEPC (NCPFEPC) and founder of the American Council on Human Rights, through his work as chairman of the Chicago Council against Racial and Religious Discrimination. As the present chapter recounts, Aronson would later be tapped to help lead the NCPFEPC and was among the LCCR's founding officials.[18]

## Civil Rights Interest Group Coalition Partners

This section follows the arc of Robison's survey of the organizational field, drawing on an array of primary and secondary sources to flesh out, clarify, and occasionally amend his impressions of the interest group sectors that composed the civil rights lobbying community. While not an exhaustive account of the many organizations that would join the LCCR and its predecessors, the section highlights a range of key players, including three sets of minority-group organizations and several peripheral group allies that were especially instrumental in postwar coalition efforts.

African American organizations were of course integral to the postwar era's civil rights coalitions, though it bears noting that two groups that would headline civil rights activity during the 1960s—the Southern Christian Leadership Conference (SCLC) and Student Nonviolent Coordinating Committee (SNCC)—had not yet been created.[19] The National Association for the Advancement of Colored People (NAACP), founded in 1909, was, as Robison wrote, the "most prominent in the struggle for equality for Negroes,"[20] and it had long pursued a well-rounded litigation and lobbying agenda.[21] The National Urban League, founded in 1910, was another long-standing national organization in this sector; however, unlike the NAACP, it generally stood aloof from the policy process, concentrating its energies and resources on social work rather than lobbying.[22]

An assortment of newer and emerging organizations rounded out the postwar set of African American organizations. Although Robison does not mention it, the National Council of Negro Women (NCNW), which Mary McLeod Bethune founded in 1935, reinvigorated and coordinated long-standing lobbying traditions by Black women's organizations.[23] The Congress of Racial Equality (CORE) was founded in 1942 and, though primarily oriented toward nonviolent direct action, it participated in several postwar interest group coalitions. The Southern Conference for Human Welfare and Southern Regional Council, founded in 1938 and 1944, respectively, were New Deal–inspired interracial organizations promoting racial equality and economic justice in the South. There was also an array of black professional and fraternal organizations that varied in size, prominence, longevity, and engagement in political activity. As studies of medical civil rights activism highlight, several black professional organizations reoriented their policy objectives and forged new ties with the NAACP and other civil rights organizations at this juncture.[24] Fraternities and sororities likewise took increasing interest in legislative affairs, and seven of them joined forces under the umbrella of the American Council on Human Rights in 1948.[25]

The Great Depression and World War II marked a turning point in the NAACP's development, solidifying its role as the lead organization in postwar efforts to secure civil rights legislation and reorienting its focus to encompass causes of import to an increasingly working-class constituency.[26] Successful collaboration with the March on Washington Movement and the United Automobile Workers during the Ford strike in 1941 enhanced the NAACP's propensity for partnership with other organizations, as did the creation of its Washington Bureau the following year. Intended as a "'watchdog' of the interests of Negroes" in the federal policy-making realm, this new unit's functions would include, among other activities, "cooperat[ion] as far as possible with other agencies or organizations interested in the same or similar objectives."[27]

The result of these developments, as August Meier and John H. Bracey describe, was a "radical transformation" in the NAACP's approach to lobbying, "from one based on personal contacts by a few top officers . . . to one that mobilized the resources of scores of civic, labor, and religious organizations."[28]

In addition to African Americans, Robison identified two other minority groups that participated in postwar collaborative efforts to secure legislative protections against racial discrimination: Jews and Japanese Americans.[29] The Jewish advocacy sector was particularly vibrant and included a number of organizations that had been active in the national policy scene since the Progressive Era, including the Anti-Defamation League of B'nai B'rith (ADL, founded 1913), the American Jewish Committee (AJC, founded 1906), the American Jewish Congress (AJCon, founded 1918), and the Jewish War Veterans (JWV, founded 1896), all of which Robison mentioned in his survey, as well as the National Council of Jewish Women (NCJW, founded 1893), which he did not. Surging anti-Semitism and Hitler's rise to power during the 1930s gave new wind to American Jewish organizations, which reaped growing membership rolls and an increase in funding for their work.[30] These developments also prompted Jewish organizations to routinize cooperation among themselves and, after a few false starts, the National Community Relations Advisory Council (NCRAC) was formed in 1944 as a coordinating agency for Jewish national organizations and community councils.[31]

Jewish interest groups' postwar engagement in civil rights promotion is undisputed; indeed, it has been claimed that "the Jewish communal agenda [of the 1950s and 1960s] was the civil rights movement."[32] This was not an inevitable outgrowth of their traditional advocacy agendas, however; rather, it marked a shift in Jewish groups' orientation—a move from "from ethnic advocacy to intergroup relations," according to Stuart Svonkin—that was undertaken deliberately by a new generation of organizational professionals who embraced unitary theories of prejudice and collaborative approaches to combating it.[33] As Cheryl Lynn Greenberg recounts, fair employment politics concretized this new propensity to collaborate with other minority groups. Insofar as Jews "constituted the majority of complainants" in some locations, preserving and strengthening the FEPC quickly became a priority for Jewish organizations, which "brought [them] . . . into frequent and productive contact" with African American and other groups working on this issue.[34]

In contrast to the preponderance of Jewish advocacy groups, just one organization, the Japanese American Citizens League (JACL), represented Japanese American interests in national politics.[35] Unlike the Jewish organizations' time-honored lobbying presence, moreover, the JACL was a newcomer to the national policy scene. Although founded in 1929—more than a decade before the U.S. entered World War II—the December 7, 1941, attack on Pearl Harbor and subsequent removal and internment of West Coast Japanese Americans brought the Salt Lake City–based JACL into contact with the civil rights lobbying community in New York and Washington, DC, for the first time.[36] Mike Masaoka, who had recently been appointed as the first national secretary of the JACL, described his first taste of this interaction when he was invited to participate in a FEPC hearing in Los Angeles in October 1941. This, he wrote, was "the first opportunity for Japanese Americans to present their employment grievances to a government agency and to ask for equality in the matter of jobs," and the JACL's inexperience relative to other testifying organizations was painfully apparent. Among other lessons, Masaoka reflected that this experience revealed that "the problems of one minority are inextricably tied up with the comparable problems of all minorities," an insight that would drive his efforts to engage the JACL in the civil rights movement well into the 1960s.[37]

In the same report, Masaoka described his first interactions with civil rights and other organizational leaders and lobbyists during his trip to Washington in the summer of 1942, when the JACL dispatched him to pursue its goal of working with the federal government to minimize the impact of the Japanese internment. In addition to helping him find his footing, they impressed on him "the necessity for keeping in daily touch with developments in government and the influential national organizations."[38] Masaoka subsequently secured approval to establish the JACL's Washington office, which included "cooperat[ion] with other organizations in the promotion of the general welfare" among its core functions.[39] By the late 1940s, Masaoka's office had participated in several collaborative initiatives in pursuit of civil rights legislation, and, owing to Japanese Americans' geographic distribution—which differed substantially from those of the African American and Jewish organizations' constituencies—he had cultivated working relationships with the offices of several western members of Congress, which would prove useful to the civil rights lobby down the line.

African American, Jewish, and Japanese American organizations accounted for about half of the fifty-two groups that would compose the original LCCR. An overwhelming preponderance of the peripheral groups that filled out the coalition were labor organizations, including both the American Federation of Labor (AFL) and Congress of Industrial Organizations (CIO) prior to their 1955 merger, as well as a number of local unions affiliated with each federation. Robison's passing mentions of labor unions belie the prevalence and central role they played within the civil rights coalitions of the postwar era; indeed, as Paul Frymer notes, "in . . . support of national civil rights causes, union efforts were quite arguably unsurpassed by any other non-civil rights organization."[40] Support for civil rights was not a long-held position of organized labor in the United States, to be sure, and there is an extensive literature documenting complex and often tense relationships among mainstream unions, black workers, and civil rights organizations.[41] Union support began to turn a corner during the mid-1930s, when the CIO was created. In contrast to the craft-based organization and traditionally politically aloof posture of the AFL, the CIO's industrial model and quick embrace of political engagement predisposed it to support—at least in principle, if not always in practice—the unionization of black workers and some civil rights causes.[42] While Baylor's and Schickler's accounts differ in some details, both cast the CIO's support for racial equality as key to the incorporation of civil rights into the mid-twentieth-century liberal agenda.[43] The creation of the FEPC cemented this development. It was a civil rights issue that related directly to concerns of organized labor, and the CIO and several of its affiliates—most notably the influential United Automobile Workers (UAW)—were quick to get involved in both solo and collaborative efforts to maintain and empower the FEPC.[44] Randolph's long-standing ties with the AFL (his own union, the Brotherhood of Sleeping Car Porters, was an AFL affiliate) and pressure to align its position on employment discrimination with the CIO brought that federation into the civil rights lobbying ambit, though its support was tepid at first and its preferences were shaped as much by a desire to keep unions free from FEPC scrutiny as by a concern for racial equality.[45]

Two additional organizations merit recognition for the central role they would play in postwar civil rights politics. The American Civil Liberties Union (ACLU), founded in 1920, had a long-standing working relationship with the NAACP, though the relationship was tempered somewhat by the ACLU's championing of free speech rights for Ku Klux Klan members and, at least with respect to litigation, typically entailed the deferral of race-related cases to the NAACP rather than collaboration between the two organizations.[46] Nevertheless, the ACLU's antidiscrimination work intensified and grew increasingly collaborative during World War II, when it took the lead in mounting legal challenges against the Japanese internment and helping Masaoka kick-start the JACL's lobbying efforts,[47] collaborated with the NAACP on lobbying and litigation strategy to strengthen the new FEPC and oppose segregation in the military, and worked with AJCon lawyers to develop model anti-discrimination legislation for enactment by the states.[48]

A much newer organization—Americans for Democratic Action (ADA)—quickly became an integral member of the postwar era's civil rights lobbying initiatives. Formed initially as the Union for Democratic Action (UDA) during World War II, the ADA sought to cultivate a robust liberal policy program, and its founders identified inattention to racial inequality as a shortcoming of the New Deal program early on. While the ADA's role in securing a strong civil rights plank in the Democratic Party's 1948 platform is frequently touted as evidence of its commitment to the cause,[49] its generally collaborative proclivities are more germane here. Though not a coordinating agency per se, the ADA (and the UDA before it) was a hub within the postwar universe of liberal, labor, and civil rights advocacy groups. Many of its officers and core members held prominent positions within organized labor and other pro–civil rights groups, and it prioritized identifying organizations that were already active in its focal issue areas and cooperating with them.[50]

Finally, Robison singled out Protestant and Catholic church groups as "deserv[ing of] special mention" for their pro–civil rights orientation.[51] Though this organizational sector would become far more vital to the civil rights lobby during the 1960s, initial forays into this policy arena were made earlier.[52] Most promisingly, the Federal Council of Churches, an ecumenical association of Protestant and Orthodox churches, adopted a progressive policy statement against segregation in 1946 and reaffirmed this position several years later in its new incarnation as the National Council of Churches (NCC).[53] A budding interracialist Catholic movement was taking shape during this time as well. While it lacked a national organizational presence during the 1940s and early 1950s and was generally more oriented to cultivating interracial understanding than lobbying for federal legislation, prominent leaders of the largest Catholic Interracial Conference chapters did participate in several postwar civil rights interest group coalitions.[54]

## Civil Rights Interest Group Coalitions during the 1940s

That the aforementioned organizations were all motivated to pursue civil rights legislation by the mid-1940s dictated neither their active collaboration nor the organizational forms any such collaboration would take. Both within and across advocacy sectors, long-standing interorganizational frictions and rivalries persisted and constrained the impulse to cooperate. Nevertheless, they did sometimes join forces, as the next section elaborates. While civil rights interest group coalitions began forming during World War II, the drive to foster new alliances and hone their operations intensified in the postwar context. By the time the Leadership Conference took shape during the early 1950s, its founders and member organizations had ample and varied experience with collaboration.

As noted at the start of this chapter, Robison observed that the earliest civil rights interest group coalitions were established in pursuit of specific legislative objectives. Two such single-issue coalitions have been identified in previous scholarship as LCCR progenitors: the National Committee to Abolish the Poll Tax (NCAPT), which Steven Lawson bills "the spiritual ancestor" of the LCCR in his history of black voting rights in the South, and the NCPFEPC, which is the first link in Kevin Schultz's genealogy of FEPC-centered coalitions culminating in the LCCR.[55] In contrast to the collaborative initiatives discussed later in this section—but like the Leadership Conference itself—NCAPT and NCPFEPC were both relatively durable, formal coordinating agencies. They also provided cautionary tales, as their organizational pathologies loomed large for would-be coalition builders in the late 1940s and 1950s.

The NCAPT was formed in 1941 at the behest of Representative Lee Geyer, a congressman who had worked with the Southern Conference for Human Welfare to introduce anti-poll-tax legislation in 1939. In Geyer's view, a new, "national, single-issue lobby" would help deregionalize and deracialize the poll-tax issue, making it more appealing to his congressional colleagues. It could also draw in the support of a wider array of lobbying groups, since its strict focus on the poll tax, as opposed to a broader civil rights agenda, "could attract organizations disagreeing on various policies to contribute financially to a special, limited campaign." As Lawson recounts, a diverse set of organizations joined the ensuing coalition organization, including "the AFL, CIO, NAACP, National Negro Congress, National Urban League, YWCA, United Jewish Youth, ACLU, National Lawyers Guild and League of Women Shoppers."[56]

The NCAPT persisted for seven years but began losing steam well before it disbanded in 1948. It did have some success early on in the form of the Soldier Voting Act's poll-tax waiver in 1942, but the coalition was unable to secure civilian relief from poll-tax requirements for voting. Several forces conspired to weaken it further after the war, including two that are especially germane here. The first was the red taint it acquired from its affiliation with organizations like the National Negro Congress and National Lawyers Guild, which were alleged to be communist fronts. These associations were damning in the emerging Cold War milieu and, by 1946, the NAACP, CIO, and ACLU had disaffiliated as part of larger efforts to burnish their noncommunist credentials. The second was the increasing untenability of the poll tax as a single-issue focus once President Harry Truman came to embrace a civil rights agenda that incentivized pro–civil rights forces to direct their attention more broadly.[57]

The NCPFEPC was also founded during the war, after a flurry of ad hoc "save FEPC" initiatives that had emerged when the new agency's survival was threatened by a move to subsume it under the congressionally controlled War Manpower Commission. Randolph invited FEPC supporters of all stripes to a conference in February 1943, where it was agreed that the FEPC campaign should prioritize preservation of the FEPC as a permanent federal agency so that gains made by minority workers would not disappear at the end of the war. The NCPFEPC grew out of this agreement and was formally established at a second conference later that year.[58] Unlike the NCAPT, which was conceived as an alliance of national organizations pursuing federal anti–poll tax legislation, the NCPFEPC operated at all levels of government to promote both a permanent federal FEPC and state-level anti-employment discrimination programs. The NCPFEPC was thus a sprawling coalition, counting numerous local affiliates and national organizations among its members.[59]

Financial and organizational challenges plagued the NCPFEPC throughout its nine-year lifespan. While the challenges were partly structural, conflicts between Randolph and Anna Arnold Hedgeman, the NCPFEPC's first executive secretary, and Randolph's leadership style more generally, were also problematic.[60] A concerted effort to address these problems was made in 1946, when a committee formed to recommend a reorganization plan and Hedgeman tendered her resignation.[61] Arnold Aronson, an NCRAC staffer who was a passionate civil rights advocate with a knack for administration, replaced Hedgeman, and new coalitional governance structures were established with an eye toward both enhancing operational efficiency and bringing the NCPFEPC's member organizations into more active participation in its affairs.[62] Further organizational adjustments were made some months later and Roy Wilkins, editor of the NAACP's *Crisis* magazine, became chairman of the NCPFEPC's Executive Committee,[63] relegating Randolph to an ex-officio role and presaging Wilkins's and Aronson's coleadership and division of labor within the Leadership Conference from its founding until Wilkins's retirement in 1977.

Still, the NCPFEPC's problems persisted.[64] Despite reorganization, it remained a "big but nebulous operation" with frequent staff turnover.[65] Fundraising to support its New York and Washington offices, maintain a staff, and repay its debts was a constant struggle.[66] The situation was particularly fraught for NAACP officials who were increasingly caught in the middle of intra-NCPFEPC conflict but could see no way out that would not harm both their own organizational reputation and the FEPC cause.[67] As a result, even as they continued to support the NCPFEPC and participate in its governance, they began experimenting with new efforts to coordinate national interest groups' civil rights advocacy without creating new organizations dedicated to this purpose. The ad hoc coalitions they initiated varied substantially in purpose, size, duration, and activity. Some were established in response to an exogenous development; others were conceived to stimulate pressure on Congress at a particular juncture in the legislative process or election cycle. While all were diverse insofar as they included a mix of civil rights, labor, religious, fraternal, professional, and civic groups, some involved the cooperation of just a handful while others had many participating organizations. And, while some consisted of a single meeting followed by a single joint action, others entailed iterative collaboration and a range of lobbying activities.

Among the earliest and most influential of these initiatives was one that came to be called the National Emergency Committee Against Mob Violence (NECAMV). Formed in reaction to a spate of lynchings during the summer of 1946, the NECAMV remained active for about a year and is credited with prompting President Truman to form his Committee on Civil Rights, a presidential advisory commission whose recommendations recast the civil rights policy agenda during the late 1940s.[68] The NECAMV got its start when NAACP executive secretary Walter White invited groups to send representatives to an August meeting in New York to discuss ten possibilities for coordinated action, ranging from meeting with President Truman and Attorney General Tom Clark to encouraging clergy to speak out against mob violence and forming a small executive committee to develop further strategy.[69] This initial meeting was fairly large—"some 40 or 50 organizations" were represented, according to Al Bernheim, who attended on the AJC's behalf, and participants included both the usual roster of liberal organizations and, to Bernheim's chagrin, "a considerable number of representatives from Communist or Communist dominated organizations."[70] White's full list of action items was adopted, albeit with the assurance that "none of the organizations represented would be deemed bound to participate in any specific activity which they would not approve"—a nod to the organizational autonomy that would remain a guiding principle for coalition activity.[71]

While White issued similar calls for collaboration several times during the late 1940s, one that stands out—not least because it is sometimes mistakenly presented as the LCCR's first incarnation—is the Joint Committee on Civil Rights (JCCR), which the NAACP initiated in December 1948.[72] Like the Committee against Mob Violence, the JCCR persisted for about a year and began with a meeting of organizational representatives invited by Walter White, though this time he exercised far greater selectivity to ensure a most well regarded—and decidedly noncommunist—set of participants.[73] There was no stated impetus or goal; rather, White's invitation indicated that the meeting would address "the pressing problem of human rights not only in the 81st Congress but in American life generally" and that attendees would "discuss an action program on which it is hoped we might arrive at an agreement for unified and cooperative action."[74] Within a few weeks of the initial meeting, however, NAACP leaders sensed that their new coalition was losing control of the effort to coordinate lobbying for civil rights legislation; in White's assessment, "neophytes are rushing into the act and muddying the waters through inexperience."[75] He noted that CIO officials had identified the NCAMV as one of the "best jobs of coordination" and proposed a second meeting at which, following the NCAMV model, a small executive committee would be appointed to "direct and coordinate" collaboration among the larger set of participating groups.⁷⁶ This second meeting was held in February 1949. Channing Tobias, a member of President Truman's Committee on Civil Rights and the NAACP Board of Trustees, was appointed to chair the reorganized alliance and its ten-member executive committee, and a separate committee of Washington-based lobbyists was established to coordinate legislative strategy.⁷⁷ The JCCR immediately embarked on an enthusiastic but ultimately unsuccessful campaign for Senate filibuster reform. Despite civil rights forces' concerted efforts, a Senate vote in mid-March made it even harder to end filibusters, and the JCCR never quite rebounded from this initial failure.

A few months after the debacle on Senate rules change, a small cadre of legislative affairs personnel representing several core organizations—that is, those with the most experience lobbying for civil rights—began collaborating more intensively than they ever had in the past to hone their legislative strategy. The initial meeting on June 2, 1949, was significant, NCRAC Executive Director Isaiah Minkoff wrote, insofar as it marked "the first occasion on which all the groups involved had come together to work out a general, overall strategy for the battle for civil rights legislation."⁷⁸ Over dinner with White House counsel Clark Clifford and Senator Hubert Humphrey, nine officers and lobbyists representing the NAACP, AFL, CIO, ADA, and NCRAC began hammering out a plan to shepherd civil rights legislation through Congress. Though alternatives were considered, including antilynching and anti–poll tax legislation and a comprehensive bill to improve the civil rights machinery of the federal government, they agreed to focus on resuscitating the FEPC despite the relative difficulty that objective would pose. As Minkoff relayed, "NAACP spokesmen insisted on priority to FEPC; the NCRAC representatives emphasized that all the Jewish organizations were committed to FEPC[;] . . . the AFL group . . . said that in the minds of trade unionists the civil rights program was a bread and butter affair . . . [and] that the AFL would rather go down fighting on FEPC than win one of the easier but less important measures . . . [and this] position was vigorously supported by the CIO spokesmen."⁷⁹

The group met several more times that summer and early fall to revisit and hone their strategy for securing FEPC legislation.⁸⁰ Its members struggled to attain favorable action in Congress, however, and, as the next section recounts, its direct lobbying efforts were soon eclipsed by a new campaign to mobilize grassroots support for civil rights legislation. But its formation attests to an increasingly palpable tension between the impulse to construct long-roster coalitions that showcased broad-based support for civil rights legislation and a recognition that smaller coteries of lobbying insiders were better suited to devising legislative strategy.

## The National Emergency Civil Rights Mobilization and Creation of the LCCR

It is generally understood that the LCCR was a byproduct of the National Emergency Civil Rights Mobilization (NECRM), an event that brought several thousand delegates representing "some fifty" organizations to Washington, DC, for three days of presentations, briefings, and citizen lobbying in January 1950.[81] The contemporary Leadership Conference counts 1950 as its founding date, and several scholarly works make the connection—albeit sometimes offhandedly.[82] But the progression from a three-day event to the establishment of a permanent interest group coalition several years later was far from straightforward. The remainder of this chapter describes the fraught interorganizational politics that ensued from the 1950 mobilization and ultimately gave rise to the Leadership Conference.

The NECRM grew out of the confluence of two organizational developments. The first was a decision at the NAACP's Fortieth Annual Convention in July 1949 to launch a broad-based campaign for federal civil rights legislation culminating in a mass conference in Washington to showcase the breadth of support for civil rights reform at the start of the 81st Congress.[83] The second came two months later, when the core civil rights lobbyists who had begun meeting earlier that year determined that an educational campaign would bolster their work on behalf of FEPC in the upcoming legislative session.[84] They agreed that, as part of this campaign, a conference should be held in Washington to mobilize a broad base of support. Wilkins, who was acting executive secretary of the NAACP during White's leave of absence and a regular participant in the legislative strategy meetings, suggested that the organizations represented at the lobbyists' meeting and "others to be agreed upon" might cosponsor the NAACP's event instead.[85]

The NAACP began working on conference plans in mid-October. After discussing the lobbying group's conversation with his top staff and inaugurating the committee he established to coordinate the NAACP's broader campaign, Wilkins reached out to the leaders of other organizations. In addition to requesting their formal cosponsorship of the event, he asked them to designate a representative to attend a planning meeting early the next month and encourage their branch affiliates to work with NAACP chapters around the country on local programming and delegate selection.[86] An overriding concern for many organizations contemplating participation in the NECRM was the fear that the unprecedented mass nature of the event would facilitate communist infiltration. The steering committee that was created in November to coordinate event planning thus took great pains to prevent this possibility. Its members developed an elaborate credentialing process for mobilization delegates and aggressively countered media insinuations that communists were involved in the initiative.[87] Still, while some organizations joined the initiative quickly, others were cautious. The AJC, for example, held out for more than a month before signing on. Internal communications among national AJC officials indicate at least two causes for apprehension: first, that organizations already signed on as cosponsors might not be "really participants" but merely "nominal" namelenders that did not intend to follow through with a strong commitment to the campaign for FEPC legislation; and second, that "with the exception of the ACLU, only Jewish and Negro organizations are really active in this campaign," which cut against the AJC's belief that nonminority group participation in such campaigns was essential to signal that civil rights is not merely a concern for minority groups.[88] As the date of the mobilization approached, moreover, AJC chapters in several cities expressed concern about their organization's cosponsorship of "mass demonstrations," and some actively refused to participate in the formation and financing of delegations to the event.[89]

As Robison noted, the NECRM was a milestone in the postwar wave of coordination among pro–civil rights advocacy groups in that it produced unanimous agreement among so many organizational representatives "not only on a single objective [i.e., to prioritize FEPC over other civil rights legislation] but also on strategy."[90] It also prompted an uneasy interalliance merger. Shortly after the event, Randolph and Wilkins convened a meeting of the "virtually identical" NCPFEPC Executive Committee and NECRM Steering Committee to discuss "the respective role of the National Council for a Permanent FEPC and the National Emergency Civil Rights Mobilization and the future relationship between these two organizations."[91] The result was the fusion of the two coalitions under the very unwieldy name "National Council for a Permanent FEPC in Cooperation with the National Emergency Civil Rights Mobilization" (NCPFEPC-NECRM) and a commitment to pursue a concerted campaign to pressure Congress for FEPC legislation.

Not all were comfortable with this arrangement. Some within the black press suspected a ruse to eliminate the NCPFEPC and place leadership of the FEPC lobbying effort firmly within Wilkins's and Aronson's hands.[92] Within the lobbying community, ADA legislative representative John Gunther advocated withdrawing. He offered several reasons for his position, including concern about the inclusion of organizations that might tarnish the ADA's well-guarded noncommunist credentials and the diversion of resources from actual lobbying activity to coalition maintenance.[93] NAACP officials, meanwhile, worried about the implications for their own organization's preeminent role within the civil rights organizational sector. The controversy came to a head in 1951 when the NCPFEPC-NECRM formed a subcommittee to consider pursuing changes to the Senate's filibuster rule as a means of improving the chances of passing FEPC legislation just as the NAACP convened a conference attended by representatives of thirty-one organizations at which it was decided that the NAACP would lead a new campaign to secure congressional rules reform.[94] "The whole situation seems to be in a mild tangle," Wilkins wrote to White, who had reassumed leadership of the NAACP. Wilkins proposed disavowing the NAACP's support for the NCPFEPC-NECRM's rules reform subcommittee and clarifying that its participation in the NCPFEPC-NECRM was limited exclusively and strictly to work on the FEPC bill. This, he thought, would "free [the NAACP] to recruit such organizations as we can secure, assuming without division or misunderstanding the responsibility for the fight to change the [Senate] rules."[95] White's response reiterated that the NAACP's role in NCPFEPC-NECRM hinged on its being "confined solely to coordinating efforts for an FEPC and not the tangential issues dealing with civil rights." To allow otherwise, he asserted, would fly in the face of his board's directive that "the NAACP lead and not follow in this fight."[96]

It was at about this juncture that the NAACP's annual convention resolved to hold a second mass conference modeled on the 1950 mobilization in advance of the 1952 election season. White wrote to seventy-six other organizational leaders in November, announcing that "In order to stimulate action on Amendment of Senate Rule XXII which must be attained in order to pass any civil rights legislation in the second session of the 82nd Congress, the NAACP will sponsor a mobilization of citizens in Washington" in February 1952. He invited other national organizations to "join in the effort," which would entail their "consultation on program and strategy," facilitating communication about the event with local affiliates, working with NAACP chapters to form local delegations for the event, and a $100 minimum monetary contribution.[97]

White's invitation was not well received. On December 7, leaders of eleven prominent organizations that had participated in the 1950 mobilization voiced two concerns with the NAACP's plan in a joint letter. The first was strategic: "We are not sure that a mobilization . . . comparable in size to that of 1950 represents the most effective technique" to achieve their shared goal of legislative action on civil rights. Indeed, they continued, "such a mobilization, planned on what is necessarily very short notice[,] . . . may defeat the very ends we hope to achieve."[98] The second, advanced more subtly, was procedural and related to a not-quite-stated concern that the NAACP was overstepping in its request for support rather than cosponsorship of the event.[99] The letter observed that "the outstanding success" of the 1950 mobilization stemmed from "the cooperation of all the participating organizations, both in the planning and in the execution of that undertaking," and contended that "it is essential . . . that an opportunity be provided for joint discussion and consideration of all the factors involved before any further steps are taken."[100]

White brought these concerns before the NAACP Board of Directors a few days later. Reporting on both the December 7 letter and a face-to-face conversation with a delegation of officers from the UAW, ADA, and NCRAC, he noted that the other organizations favored a smaller event for organizational leaders rather than a mass mobilization of several thousand participants. The ensuing discussion was heated. Some board members questioned the merits of a leadership event as opposed to a mass meeting, but they raised other concerns, as well: One wondered whether simply allowing more time for planning a mass mobilization would mollify the strategic concern raised in the December 7 letter; another asked whether the NAACP could shoulder the cost of a mass mobilization alone should other organizations withhold their support; and a third posed the rhetorical question, "Since when does the NAACP go along with the thinking of other organizations, when its own convention has spoken?"[101]

Ultimately—though not unanimously—the board voted to hold "a junior mobilization of four to five hundred leaders rather than attempt to have a mass mobilization of 5,000."[102] Four days later, White and nine other NAACP staff members were joined by representatives of twenty-three labor, religious, fraternal, professional, and civic groups for a preliminary planning meeting.[103] They reviewed the decision to go ahead with a smaller conference for organizational leaders and set February 17–18, 1952, as the dates for the event. Wilkins and Aronson were appointed as cochairs, and it was proposed that the steering committee that had organized the 1950 mobilization be reconvened to coordinate the 1952 conference program.[104] Sponsorship shifted from the NAACP to the alliance of organizations collaborating in support of the event, and those who had expressed concern about the limited role initially envisioned for the NAACP's allies were satisfied that "plans for the Conference were evolved in a truly democratic fashion by a representative Steering Committee."[105] It was also at about this point that the LCCR's name was born. Although it was not named at the December 14 meeting,[106] Aronson's December 17 memorandum inviting the NECRM steering committee to reconvene billed the upcoming event as "a two day *Leadership Conference* in Washington."[107] By early January, stationery emblazoned with "1952 Leadership Conference on Civil Rights" in the letterhead and a list of "Participating Organizations" on the reverse side had been printed and was used for subsequent communications.

Despite the short lead time and some logistical confusion, approximately eight hundred individuals representing about fifty organizations attended the February 1952 conference. Their registration fees and donations from many of the sponsoring organizations yielded a few thousand dollars for follow-up activities.[108] Substantively, the conference delegates produced a resolution that called for fair employment, antilynching, and anti–poll tax legislation; urged the Senate to revise its filibuster rule; and exhorted the Democratic and Republican Parties to "include in their platforms a plank advocating a rule which will make it possible to curb filibusters by the vote of a majority of senators present."[109] The Steering Committee capitalized on this momentum to mount a two-pronged campaign to influence the Republican and Democratic Parties' 1952 platforms and pressure Congress for rules reform at the start of the 83rd Congress. Its members met periodically in the ensuing months to develop both initiatives and update their plans as the election season played out. They secured the consensus of all fifty-two organizations that had cosponsored the conference on a nine-point civil rights platform plank that was sent to the delegates to the Republican and Democratic National Conventions, and spokesmen for the Leadership Conference and its sponsoring organizations participated in platform proceedings at the conventions themselves.[110] After the election, they devised a strategy for coordinating direct lobbying and mobilizing cosponsoring organizations' grassroots members in support of reforming the filibuster rule.[111]

This effort was unsuccessful, and the Steering Committee met once more on February 10, 1953, to debrief. After reporting on the rules reform campaign, Wilkins raised the question of whether to maintain the coalition. Because the charge established at the previous year's conference was no longer operative, he pointed out, "it was for the Steering Committee to determine whether the Conference should continue and, if so, the nature of its future activities."[112] In the ensuing discussion, only Clarence Mitchell, the NAACP's Washington Bureau director, spoke against maintaining a permanent interest group coalition. His concern was about free riding by less active members. According to the minutes, he noted that "although the Conference boasted of 53 national organizations[,] . . . the brunt of the activity was carried on by only 3 or 4." This, he worried, "conveyed a false impression of unity and strength."[113] Other Steering Committee members pushed back. It would be "unrealistic," they maintained, "to expect all [member organizations] to proceed at the same pace or with the same intensity" in light of their disparate "structure, function, and resources." Indeed, they maintained, "the fact that more than 50 national organizations of diverse interest and viewpoints were united in a demand for civil rights . . . was in itself of inestimable value in impressing on legislators and the public generally that the expansion of civil rights was the concern not only of minority groups but of the community at large." They pointed to the previous year's activities as proof of the coalition's impact: Their "agreement on a proposed civil rights platform" and "unified presentations" to the Republican and Democratic platform committees "had considerable impact," they argued, and "the attempt to change the Senate rules at the opening of the present Congress would not have taken place had it not been for the concerted and coordinated efforts of all the organizations through the Leadership Conference." Finally, they warned that dissolving the coalition would be especially ill advised in the post-1952-election milieu: "it would be a distinct disservice to disrupt our ranks and dissipate our strength in the face of the growing trend toward conservatism."[114]

Ultimately, a motion to maintain the Leadership Conference passed unanimously.[115] But even as the Steering Committee members were united in their sense that the incipient interest group coalition was worth preserving, they envisioned a light-handed approach to coordination. The rejoinders to Mitchell's concern about imbalance in organizations' contributions to the joint effort set the tone: The Leadership Conference, it was asserted, "does not purport to be an authoritative organization with binding powers. . . . It is, rather, an instrumentality for facilitating cooperation and coordination among the participating organizations, each of which reserves for itself the right to determine its own course of action."[116] It is perhaps telling that practically no attention was given to demarcating the LCCR's organizational and operational parameters at this historic meeting. Only the matter of financing LCCR activities was addressed when Wilkins noted that the previous year's revenue, which had come largely from delegate registrations and organizational donations to the February 1952 conference, was practically exhausted. A motion to assess mandatory annual dues on member organizations was rejected in favor of soliciting voluntary donations and in-kind contributions—a policy that would remain in place until 1967.[117]

## Conclusion

As this chapter has documented—and as participant-observers like Joe Robison recognized at the time—coalition building became a hallmark activity of pro–civil rights interest groups after World War II. Seeking to preserve tenuous wartime policy gains and energized by changing realities that made the achievement of civil rights reform seem more attainable than ever before, civil rights organizations and their allies grew increasingly cooperative. They invested a good deal of time, energy, and resources in formal and ad hoc initiatives to coordinate their responses to emergent political developments, identify common legislative priorities, and craft joint strategies for achieving shared policy goals. Though not generally successful from a policy standpoint, their efforts were instrumental in other ways. They were an early, if sometimes clumsy, signal of broadening support for civil rights reform; they helped interest group officials and lobbyists appreciate the benefits and frustrations of collaboration; and they offered an initial set of dos and don'ts for would-be coalition leaders from the late 1940s on.

The Leadership Conference was an outgrowth of these developments. Though hardly inevitable—and though perhaps not perceptible to participants at the time—its emergence during the early 1950s represented a culmination of sorts. The NCPFEPC and other remnant 1940s coalitions had disbanded by 1953 and, while new collaborative initiatives occasionally took shape in the years after its founding, the Leadership Conference quickly became the principal coalition player in national civil rights lobbying. Yet, even as it brought a critical experimental phase to a close, the LCCR's creation marked a new beginning for coalition leaders, who were thoroughly sensitized to the promises and pitfalls of interorganizational collaboration in the preceding decade. As the next chapter details, the lessons they took from their early postwar experiences informed their approach to administering the Leadership Conference and shaped the new coalition's operations and activities well into the next decade.

# 3

## We Have No Formal Structure

The Leadership Conference marked its twenty-fifth anniversary in 1974 in part by forming a committee to identify an archival repository for its records and commission an official history of the coalition.¹ Norma O. Leonard, associate director of the Civil Rights Documentation Project, was among those considered to write the history and, in a letter describing the legwork it would entail, she recalled "the early years of the LCCR when it operated out of one or two drawers in New York."² Though there was a bit more to the early Leadership Conference than a small filing cabinet, Leonard's comment captures the young coalition's limited organizational apparatus in the decade after the February 1953 decision to maintain the LCCR as a permanent coordinating agency. This state of affairs would change during the mid-1960s, as Chapters 4 and 5 recount. But for ten critical years—years spanning the momentous *Brown v. Board of Education* ruling, the Montgomery Bus Boycott, the first sit-in campaigns, and passage of the first federal civil rights legislation since Reconstruction—the Leadership Conference practiced a rudimentary and ad hoc style of operation.

This chapter unpacks these organizational dynamics and explores their implications for the LCCR's efforts to influence the legislative process during the 1950s and early 1960s. Though sometimes mentioned in passing, the Leadership Conference rarely appears in scholarly treatments of this period's civil rights policy developments, which tend to center on partisan and institutional forces that conspired both to permit previously elusive legislative breakthroughs and to limit their effectiveness and prevent more substantial reform from coming to fruition.³ It shows up instead as a fully formed player in key legislative episodes during the mid-1960s or later; any references to its prior incarnation in these accounts evince some descriptive ambiguity. In assessing the LCCR's readiness to coordinate lobbying for the Civil Rights Act of 1964, for example, Clay Risen suggests that the pre-1963 Leadership Conference was "an ad hoc operation, existing more on paper than in practice" but adds that it had nevertheless managed to establish "a proven record of coordinating lobbying efforts across a wide variety of groups." Yvonne Ryan's biography of Roy Wilkins similarly suggests that despite "meeting intermittently . . . without any formal constitution, organizational structure or even budget . . . [and] no successes," the LCCR "presented an impressive front to Congress and the main political parties" during the 1950s.⁴

My account of the early LCCR's organizational wherewithal goes to the heart of this ambiguity—not to dispel it so much as to lay bare how the Leadership Conference embodied this tension and to clarify the implications for its lobbying activity prior to 1963. In doing so, it illustrates how interest group coalitions' organizational characteristics constrain their capacity to capitalize on the signaling potential of a diverse membership roster. Even at this early stage in its development, the Leadership Conference comprised a variegated coalition of some fifty organizations representing racial and ethnic minority groups, assorted faith traditions, labor unions, civic groups, and fraternal and professional associations.⁵ In addition to sectoral diversity, member groups varied in their resource endowments, grassroots constituencies, legislative connections, and tactical orientations. By all measures, their coalition was compositionally poised to showcase broad-based support for civil rights legislation—a feature LCCR officials routinely touted in press releases, legislative testimony, and communications with public officials. Organizationally, however, they struggled to bring the full force of their diverse membership to bear on the legislative process. Though well suited to preserving a long-roster alliance with low administrative and maintenance costs, their barebones operation made it difficult to negotiate coalition priorities and positions, implement decisions that entailed broad resource mobilization, and sustain the limited coordination they did muster over long policy-making episodes.

The Leadership Conference did not codify its bureaucratic structure or operating procedures until 1967, when it finally adopted its first official statement of purpose and bylaws. Therefore, I draw on a variety of archival sources to reconstruct its organizational parameters in the first half of the chapter. The second half explores the implications, both for the organizational development of the Leadership Conference itself and for its legislative activities during the mid-1950s and early 1960s. In addition to general observations about the early LCCR's coordination capacity, it takes a deep dive into the coalition's work during three legislative sessions spanning the 84th and 85th Congresses—essentially from the initial aftermath of the *Brown v. Board of Education* ruling through passage of the first federal civil rights law of the twentieth century in 1957.

## "A Permanent Ad Hoc Body"[6]

The early LCCR's bureaucratic structure was embryonic. Walter White, executive secretary of the NAACP, served briefly as its first chairman, Arnold Aronson of the National Community Relations Advisory Council (NCRAC) was its secretary, and the NAACP's Roy Wilkins was chairman of the Executive Committee, a board of organizational officials representing about a third of the coalition's membership roster. The size and composition of the Executive Committee were somewhat variable. Early on, its members were handpicked by White, Wilkins, and Aronson with substantial carryover from the Steering Committee of the 1952 Leadership Conference and some effort to ensure that the most prominent member organizations were represented.[7] Correspondence from the early 1960s, however, indicates that the Executive Committee's composition was "not rigidly fixed" and suggests that any member organization could ask to join it.[8]

After White's death in 1955, Wilkins succeeded him as both executive secretary of the NAACP and chairman of the LCCR. He continued to serve as chairman of the Executive Committee, as well, and the Leadership Conference persisted with him and Aronson as its only officers through the mid-1960s. For the entirety of this period, moreover, the Leadership Conference had no hired staff or headquarters of its own. Wilkins and Aronson lived and worked in New York City, and they ran the coalition's clerical operations out of their NAACP and NCRAC offices in Midtown Manhattan. The LCCR's letterhead stationery listed the NAACP's New York office address, where Wilkins's assistant John Morsell would intercept correspondence directed to the Leadership Conference and either handle it himself or refer it to Aronson for resolution. Temporary staff were occasionally brought in to assist with special events, but for the most part it fell to Aronson and Morsell to carve time from their official work to keep the Leadership Conference running. "Between the two of us," Morsell wrote in 1959, "Arnold and I manage to comprise a parttime secretariat."[9]

By the late 1950s a second committee that dealt with the finer points of legislative strategy operated in tandem with the Executive Committee. Based in Washington, DC, and led by Clarence Mitchell, the NAACP's Washington Bureau director, this unnamed group of lobbyists developed organically in the months leading up to passage of the Civil Rights Act of 1957.[10] As the 85th Congress got underway early that year, Mitchell proposed a periodic rendezvous of pro–civil rights interest groups' Washington representatives. In response to his concern that these meetings be limited to "those individuals who will really do some work," John Gunther, a legislative representative for the ADA, offered a list of lobbyists for twelve LCCR member organizations and the Friends Committee on National Legislation (FCNL), a group that routinely participated in Leadership Conference initiatives but did not formally affiliate as a matter of Quaker principle.[11] As Table 3.1 shows, the organizations represented in this group overlapped substantially with those represented on the Executive Committee; indeed, its members often stood in for the heads of their respective organizations when Executive Committee meetings were held in Washington. This and other considerations—for example, the group's unofficial status, its members' proximity to each other and their distance from the coalition's executive leadership, the nature of their direct lobbying work, and longstanding working relationships among them—meant that this committee operated with relatively little oversight.[12] Its members' expertise, relationships with policy makers, and access to day-to-day legislative proceedings further meant that this group sometimes assumed an advisory role to Wilkins, Aronson, and the Executive Committee.

Executive Committee meetings were held, sometimes in New York and sometimes in Washington "as occasion requires," Morsell wrote in 1961.[13] Long intervals sometimes separated these meetings. The Executive Committee met just once in 1953 after the decision early that year to maintain the Leadership Conference as a permanent lobbying coalition. This mid-April meeting featured robust discussions of several policy initiatives, and the minutes Aronson took suggest that those in attendance anticipated at least one additional meeting to address administrative concerns that went undiscussed because of time constraints.[14] None was called, however, prompting one Executive Committee member to write of concern for "the failure of the Leadership Conference on Civil Rights to show any signs of activity." His suggestion at the start of the 1954 legislative session that the Executive Committee meet "as soon as possible to assess the [legislative] situation and to map out a course of action for the next six months" appears to have gone unheeded, as the next meeting for which I could find any record was held nearly a year later.[15] The frequency of Executive Committee meetings did pick up after 1954, as Figure 3.1 shows; nevertheless, they remained few and irregular.

It bears emphasizing that the Executive Committee was the sole venue for deliberation within the LCCR during the 1950s and early 1960s. Short of convening special events like the 1952 Leadership Conference—a possibility that was periodically floated in Executive Committee meetings but rarely carried into fruition and, in any case, unfeasible as a routine mode of con-

TABLE 3.1  ORGANIZATIONAL REPRESENTATION IN LCCR LEADERSHIP, EXECUTIVE COMMITTEE, AND LOBBYISTS' COMMITTEE

| Organizations represented in LCCR Leadership and Executive Committee | Organizations invited to participate in the Washington lobbyists committee |
|---|---|
| American Civil Liberties Union | American Civil Liberties Union |
| American Council on Human Rights | American Council on Human Rights |
| American Federation of Labor *and* Congress of Industrial Organizations (represented separately before their 1955 merger) | American Federation of Labor-Congress of Industrial Organizations |
| American Jewish Committee | American Jewish Committee |
| American Jewish Congress | American Jewish Congress |
| American Veterans Committee | American Veterans Committee |
| Americans for Democratic Action | Americans for Democratic Action |
| Anti-Defamation League | Anti-Defamation League |
| Brotherhood of Sleeping Car Porters | |
| Catholic Interracial Council | |
| | Friends Committee on National Legislation |
| Improved Benevolent and Protective Order of the Elks of the World | |
| International Union of Electrical, Radio and Machine Workers | International Union of Electrical, Radio and Machine Workers |
| Jewish Labor Committee | |
| National Alliance of Postal Workers | |
| National Association for the Advancement of Colored People | National Association for the Advancement of Colored People |
| National Baptist Convention | |
| National Community Relations Advisory Council | |
| National Council of Jewish Women | National Council of Jewish Women |
| National Council of Negro Women | |
| United Automobile Workers | United Automobile Workers |
| United Steelworkers of America | |

*Note:* For purposes of this table, membership in the Executive Committee is determined by (a) listing on the LCCR's 1952 letterhead, the only version of its stationery that listed Executive Committee members, or (b) attendance at two or more of the Executive Committee meetings held during the first session of the 84th Congress in 1955. Organizations invited to participate in the Washington lobbyists committee are gleaned from John Gunther's January 15, 1957, letter to Clarence Mitchell, Part IX, Box 117, Folder 2, NAACP Records.

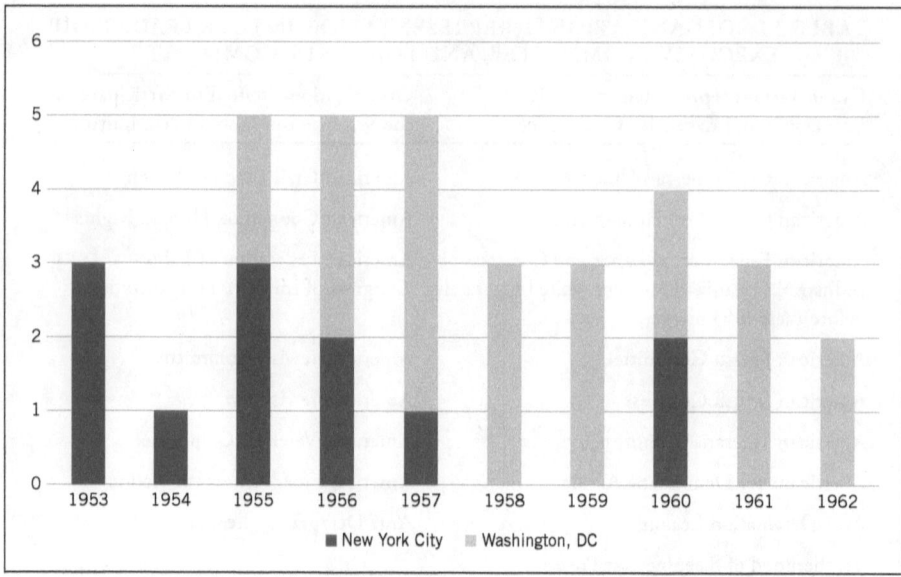

**Figure 3.1** Frequency and location of LCCR Executive Committee meetings, 1953–1962.

sultation—the coalition's limited organizational means effectively precluded collaborative agenda setting and strategizing by the full set of coalition partners. More generally, there were few expectations for member organizations' participation in the Leadership Conference.[16] Criteria for entry or continuing membership were not codified. Informally, however, any group that was organized at the national level, interested in the achievement of civil rights reform through legislation, and not communist was eligible for LCCR membership, subject to Executive Committee approval. While voluntary contributions, whether monetary or in-kind, were accepted and occasionally solicited, there were no mandatory donations or dues. Nor were member organizations obligated to participate in any LCCR initiative, though they were invited and encouraged to do so. Apart from the February 1952 Leadership Conference itself, there were just three gatherings for the full membership during the LCCR's first decade: a National Delegate Assembly in March 1956, a National Civil Rights Rally in April 1962, and a conference at the culmination of the LCCR's Senate rules reform campaign in January 1963. All three events met in Washington, DC, and focused primarily on raising awareness of legislative opportunities and hurdles, showcasing the breadth of support for civil rights legislation, and engaging participants in meetings with their congressional representatives—not on deliberating over coalition priorities or legislative strategy, which remained the purview of the Executive Committee.

Some of the Executive Committee's determinations were purely organizational—that is, they pertained strictly to LCCR operations—and were simply made and conveyed to member organizations as needed for implementation, if at all. Similarly, coalition leaders sometimes identified grassroots action steps to facilitate achievement of their legislative goals and these, too, were simply communicated in memorandums to member organizations. Sometimes, though, the Executive Committee met to address emergent political developments and crafted responses that involved the issuance of joint public statements, letters to public officials, or testimonies for congressional hearings. In these cases, and more generally when engaging in corporate position-taking, the Executive Committee would prepare the document in question and circulate it to member groups with a request to indicate whether their names should be included in a list of endorsing organizations. Feedback was not typically solicited; rather, member groups were asked simply whether they would lend their name to a position the coalition leadership had already finalized.

But even while the Executive Committee retained all decision-making authority, the overarching principle guiding their work was deference to member organizations' autonomy. The refrain was constant in official correspondence about the coalition throughout this period. "The Conference does not act as an independent body," Aronson averred in 1956; similarly, he assured the general secretary of an organization whose membership Wilkins had solicited earlier that year that "the Leadership Conference does not presume to speak for the supporting organizations without their expressed consent, and each organization is free to accept or reject the recommendations of the Executive Committee."[17] Three years later, Morsell informed a member group's public affairs director that "the Leadership Conference may not bind any participating organization to any course of action" and, when Mathew Ahmann, the executive director of the National Catholic Conference for Interracial Justice, asked for a description of the Leadership Conference to share with other Catholic organizations in 1962, Aronson's response emphasized that "the autonomy of each participating organization is recognized and respected. The Conference takes no action which is in any way presumed to be binding on the participating organizations."[18] While the Executive Committee sometimes did act in its own name without broad consultation, it was understood that positions taken in the name of the Leadership Conference as a whole should reflect the consensus of its member organizations, which was in turn understood to entail their explicit agreement—a high, if not impossible, bar to reach without robust means for consultation with constituent groups.

A full-throated articulation of this understanding of consensus and its centrality to early Leadership Conference operations was expressed when civil rights activists in Baltimore announced the creation of a state-level division of the Leadership Conference after their participation in the LCCR's National Delegate Assembly in 1956. Several member organizations got wind of this initiative and objected to the use of their names in a list of "supporting organizations" on the Maryland division's stationery.[19] "Cooperation cannot be declared," Aronson wrote in response to the Maryland organizers' request for assistance in sorting out the controversy; rather, "it must be achieved through the consent of the groups involved." He described the Leadership Conference as "a voluntary association of independent autonomous organizations . . . [whose] cooperation and coordination . . . derive essentially from the fact that each organization has an equal voice in determining . . . the policies and programs that have been pursued and the extent of its own participation." Therefore, a state-level affiliate could be approved only if authorization is "granted by the organizations comprising the [Leadership] Conference." Absent such authorization (and with no offer to facilitate it), Aronson concluded, "we must ask you to desist from identifying your organization as the Maryland Division of the Leadership Conference on Civil Rights and from listing our cooperating agencies as 'supporting organizations.'"[20] Morsell offered a similar assessment in a letter to one Maryland activist: "it is of the utmost importance that the Leadership Conference . . . be able to count on the continued interest and support of its constituent organizations . . . [which] it can only do if they . . . remain convinced of its responsibility and judgement." He suggested that the Executive Committee could take up the matter, but even its approval of the Maryland Division's creation would still not permit listing the national member organizations on its stationery without each one's express permission. "It must be borne in mind always," he added, "that the sponsorship [of the LCCR by its member organizations] was often hard-won and subject to very explicit limits; but the overriding importance of having the broadest possible supporting base was felt (in 1950 as now) to justify the relatively restricted area of joint activity on which there could be consensus."[21]

Aronson made the case similarly when Joseph L. Rauh Jr., an attorney affiliated with the ADA and a core figure within Clarence Mitchell's inner circle of lobbyists, testified on the LCCR's behalf at a subcommittee hearing on civil rights bills that had been introduced in the Senate in 1959.[22] Upon learning that Aronson felt his testimony had not been properly authorized, Rauh clarified that Mitchell had encouraged him to testify in the LCCR's name and described the sequence of events as follows:

> I agreed to do this *if* this were cleared with Roy [Wilkins] and you. . . . About a week or so later, Clarence called me to give me the exact date for the testimony and I reraised with him the problem of my authority

to testify. Clarence said that Roy thought it was a fine idea and also that either Roy or John Morsell were [*sic*] going to clear it with you.

He added that he had worked with Mitchell and other core civil rights lobbyists to edit his testimony "to make certain that [he] didn't say anything that would offend anybody in the Conference" and assured Aronson that its contents "more or less followed the Leadership Conference Executive Committee release" that had been issued some weeks earlier.[23] Aronson pointed out that Rauh's appearance ran counter to a decision at the last Executive Committee meeting to have organizations submit testimony individually rather than "make a unified presentation." Moreover, he wrote, had Wilkins's office in fact reached out to him, "I would have voiced my strong opinion regarding the necessity of seeking prior approval from the cooperating organizations." As in his response to the Maryland division controversy, Aronson justified this view in terms of an overriding need to protect member groups' autonomy. Acknowledging the "cumbersome and tedious" nature of the LCCR's approval-seeking process, he maintained that this process was nevertheless "prerequisite to the success of any mechanism which seeks to coordinate, as does the Leadership Conference, a number of organizations, each of which jealously guards its autonomy." His concern, in other words, was less that Rauh may have departed from the coalition position in the substance of his testimony than that "the failure to follow our customary procedures might have repercussions that would be damaging to the future of the Leadership Conference."[24]

For Aronson in particular, such deference to member organizations' autonomy may have been influenced by developments within his home organization. NCRAC had been founded as a coalition of Jewish community councils and national organizations during the mid-1940s and, in 1950, its leadership commissioned a study of the American Jewish organizational sector and NCRAC's role as a coordinating agency within it. The ensuing report made several controversial recommendations, including the designation of specialized roles to each national organization and a greater centralization of authority within NCRAC with decisions made by a majority vote of its participating organizations. The AJC and ADL, two of the most prominent national Jewish organizations (and, incidentally, founding members of the LCCR with Executive Committee representation), disaffiliated from NCRAC, citing a desire to preserve their autonomy to determine their own agendas and activities. While other national organizations remained in NCRAC and some even applauded the recommendations, the prevailing sense was that this effort to promote efficacy and unity within Jewish organizational life had backfired—that, if anything, it had exacerbated interorganizational tension and made groups even more prone to duplicate each other's activities rather than collaborate.[25]

But Aronson was not alone in upholding the LCCR's strong commitment to member organizations' autonomy, and even he seems to have been optimistic at first about the possibility of broad-based unity and consensus negotiation among the full roster of participating groups. As mentioned in Chapter 2, a campaign to pressure the Republican and Democratic Parties to adopt strong civil rights platform planks was the first major initiative to grow out of the February 1952 conference that gave the LCCR its name. The Leadership Conference Steering Committee began working on proposed platform language in March of that year and, in May, Aronson circulated a draft for consideration by all of the conference's cosponsoring organizations. "It is our hope," he wrote in a cover memo, "that the 52 organizations participating in the Leadership Conference can be united around an agreed upon plank in order that we may be able to exert maximum pressure in support of our organization." To this end, he requested "comments and suggestions" on the draft, along with "an indication as to whether your organization may be listed among those endorsing it."[26]

Subsequent developments dashed his initial optimism. A few weeks after Aronson circulated the draft platform plank, Mike Masaoka, the JACL lobbyist, noted that his organization would not accede to any proposal that denounced the controversial Immigration and Nationality (McCarran-Walter) Act of 1952, as its path to citizenship for Asian immigrants was a "definite improvement" over their long-standing exclusion from naturalization.[27] With just over a month to the Republican National Convention, time was of the essence and other member organizations would have opposed anything short of an outright condemnation of the law, which promised to further entrench the discriminatory principles that informed the national origins immigration quotas that had been adopted during the 1920s.[28] Rather than attempt to develop platform language that would be acceptable to all parties, immigration was dropped from the proposed civil rights plank altogether and a separate, rephrased "Immigration and Naturalization" statement that both supported naturalization for Asian immigrants and decried the quota system without naming the McCarran-Walter Act was circulated to member organizations "for informational purposes only."[29]

Plans for the February 1952 conference and the LCCR's subsequent campaign for congressional rules reform likewise elicited reactions from member organizations that tempered coalition leaders' ambitious plans for mobilizing a united front. Concerned for their tax-exempt status, two organizations that had already signed on as cosponsors of the February event signaled they might withdraw when a letter from Walter White indicated that the upcoming conference would seek to "make known to the members of Congress and to the political leaders our firm intention of holding them accountable in the 1952 election, both as individuals and as parties."³⁰ Sol Rabkin, director of the ADL's Legal Department, and Ed Lukas, the AJC's Civil Rights Program director, both replied with concern about this wording. According to Rabkin, the ADL "consistently followed a policy of not involving ourselves in political [as opposed to educational] activity, as well as taking a position which might in any way be interpreted as a partisan political one." It "shall be unable to participate," he added, if the conference's purpose was in fact as White had stated.³¹ Lukas similarly wrote that the AJC has "scrupulously avoided, and will continue to avoid, any political activities in connection with civil rights" and that it "would be unable to engage . . . in the conference . . . as a sponsor or otherwise, so long as the purpose of that conference continues to be described in the manner contained in [White's] letter."³² Subsequent communications took pains to assure them and others that participation in the conference would not entail political action. Wilkins's reply clarified that "the purpose of the 1952 Leadership Conference on Civil Rights is strictly an educational one" and that its "primary objective . . . is to assemble, discuss, and disseminate the kind of educational information . . . that will accomplish a change." He added that "the conference itself will not deal with political action" and that "whatever political activity is decided upon by those organizations which are free to engage in it, will be a matter for their individual group action after the conclusion of the conference and wholly apart from its deliberations."³³ A letter thanking organizations for their sponsorship a few weeks after the event reaffirmed that "the Conference was strictly an educational phase of the campaign for the entire civil rights program" and that the ensuing "political action phase" would "be undertaken by those sponsoring organizations whose programs permit such activity."³⁴

Finally, experience with other postwar civil rights coalitions, especially the perpetually frustrating NCPFEPC, was still fresh in LCCR officials' minds as they embarked on their new coalition building project during the mid-1950s. The structure and operating principles of the early LCCR were in some ways a pendulum swing away from the NCPFEPC's most aggravating features. In contrast to the NCPFEPC's sprawling federated structure and split focus on federal and state-level FEPC laws, for example, the Leadership Conference maintained a strict focus on national civil rights legislation, limited its membership to national organizations, and resisted suggestions that it establish state-level branches. Similarly, the decision to administer the Leadership Conference on a voluntary basis without headquarters or staff obviated the perpetual fund-raising and personnel management challenges that plagued NCPFEPC officials throughout the late 1940s.

## Implications for Civil Rights Lobbying

As far as Leadership Conference officials were concerned, the state of affairs described in the last section was on balance beneficial. In contrast to the minutes of top-level NCPFEPC meetings during the mid- to late 1940s, records of the LCCR's Executive Committee interactions suggest that they were not bogged down by fund-raising or administrative concerns. With no dedicated personnel to manage or headquarters to maintain, coalition leaders could concentrate on substantive matters. They likewise saw little need to seek contributions from member groups or otherwise pressure them to partake in coalition maintenance, facilitating a win-win scenario for the Leadership Conference: coalition membership was effectively costless and hassle-free for most organizations, giving them little incentive to reconsider their membership on a roster that coalition leaders could—and frequently did—point to as evidence of broad-based support for civil rights legislation. As a result, and despite a somewhat abashed tone in describing the extent of the LCCR's informality in his March 1962 letter to Ahmann, Aronson defended the status quo: "I believe that our success in working together for almost 13 years now derives in large measure from the informal nature of the Leadership Conference."[35]

But even as Aronson asserted that "any attempt for a more formal structure and method of procedure would . . . make it difficult for many of the organizations which have been cooperating to affiliate," he acknowledged that the status quo was "rather inefficient."[36] As might be expected, noncolocation of LCCR officers, geographic distance between administrative and legislative affairs leadership, and the lack of codified procedures, headquarters, and clerical staff yielded some administrative strain and confusion. Many member organizations were oblivious, or at least relatively untouched, by this circumstance. It was disconcerting for some that were more centrally involved, however. Indeed, frustration stemming from the LCCR's lack of standard operating procedures was at the heart of the National Council of Jewish Women's decision to disaffiliate from formal membership in the coalition despite its active role in the Executive Committee and coalition lobbying efforts during the mid-1950s.[37]

The LCCR's structural and operational limitations also affected its substantive work. Limited manpower and lack of robust means for consultation with member organizations meant that the Leadership Conference maintained a fairly circumscribed lobbying agenda.[38] Though in principle committed to the advancement of civil rights generally, in practice the LCCR of the 1950s and early 1960s focused exclusively on racial civil rights—and then only on selected legislative initiatives within that ambit. As recounted earlier, this narrowing began early on, when immigration reform was dropped from the LCCR's proposed party platform plank in 1952 because of member organizations' incompatible positions on the McCarran-Walter Act. The plank it submitted to the parties four years later reflected a similar tendency to restrict the LCCR's purview rather than negotiate common ground among its members. Two priorities that had been included in 1952—Alaska and Hawaii statehood and home rule for Washington, DC—were quickly eliminated from the 1956 proposal in light of some Executive Committee members' sense that they were "not truly civil rights measures."[39] A draft plank without these provisions was completed in late May and circulated to all member groups for feedback about a week later.[40] Even after this rare attempt at consultation, however, Executive Committee members remained leery of extrapolating policy details from general pro–civil rights positions without member organizations' express consent.[41] The fourth of the draft plank's eight points—a call for "congressional action to reduce the representation in Congress of those states that arbitrarily abridge the right to vote on account of race or color"—drew particular concern because the Executive Committee sensed that many member organizations did not maintain an official position on the issue, and it was excluded from all subsequent versions.[42]

The LCCR's quadrennial efforts to influence the national parties' civil rights platform planks were its most intensive campaigns during this period. In 1960 in particular, its work paid off in the form of platforms that, according to Aronson, were "by all odds the strongest in history"—an outcome he attributed in part to LCCR members' "united support of a single comprehensive and detailed set of proposals."[43] But while the Leadership Conference did have some success at shaping the parties' platform positions, it was consistently less equipped to influence which bills pro–civil rights senators and representatives would prioritize during the long periods between party conventions. With limited manpower, irregular Executive Committee meetings, and a long-standing commitment to advocate for rules reform as a means of making Congress institutionally hospitable to civil rights legislation, the LCCR was always behind the curve when it came to identifying a substantive lobbying agenda at the start of a legislative session. Nor was the Leadership Conference of this period prepared to spring into action in response to emergent legislative developments. It typically took at least a week to convene the Executive Committee, as Wilkins and Aronson would have to identify a mutually agreeable date and time to meet, secure a meeting location in New York or Washington, and circulate announcements with enough notice for committee members to plan their own attendance or designate a representative to attend on their behalf.[44]

While the Executive Committee did occasionally act immediately in its own name after meeting, there was usually additional lag time between the Executive Committee's decision to act and the implementation of its plans. Some activities—for example, producing new educational materials or staging broad-based lobbying events—would obviously take time, but even releasing a prepared statement required at least several days to solicit endorsements from member groups. An inevitable trade-off would ensue: signaling broad support for Leadership Conference positions would entail gathering as many endorsements as possible, but rarely could much additional time be spared to wait for fifty-odd groups, each with its own internal process for appraising such requests, to weigh in. As a result, rarely if ever did more than half of the LCCR's member organizations sign on to press releases, legislative testimonies, or other public position statements.

More generally, the early LCCR's capacity to activate member organizations for concerted action was limited. There were, in effect, two LCCR coalitions: the select group of organizations represented by officials and lobbyists who collaborated with some frequency—however variable—to administer the coalition, identify coalition legislative priorities, craft responses to emergent developments, and engage in direct lobbying; and the long roster of fifty-odd member groups that officially participated in the Leadership Conference but were rarely engaged in its decision-making or advocacy activities. There was no organizational infrastructure connecting the top-level and broader coalitions. Consequently, while the Leadership Conference could always—and often did—point to a large, heterogeneous set of allies committed to civil rights reform in principle, it was not well poised to coordinate their position taking on specific legislative proposals or mobilize their professional and grassroots lobbying resources for concerted action.

## Civil Rights Lobbying from *Brown* to the Civil Rights Act of 1957

While most efforts to secure civil rights reform through legislation during the LCCR's first decade were frustrated, there was one significant legislative achievement: the Civil Rights Act of 1957, which empowered the attorney general to seek injunctions to protect voting rights, established a Civil Rights Division within the Department of Justice, and authorized a new Civil Rights Commission to investigate and make recommendations to mitigate civil rights infringements.[45] The Civil Rights Act of 1957 was a far cry from civil rights advocates' ideal legislation, to be sure. Even in its most robust prepassage form, its focus on bureaucratic capacity to enforce voting rights meant that it addressed just a small slice of the legislative agenda pro–civil rights legislators and lobbyists had promoted since the late 1940s. It passed in substantially weakened form, moreover, with two changes in particular undercutting the original thrust of the bill: a jury trial amendment and the removal of Part III, which would have granted broad authority to the attorney general to file civil rights suits. But, despite these limitations, it was the first federal civil rights law passed in the twentieth century, and its passage marked a momentous breakthrough—both in the development of civil rights policy generally and for the Leadership Conference and its member organizations, who finally enjoyed their first legislative victory after years of fruitless lobbying.

The remainder of this chapter examines the LCCR's activity leading up to the Civil Rights Act of 1957's passage. As Morsell acknowledged in response to a query about the LCCR's achievements, "estimates of success in legislation, and particularly of the importance of relative contributions to success, are hazardous."[46] The goal of this discussion, therefore, is less to attribute credit or blame for legislative outcomes than to illustrate how the early LCCR's organizational style shaped its capacity for marshaling the resources of its member groups in pursuit of their shared interest in securing civil rights legislation.

As others have detailed, efforts to achieve this legislative breakthrough spanned two Congresses: During the 84th Congress (1955–1956), the House of Representatives passed H.R. 627, a bill containing the Dwight D. Eisenhower administration's proposal for four provisions to protect voting rights and shore up the civil rights machinery within the federal bureaucracy, but it succumbed in the Senate as the 1956 legislative session came to a close. The 85th Congress (1957–1958) enacted H.R. 6127, an ultimately weakened version of the administration bill, during its first session.[47] The discussion here begins at the start of the 84th Congress. It considers, first, the LCCR's generally aimless struggle to identify coalition priorities and pressure legislators to act in support of civil rights during the 1955 congressional session. It then turns to the legislative developments of 1956 and 1957 to examine how the Leadership Conference sought to mobilize member groups for collaborative lobbying once consideration of the bills that would become the Civil Rights Act of 1957 was underway.

## *Lobbying for Civil Rights during the 1955 Legislative Session*

Nearly two years had passed since the decision to maintain the Leadership Conference as a permanent interest group coalition when the 84th Congress convened for its first session in January 1955. It was the first legislative session after the Supreme Court's historic ruling in *Brown v. Board of Education* and, in addition to its broader legal significance, the decision to overturn the long-standing "separate but equal" doctrine recast the possibilities for civil rights reform through legislation. "If the Court was correct in holding the fourteenth amendment does not prohibit segregation," AJCon lawyers Will Maslow and Joseph B. Robison wrote about a year prior to the ruling, "Congress apparently has no power to take such action." In turn—and in contrast to litigators—legislative lobbyists could pursue only "a limited fight against segregation."[48] The LCCR's platform plank proposal in 1952 reflected this understanding. In contrast to its unqualified calls for the parties to endorse federal legislation to end employment discrimination, lynching, and poll taxes (that is, civil rights violations that did not rely on separate facilities for their perpetration), the section on segregation advocated limited reform that would not run afoul of the judicially sanctioned status quo:

> We pledge our efforts to the prohibition by law of segregation in *interstate* transportation and the elimination of segregation by legislative or executive action in all *activities of the Federal Government* and in all *areas to which Federal authority extends*, including among others: the armed forces, all federal agencies, the District of Columbia and the Panama Canal Zone and all other territories and possessions.[49]

*Brown* opened the prospect for a broader range of possibilities—and a potential opportunity for the LCCR to set the tone for a new civil rights legislative agenda. As this section shows, however, Executive Committee members struggled to gain traction in their efforts to identify coalition priorities and urge Congress to act on any of the proposals pro–civil rights senators and representatives put forward on their own.

The Leadership Conference had been basically inactive from mid-1953 until the end of 1954, when the Executive Committee finally met to consider "plans and programs in connection with the 84th Congress."[50] For about a month after this meeting, they concentrated their energies on an intensive but ultimately ill-fated push for Senate rules reform at the start of the 84th Congress.[51] By the time the Executive Committee came together again on February 2, 1955, to plan their next steps, a bipartisan group of senators had already introduced a package of eleven civil rights bills.[52] As the agenda that was circulated several days prior to the bills' introduction indicates, the main focus of the meeting was to be "the strategy and program of the Leadership Conference in the 84th Congress."[53] But the Senate civil rights package was introduced in the interim, preempting any agenda-setting intentions and posing a conundrum to the Executive Committee. On the one hand, its members felt bound to support the proposed bills, which promised significant reform. Withholding support, moreover, would alienate precisely those senators on whom they relied most to advance their legislative goals. On the other hand, they feared a repeat of the 83rd Congress's failure to act on any of the civil rights legislative proposals that had been introduced in 1953 and worried that simply endorsing the Senate civil rights package would not generate sufficient pressure to produce a better outcome.[54]

The meeting participants staked out a rhetorical position that conveyed this sentiment readily enough. The statement they sent the bills' sponsors observed that the 1955 package encompassed "the same bills introduced in previous Congresses" and offered that the LCCR would support them as it had in the past but added that "the task is not the introduction of this legislation, but the getting of it to the floor of the Senate for debate and passage." It further emphasized that the Leadership Conference advocated "not merely the holding of hearings and the issuance of favorable reports by committees, but action on the floor of the House and the Senate, and the actual passage of needed civil rights legislation."[55] They were far less decisive about how to proceed in more practical terms, however. Nathaniel Goodrich, who represented the AJC at the meeting, reported that the discussion "seemed to be headed for deadlock after three hours of talk."[56] The focus was less on legislative strategy—indeed, Goodrich noted, "after all the talk little had been said on strategy and tactics"—than on a felt need to restore a sense of urgency to the pursuit of civil rights reform among LCCR members.[57] Various approaches were proposed and debated and only a "tentative agreement" to convene a strategy conference for organizational leaders "sometime in April" had been reached by the end of the meeting.[58] In the meantime, a subcommittee would draft "a document setting forth the overall civil rights picture," and the full Executive Committee would regroup on February 23 to review their draft and begin making arrangements for a spring event.[59]

The February 23 meeting was postponed "due to a delay in preparing the document,"[60] and when the Executive Committee finally did reconvene on March 3, the subcommittee's products sparked heated debate. An eight-page memorandum noted at the outset that there had been "strong difference of opinion" among subcommittee members with respect to some contents, including the basis used to prioritize the listing of various civil rights measures and the inclusion of Washington, DC, home rule and Alaska and Hawaii statehood as legislative priorities.[61] The memorandum went on to review pertinent legislative developments, including both the failure to achieve filibuster reform and procedural and other hurdles that had felled the various civil rights measures that had been proposed since the 1940s, and it concluded with a call for electoral pressure:

> The individuals and groups who favor civil rights legislation must make it clear to those who seek their votes and support in elections that they view civil rights as important. . . . Roll call votes on the measures in the eleven part civil rights package should be demanded . . . [since] these roll-call votes are needed to assist voters in the 1956 elections in telling their friends from their enemies.[62]

Sandy Bolz, Washington counsel for the AJCon and a member of the subcommittee, prepared a separate document that offered what he called a "realistic evaluation of the political situation on civil rights legislation."[63] While not quite a dissent from the largely nonprescriptive subcommittee memorandum, Bolz's addendum argued forcefully that the LCCR "should *now* make a complete reappraisal" of its legislative priorities, "with a view to shifting our strategy from all-out insistence on an all or nothing program of compulsory FEPC etc. etc." to a more limited one focused on "moderate civil rights measures . . . for the purpose of achieving . . . at least some accomplishment . . . instead of retaining all civil rights measures as unenacted issues."[64]

While some at the meeting agreed that even minuscule legislative success would boost lobbying momentum and make it easier to sustain enthusiasm for civil rights, others feared that advocating a scaled-back legislative package would imply that previous failures had been due to advocacy groups' intransigence rather than obstructionism in Congress. Still others worried that failure to specify coalition priorities because of this disagreement would lead to "everyone . . . pushing in different directions."[65] Effectively back at square one, the meeting participants determined that the LCCR should maintain support for the Senate civil rights package, but that it should simultaneously "seek to fix responsibility for determining the order in which the various measures . . . should be pursued, the legislative strategy to be employed, and the methods for overcoming the filibuster, on Congressional leaders and those who . . . had opposed any effort to adopt new Senate rules." To this end, the Executive Committee would delegate the coalition's most esteemed organizational officials to meet with congressional and party leaders and, in the context of a broader campaign to bolster grassroots support for civil rights reform, they would subsequently convene the April conference that had been suggested at the previous month's meeting.[66]

Implementation of these plans was uneven. A promotional pamphlet to raise public awareness of the legislative situation was drafted fairly quickly,[67] but printing was delayed for several months after objections were raised by the AJC's Publications Division staff, who had been commissioned to produce it.[68] Meanwhile, the top-level meetings with legislative and party leaders never materialized. Wilkins attributed the failure to convene these meetings to "the unavailability of the heads of some of the major participating organizations,"[69] but regardless of the reason, it meant that the Leadership Conference effectively forfeited its plan to take this first step toward developing a coalition lobbying agenda. No convocation of member organizations was held in April—or anytime that year—and the Executive Committee itself did not meet again until mid-July, when the 1955 legislative session was nearing a close.

The Senate package and other civil rights bills that had been introduced at the start of the Congress saw practically no progress in the meantime. While some groups did work individually to wrestle them out of committee, there is no evidence of LCCR-led collaboration to lobby on their behalf. A new opportunity emerged in May 1955, when Representative Adam Clayton Powell Jr. succeeded at amending a bill to strengthen the military reserves (H.R. 5297) with a provision that would restrict proposed personnel transfers to National Guard units that did not "exclude or segregate against any person on the basis of race, creed, color, or national origin."[70] This amendment resembled other "Powell amendments," which sought to condition federal funding on racial integration, and which were divisive for liberals who were otherwise supportive of civil rights.[71] The Leadership Conference did not get involved until the issue was broached at President Eisenhower's June 8, 1955, press conference, where the president deemed the amendment "extraneous" to the bill's substantive purpose and contended that "it is entirely erroneous" to seek civil rights reform in such a manner.[72] Two days later, the LCCR released a statement in the name of the Executive Committee. Carefully worded to avoid taking a stance on the Powell amendment strategy per se, the statement disputed Eisenhower's negative assessment of the amendment's substantive relevance. In line with concerns that had been raised at the February and March 1955 meetings that civil rights advocates would be blamed for obstructionism, it also stressed that responsibility for Congress's failure to act lay with "the bloc of Senators and Representatives that . . . says it will kill any bill for military reserve service that bars social segregation." Notably, the statement did not call for any particular action on the part of Congress or the president; its focus was squarely on assigning blame for inaction to "the die-hard pro-segregationists in the Congress."[73] Nor did the Leadership Conference take further action on the matter. A few days after the statement was released, John Gunther suggested that the Executive Committee meet "to work out a plan of action so that there will be no doubt as to where the responsibility lies if Civil Rights issues are buried in political expediencies."[74] No meeting was held, however, and H.R. 2597 was scuttled in favor of H.R. 7000, a similar bill that did not contain the National Guard provision and was therefore less susceptible to Powell's attempt at amendment.[75]

The Executive Committee's meeting on July 19, 1955, was prompted by invitations to several LCCR member organizations to participate in subcommittee hearings on forty-four civil rights bills that had been introduced in the House earlier that year. It was roundly understood that the hearings would not yield enacted legislation that late in the legislative session; in one UAW lobbyist's vivid assessment, "this political raz ma tazz will probably have little more meaning than the antlers on a cast iron deer."[76] Nevertheless, the hearings did present an opportunity for organizations to showcase the breadth of support for civil rights reform and, perhaps, to reinvigorate the issue after a frustrating year without progress on the legislative front.

Aronson's summary of the meeting records "a clear consensus . . . that ground [had] been lost" since the Executive Committee's last meeting more than four months earlier and a sense that, while partisan wrangling in Congress was surely to blame, civil rights allies more broadly—including "many of the participating organizations" of the LCCR—had deprioritized the achievement of civil rights in favor of other legislative goals.[77] The meeting participants devised an action plan that reflected this diagnosis but also underscored their continual failure to identify the coalition's legislative priorities. For example, they agreed that "as many organizations as possible" should seek to testify before the subcommittee "in order to demonstrate the continued and widespread concern for civil rights legislation." Rather than endorse any particular legislative proposal, however, testifying organizations should reiterate the theme the Executive Committee had sounded earlier that year in its response to the eleven-bill civil rights package that had been introduced in the Senate; in Aronson summary:

> it was recommended . . . that organizations not attempt to provide detailed analyses of the many bills before the subcommittee or to designate priorities among them. Instead, it was suggested that the testimony emphasize that all of the bills before the subcommittee have been repeatedly endorsed . . . [and] that the goal of the organizations comprising the Leadership Conference is not the introduction of civil rights legislation, nor the holding of hearings . . . but action on the floor of the House and the Senate and the actual *passage* of overdue and needed civil rights legislation *in the 84th Congress.*[78]

Outside lobbying initiatives would likewise highlight the extent of support for civil rights without focusing on any specific legislative objectives. A statement for release to the press at the conclusion of the legislative session "over the signatures of the heads of as many of the participating organizations as possible" would urge "floor debate and a vote in both the House and Senate early in the 2nd session as a test of individual and party sincerity on civil rights," but no particular bill or policy goal was identified as the object of these actions. State and local events with "sponsorship . . . as broadly based as possible" would be staged during the intersession recess "as a demonstration of grassroots disappointment at congressional inaction on civil rights and of the demand for such action at the beginning of the next session," but here again, the nature of "such action" was unspecified.[79]

## Lobbying for Civil Rights in 1956 and 1957

Despite its failure to identify concrete legislative objectives, the Executive Committee's July 1955 plans did lay the groundwork for a series of awareness raising activities well into the next year. Twelve cities hosted LCCR-sponsored Bill of Rights Day rallies on December 15, 1955, which sought to "demonstrate the breadth and the intensity of the demand for civil rights legislation in the next session of the Congress."[80] And, as 1956 got underway, Leadership Conference officials began planning a three-day conference akin to the NECRM event its charter organizations had cosponsored in 1950. Some were discouraged enough by low turnout at the Bill of Rights Day events to question the advisability of planning a mass gathering that could backfire if poorly attended; nevertheless, the Executive Committee elected to forge ahead with plans to convene organizational delegates representing as many states and congressional districts as possible in early March "as a public demonstration of support for whatever legislation has been reported or is about to be reported . . . at that time."[81] The National Delegate Assembly for Civil Rights, as the March 4–6, 1956, event was called, ultimately brought about two thousand organizational delegates to Washington for meetings with their representatives and plenary sessions featuring legislative briefings by core lobbyists, a board of inquiry into the abridgment of constitutional rights in recent episodes of racial violence in the South, and presentations by national party and congressional leaders.[82] It also revitalized the Executive Committee's stalled efforts to identify a substantive program for the coalition. Bert Seidman, who attended on behalf of AFL-CIO Civil Rights Director Boris Shishkin, reported that "there was considerable discussion of plans for follow-up on the Civil Rights Assembly" and that there was an emerging consensus that "the Leadership Conference could function most effectively on legislative issues and related administrative policies of the Executive agencies."[83] Shortly after the event, Aronson invited Executive Committee members to a long meeting on March 20 and 21 to develop a plan for facilitating action on several bills that were making headway in Congress and begin preparing to pressure the Republican and Democratic Parties to adopt strong civil rights platform planks at their upcoming national conventions.[84]

The timing of these events was unfortunate, as the Eisenhower administration finally put forth its own civil rights legislative proposal on April 9, 1956, just over a month after the National Delegate Assembly—and so just over a month too late for the assembly to have been of use as a coordinating device for lobbying on what would soon become the centerpiece of civil rights legislative activity. Leadership Conference officials could not have anticipated this development, to be sure. As John Weir Anderson recounts in a case study of the Civil Rights Act of 1957's origins, the four bills that composed the administration's proposal were "written entirely within the [Justice] Department; not only did the Department decline to ask for congressional advice, but it gave congressmen no hint of the direction in which its draftsmen were moving. . . . Nor did the Department consult lobbying organizations in the field."[85] As a result, the administration bills came generally as a surprise—not only to the LCCR and its affiliated lobbyists, but also to pro-civil rights members of Congress, some of whom were still trying to gain traction on other bills they had introduced earlier; in fact, on the same day the administration bills were delivered, Representative James Roosevelt had assembled some thirty-five organizational lobbyists to discuss how they might help achieve progress on pending civil rights legislation.[86]

Once introduced in the House of Representatives, the administration bills were referred to the House Judiciary Committee, which elected to combine and substitute them for the original contents of H.R. 627, an omnibus civil rights bill that had covered similar ground among other sweeping provisions. By late May, the consolidated bill was reported out and referred to the Rules Committee, where it seemed set to languish indefinitely. The need for extraordinary measures to wrest civil rights legislation from the Rules Committee was well anticipated and coordination among civil rights lobbyists to secure discharge petition signatures began weeks in advance, but all records indicate that this was at Roosevelt's behest rather than a Leadership Conference initiative.[87] The only evidence of any LCCR-led effort to mobilize coalition resources for this purpose is a lone telegram sent to member groups' national offices on June 5, when the discharge petition was filed, requesting they "advise local units" that "every [House] member should be urged immediately by wire or by special [delivery] to sign petition."[88] On June 13, a day before the deadline to secure the requisite signatures for House floor consideration of the bill that month, the Leadership Conference released a statement announcing that it was "polling all members of the House of Representatives to determine who has signed Petition #5 to discharge the House Rules Committee from further consideration of H.R. 627" and reported the names of those "who have informed the organizations affiliated with the [Leadership] Conference that they have signed the petition."[89] But while this last-ditch statement did highlight the size of the LCCR's roster and attendance at its recent delegate assembly, there is no record of any concerted campaign to enlist member organizations in securing petition signature commitments either before or after its release.[90] Aronson's notes on an Executive Committee meeting the next day suggest that LCCR leaders were preoccupied with finalizing their platform plank proposal for review and endorsement by member organizations; while John Gunther did provide an update on the status of H.R. 627, discussion both before and after his report focused on the upcoming party conventions.[91]

This approach continued when H.R. 627 finally returned to the House floor in mid-July. Apart from a single memorandum informing member organizations of the bill's contents and exhorting that "all members of the House should be urged to vote for H.R. 627 in its present form and be present on the floor throughout the debate in order to prevent the adoption of crippling amendments," there does not seem to have been any real drive to engage groups in the lobbying effort.[92] A detailed chronology prepared by UAW legislative representative Paul Sifton notes that "the same groups [that had participated in lobbying for discharge petition signatures] continued to urge House Members to vote for the bill"; his account clearly states, however, that collaboration among lobbyists for these groups was "at the request of Representative Roosevelt (D., Cal.) and [Hugh] Scott (R., Pa.)" rather than the Leadership Conference.[93]

House passage of H.R. 627 was all but assured,[94] as was its subsequent failure in the Senate, which proved divisive for civil rights supporters. With mere days left before the end of the session, some—including three stalwart senators and a number of LCCR member organizations, including the NAACP, ADA, and UAW—were determined to force "some sort of Senate roll call showdown" on the bill.[95] But others, including the AFL-CIO and many senators who could normally be counted on to support civil rights legislation, were reluctant to jeopardize other bills for what would ultimately be a symbolic vote on the civil rights measure. With such a short time to act and substantive disagreement among core member organizations, the Leadership Conference was not in a position to coordinate lobbying at this point in the legislative process. An LCCR press release on July 25 announced that fifteen organizations, including "national labor, veterans, minority and civic groups," had sent a telegram urging senators to "take up the House-passed civil rights bill" and asserting that "votes on procedural motions to bring up the bill are votes on civil rights."[96] But this initiative was not a product of Executive Committee deliberation, nor was it circulated to all member groups for approval; rather, as Sifton's chronology reports, "organizations actively working for Senate action on HR 627 met and agreed to recommend to their organizations joint signature of the . . . short wire to Senators."[97]

The bill succumbed in the Senate later that night to a 76–6 vote against a motion to adjourn briefly so as to usher in a new legislative day, which would have provided an opportunity to bring it to the floor. As others have highlighted, this was the culmination of a procedural standoff between Senate Majority Leader Lyndon Johnson, who was intent on holding intraparty conflict over civil rights at bay, and Paul Douglas of Illinois, one of the three senators pushing for floor action on the civil rights bill.[98] But Sifton's timeline suggests that division within liberal ranks—including among civil rights lobbyists—compounded Douglas's challenge. Active lobbying by the AFL-CIO against bringing the bill to the floor, he wrote, "gave wavering Senators a pretext for abandoning action on HR 627."[99] In a cover memorandum to UAW President Walter Reuther, Sifton offered this final analysis:

> Because inside and outside the Senate forces usually considered liberal were divided, Senators Douglas, Lehman and Hennings received less support than they should have had. . . . Sheer lack of manpower inside the Senate made it impossible to . . . get a vote, except on the snap roll call into which the three Senators were trapped by Johnson late Tuesday night.[100]

Though disheartening, H.R. 627's failure helped to finally concretize the LCCR's lobbying agenda going into the 85th Congress. In contrast to 1955 and 1956, when Leadership Conference officials had struggled to chart a substantive course forward, the bill's success in the House coupled with a relatively favorable reception for the Senate rules reform campaign at the start of the 85th Congress empowered them to assert a clear legislative mission in 1957: namely, to secure legislation at least as strong as the civil rights bill the House had passed the previous year. It was also at this juncture that Mitchell and Gunther began convening regular meetings of the fifteen most active civil rights lobbyists, who quickly developed a working system for an ongoing division of labor and information sharing.[101]

Otherwise, though, the LCCR's structure and operating procedures remained as they had been since the coalition's inception; in turn, its central leadership was still poorly equipped to react quickly to emerging legislative developments and to mobilize member organizations' resources for concerted action. Early evidence of this continued state of affairs came soon after the 85th Congress got underway. House subcommittee hearings slated to begin in the first week of February were announced on January 23. The next day, Aronson circulated a notice announcing that a meeting of the Executive Committee would take place a full week later, on January 30.[102] A memorandum sent to member organizations two days after this meeting summarized the Executive Committee's view that organizations should not request time to testify individually to "avoid giving opponents any pretext for extending the hearings." Instead, Wilkins would testify "in behalf of as many of the organizations in the Leadership Conference as are willing to associate themselves in a joint statement," a draft of which was appended to the memorandum. Individual groups could still submit their own written testimony and, in these statements, should "express support for a bill similar to H.R. 627 as a *minimum meaningful civil rights measure*."[103] With just a long weekend to edit, print, circulate, and secure member groups' endorsements of Wilkins's statement prior to his scheduled appearance before the subcommittee, Aronson sent advance telegrams to key organizational personnel, informing them of the impending need for them to sign on: "Urge you be prepared to notify us by wire or telephone Monday [February 4] if your organization can join. Severe time shortage necessitates this procedure."[104] Nevertheless, just twenty-two groups—fewer than half of the LCCR's members—were prepared to endorse the joint statement in time for Wilkins's testimony, and just four others filed independent statements.[105] Only three more organizations added their names in time for Wilkins's testimony before the Senate Judiciary Committee's Constitutional Rights Subcommittee ten days later.[106]

Correspondence between Mitchell's Washington Bureau office and the legislative chairperson of one NAACP chapter who sought clarification on Wilkins's testimony suggests that organizational procedure rather than substantive disagreement was to blame for LCCR members' tepid response to the request for participation in the hearings. "News dispatches quoting Roy," she wrote, "refer to twenty-five cooperating organizations. We assume these to be the same group[s] that joined the 'Leadership Committee for Civil Rights' or whatever it was called. (We thought there were more than twenty-five.)"[107] Mitchell's secretary replied with lists of all LCCR members and of the twenty-two that endorsed both the House and Senate statements and offered this explanation: "The reason there were only 22 organizations which supported Mr. Wilkins's testimony is that . . . there was not enough time to contact all of the organizations and receive their answers before he testified."[108] It also yielded a quieter-than-expected signal of the extent of support for the Leadership Conference position, as suggested by this exchange at the start of Wilkins's testimony in the House:

> *The Chairman.* We will now hear from Mr. Roy Wilkins, executive secretary of the National Association for the Advancement of Colored People. It is my understanding, Mr. Wilkins, that you speak also for some 40 different organizations; is that correct?
> *Mr. Wilkins.* Twenty two, Mr. Chairman, to be accurate.[109]

While protracted Judiciary Committee consideration continued in the Senate, the House Judiciary Committee reported out H.R. 6127, a bill that, after some wrangling, was essentially the same as the version of H.R. 627 the House had passed in 1956. Unlike the previous year, LCCR officials did try to mobilize member organizations for participation in House floor debate on H.R. 6127. Soon after Rules Committee hearings began in early May, a memorandum from Aronson apprised member organizations of the legislative situation. In addition to suggesting that contact be made to encourage discharge petition signatures, the memorandum indicated—however optimistically in hindsight—that House floor debate seemed set to begin on May 20 and asked groups to identify delegates to assist with the direct lobbying effort at that time:

> It is most important that two or three individuals from each state be present, in order to help assure that [House] members remain on the floor during debate in the Committee of the Whole, to check on teller votes, and to help prevent the adoption of frivolous, as well as substantive amendments. Please send me immediately the names and addresses of persons from your organizations, and the states from which they come, who could be in Washington during floor debate.[110]

The Rules Committee finally voted to grant a rule on the civil rights bill on May 21, and lobbyists from the NAACP, ADA, UAW, and American Veterans Committee (AVC) met with House leaders the next day to negotiate the timing of H.R. 6127's arrival on the House floor. Per Gunther's report, the bill would be brought to the floor on June 5, with voting on amendments likely to take place "on the 11th or 12th." Eager to avoid "extensive delay through quorum calls" and the possibility of "frivolous amendments" to the bill, he suggested that Aronson "get a memorandum out immediately to the groups so that sufficient mail from home and individuals to help with the lobby job will be made available."[111]

The second memorandum, this time addressed from Wilkins and sent just a day before House floor consideration was set to begin, reiterated the call: "*It will be especially important* to have representatives of the participating organizations on hand in Washington for the two days of voting, for the purpose of aiding in the check-up on the teller vote. You are urged to arrange to send representatives to Washington." Wilkins added that arrangements were underway to ensure that those who took part in the effort would collaborate effectively:

> To coordinate this effort, the Leadership Conference on Civil Rights has secured a room at the Congressional Hotel . . . beginning Monday, June 10. A breakfast conference will take place there at 9 o'clock that morning, and the room will constitute a headquarters for the duration of the voting. Your representatives should make it their first contact upon arrival in Washington.[112]

The response was underwhelming, however. According to Gunther's report, only a handful of organizations ended up participating:

The UAW brought in a couple of guys from Michigan and one each from Illinois, Ohio, Pennsylvania, Massachusetts, Maryland and New Jersey. The AFL-CIO gave one man. . . . Ken Peterson worked all the time for the IUE [International Union of Electrical Workers], and they donated a couple of girls to work in the office. The NAACP had Mitchell and [Frank] Pohlhaus at the barricades all the time. Others who worked a good part of the time were [Kenneth] Birkhead from AVC and [Herman] Edelsberg from ADL, and that was that.

While the failure to drum up more organizational participation did not harm the bill's chances in the House—"everyone who knew anything about [the House fight] was confident at the outset," Gunther wrote—the Senate situation was far less auspicious. "If we are going to get any play in the Senate," Gunther concluded, "we really have to do better than this."[113]

There was some initial effort to "do better" in the Senate, which was well understood to be the site where H.R. 6127 might die (as H.R. 627 had in 1956) or emerge severely emasculated as a result of southern obstruction. Indeed, while southerners' designs to eliminate Part III and insert a jury trial amendment if they could not kill H.R. 6127 entirely had been made apparent early in the legislative process, it was only in the Senate that the threat became acute. As Senate consideration of the bill grew imminent, Wilkins invited LCCR member organizations to participate in "a special and urgent two-day session . . . to take stock and formulate plans and assignments which will promote successful Senate action on the civil rights bill." Urging groups to send those "from the highest feasible levels of their organizations" to the meeting, the invitation emphasized the need to give "assurance" to senators that "organizational support for the bill *as it stands* is positive and uncompromising." "It may be," Wilkins concluded, "that, when the record of the next several weeks is all in, this gathering of Leadership Conference organizations will turn out to have been the most important in its history."[114]

Correspondence prior to the event shows extensive coordination between LCCR leaders in New York, lobbyists on the ground in Washington, and key senators to maximize its effect. The program—which would engage participants in outside lobbying planning on July 17 followed by "strategic visits to certain senators" on the 18th—was the product of consultation by Aronson, Mitchell, and a staffer from Senator Douglas's office.[115] Mitchell's lobbyist committee met few days before the event was to begin and, in collaboration with Senator Douglas, arranged for a bipartisan group of pro–civil rights senators to meet with attendees and developed a carefully prioritized list of senators to target for visits by top organizational officials "who know them personally or represent groups with political strength in their states."[116] Nevertheless, while this event does appear to have generated several publicity-oriented outside lobbying initiatives,[117] there is no record of how many or which groups participated in the meetings and no evidence of any further attempt to engage LCCR members in the legislative process. The only coalition call to action against the proposed jury trial amendment was issued on July 16—that is, just prior to the July 17–18 meeting and well before debate and adoption of the amendment in August.[118] Two press releases subsequently announced organizational support for Senate passage and for swift resolution to any impasse over the bill's contents in conference committee; like the telegram sent at the end of the 1956 push for Senate action on H.R. 627, however, these statements were produced by the Washington committee rather than the LCCR leadership and bore the endorsements only of the sixteen organizations whose lobbyists participated in Mitchell's weekly meetings.[119]

LCCR officials did finally prepare a statement for release as congressional action on H.R. 6127 was completed. Asserting that the newly enacted legislation "can mean much or little depending on the people President Eisenhower appoints to carry out its provisions," the statement called on the president to act swiftly in appointing the new Department of Justice and Civil Rights Commission personnel so that voting rights enforcement "can be commenced at once." It affirmed the LCCR's commitment to "wholehearted cooperation" in these enforcement efforts but also emphasized its hope that the Civil Rights Act of 1957 would be merely "the beginning of a new era—an era in which the Congress of the United States will move steadily forward" with additional legislative civil rights reforms, for which the Leadership Conference would "continue unceasingly" to advocate.[120] As with previous such actions, the statement was circulated to coalition members with barely two days for them to review and sign onto it.[121] When the statement was released on September 1, it had been endorsed by just twenty-two organizations—fewer than half the roster of groups then affiliated with the Leadership Conference.[122]

## Conclusion

Soon after passage of the Civil Rights Act of 1957, its excised Part III became a rallying point for the Leadership Conference, whose core lobbyists and officers quickly turned their attention to making its achievement a priority for the 1958 legislative session.[123] These efforts were not successful. A proposed Civil Rights Act of 1958 gained little traction, and Part III was excluded once again from the Civil Rights Act of 1960, a severely emasculated enactment that barely enhanced the voting rights protections of the 1957 legislation. These efforts did, however, show a new assertiveness in the LCCR's efforts to shape the contents of civil rights legislative proposals. And, as the next chapter shows, the vaunted prioritization of Part III would be consequential several years later, when the Leadership Conference began advocating for strengthening amendments to the bill that would become the Civil Rights Act of 1964. But even while this initial legislative breakthrough gave shape to the civil rights lobbying agenda, its impact on the LCCR's organizational development was limited. As this chapter has shown, the Leadership Conference initially operated on an informal and ad hoc basis. In turn, it lacked capacity to mobilize groups for coordinated lobbying activity or otherwise capitalize on the resource potential of its large and diverse membership roster, undermining the sense of a broad united front in support of civil rights legislation. This did not change during the long fight to secure passage of the Civil Rights Act of 1957 or its aftermath; with the exception of the new Washington lobbyists committee, the Leadership Conference continued to operate as it always had well into the 1960s.

The early LCCR was not unique in this regard. In fact, the organizational structure and operating procedures reconstructed in this chapter resemble elements of the two late-twentieth-century arms-control lobbying coalitions Will Hathaway and David S. Meyer describe. Like the Leadership Conference of the 1950s and early 1960s, the Monday Lobby Group of the 1980s was "an informal entity with no offices, staff . . . and, most importantly, no fundraising of its own which might threaten member organizations." The Coalition for Arms Control likewise rejected a formal approach to coalition management two years after its 1983 founding. Despite a "growing realization that goals of the peace movement required a long-term struggle and a recognition that the coalition should be structured as a permanent organization rather than an ad hoc alliance," the Coalition for Arms Control opted "to defer such issues as office space and staff to the future" and "resisted momentum carrying the organization in the direction of institutionalization and instead placed limits on the coalition which left decision-making power with the individual organizations."[124] As these quotes intimate, concern with coalition survival was at the heart of the Monday Lobby Group and Coalition for Arms Control's organizational decisions of the—just as it was for the Leadership Conference officials who defended their own coalition's limited administrative wherewithal and overriding deference to member group autonomy. As Aronson and others saw it, a more robust operation would entail high maintenance costs and other demands that might lead groups to disaffiliate.

As this chapter has shown, however, sustaining a diverse interest group coalition by limiting its administrative apparatus and minimizing expectations for member groups' participation can also undercut its capacity to coordinate lobbying activity. Much as LCCR leaders could point to a motley listing of some fifty organizations whose coalition membership indicated their general agreement with the civil rights cause, they could not readily enjoin these groups to endorse coalition statements in support of specific legislative initiatives or otherwise mobilize their resources in pursuit of coalition objectives. To the extent that interest group coalitions' policy influence hinges on their capacity to mitigate legislative uncertainty by signaling broad, unified support for reform,[125] this limitation may be quite consequential. Instead of reassuring risk-averse policy makers, it may suggest—however inadvertently—that even those groups that are broadly supportive of reform are not convinced that a particular course of action is politically salable. Coalition leaders thus face a tradeoff in balancing survival and purposive goals. For the Leadership Conference of the 1950s and early 1960s, the balance tilted strongly in favor of the former. But as the next chapter recounts, the balance would change midway through 1963, when President John F. Kennedy's support for ambitious omnibus civil rights legislation precipitated significant changes to LCCR operations.

# 4

# The Unity among These Groups Is Truly Tremendous

Three days before the Civil Rights Act of 1964 was signed into law, Mike Masaoka recounted his participation in an intensive lobbying campaign for its passage in his biennial report as Washington representative for the Japanese American Citizens League (JACL). Apart from its substantive significance as "a meaningful and comprehensive civil rights package far beyond the expectations of even most civil rights advocates two years ago," Masaoka wrote, the new legislation marked a turning point within the interest group sector. "The National Leadership Conference on Civil Rights, bringing together almost a hundred national organizations representing almost every sector of American society—labor, veterans, business, civic, civil rights, religious, women, nationality, etc.," he asserted, "proved that different groups with generally different objectives and purposes, with varied organizational structures, can mobilize their total resources for a massive effort on the national legislative front."[1]

As a longtime participant in LCCR activities and an Executive Committee member during the early 1960s, Masaoka surely knew that the Leadership Conference had coordinated civil rights lobbying since the early 1950s and maintained a diverse membership roster throughout its existence.[2] His report to the JACL, rather, alludes to a transformation in the coalition's coordination capacity during its year-long campaign to strengthen and secure passage of the Civil Rights Act of 1964. The LCCR's first decade had been characterized by organizational limitations, as the last chapter describes. As Arnold Aronson wrote to the head of the National Catholic Conference for Interracial Justice in 1962, the Leadership Conference of the 1950s and 1960s had "no Constitution or Bylaws, no fixed dues schedule, no staff, and, indeed, no formal structure."[3] Its efforts to coordinate civil rights lobbying prior to June 1963 reflected this inchoate state of affairs. Episodic and slow to get off the ground, they were a far cry from the "total" resource mobilization for a "massive national effort" Masaoka's memorandum recounts. In contrast, the LCCR's campaign for the Civil Rights Act of 1964 was, according to one political scientist, "probably one of the . . . most powerful lobbies ever organized in United States political history."[4] As this chapter describes, new organizational practices implemented during the summer of 1963 facilitated this impressive showing. LCCR leaders' decision to open a Washington office and hire a professional staff both enhanced the coalition's administrative capacity and supported new coordinating mechanisms that enabled the Leadership Conference to engage member groups' professional lobbyists and grassroots supporters in a well-concerted struggle to strengthen the Civil Rights Act's provisions and shore up legislative support for its passage over the course of its yearlong journey through Congress.

The LCCR's new approach to coalition management was precipitated by President John F. Kennedy's decision to submit an omnibus civil rights bill to Congress in June 1963. As the first half of this chapter recounts, the Kennedy administration's outreach to interest groups for support of its newfound commitment to achieving civil rights reform through legislation prompted LCCR officials to invest in coalition infrastructure and develop new operating procedures that facilitated robust coordination on a sustained basis. The second half of the chapter turns to the lobbying campaign itself. This is not an exhaustive account of the Civil Rights Act's legislative odyssey or even of the activities the Leadership Conference pursued in support of its passage; rather, its purpose is to illustrate how the LCCR's organizational changes facilitated and sustained unprecedented coordination in pursuit of coalition goals.

## The Prospects for Civil Rights Legislation in the First Half of 1963

The year 1963 did not at first seem auspicious for civil rights lobbyists. Civil rights movement leaders were generally pessimistic as they reflected on the recent lack of progress on the legislative front, a sentiment Martin Luther King Jr. captured well in musing that 1962 had been "the year that civil rights was displaced as the dominant issue in domestic politics." Allowing that "the legislative struggle need not be a quixotic exercise in futility," he was nevertheless doubtful about its prospects and emphasized that that any favorable outcome would entail renewed commitment by public officials who had turned their attention to other issues. "If . . . the President is lethargic," he wrote, "the Republicans [in Congress] can be tranquil. They can content themselves merely with criticizing the President in absence of real challenge. If [and only if] civil rights is elevated to the urgency that trade, tax and military legislation enjoys, 1963 can be a year of achievement and not another annual experience with frustration."[5]

For the Leadership Conference, 1963 began with a mostly unsuccessful campaign for congressional rules reform. Hoping to succeed at last at eliminating procedural obstacles to the achievement of civil rights legislation—a priority since the coalition's founding a decade earlier—the Executive Committee met late in 1962 to sketch out plans for a nationwide lobbying campaign culminating in a rally in Washington, DC, at the start of the new Congress.[6] Ted Dudley, the AFL-CIO Speakers Bureau director, was assigned to lead this effort and, with a small cash advance from the NAACP and an office-space loan from the American Veterans Committee, he established a temporary headquarters in Washington's Dupont Circle neighborhood and began implementing the Executive Committee's plans.[7] A series of memorandums to member organizations set out the broad outlines of the campaign. The final weeks of 1962 would be dedicated to "nose counting" likely Senate votes for filibuster reform and House members' support for curbing the power of the Rules Committee. Dudley urged member groups to encourage state and local branches to contact legislators during the Christmas recess and report back so that he and other Washington-based lobbyists could target direct lobbying strategies appropriately. Small delegations of organizational representatives from each state would then convene in Washington for a Sunday evening briefing followed by two days of lobbying before the opening of the 88th Congress on Wednesday, January 9.[8]

Though more elaborate than previous rules reform drives, the 1963 effort was not much more successful. The House did vote to maintain the enlarged fifteen-member Rules Committee it had adopted for the 87th Congress, a modest and unexpected victory Dudley attributed to intensive lobbying by state delegations during the LCCR conference on January 7 and 8.[9] But the more significant procedural changes the Leadership Conference sought in the House—reinstatement of a 21-day rule to limit the Rules Committee's power to withhold favorably reported legislation from floor consideration and adoption of a 7-day rule to ensure timely authorization to send House-passed legislation to conference committee—were not even considered. A protracted fight over the vote threshold to invoke cloture was still ongoing in the Senate when Dudley closed the Washington headquarters in mid-January, and his report at that point described "very uncertain" prospects for achieving filibuster reform.[10]

The outlook for substantive civil rights legislation was barely more promising. Much as it had not been during his first two years in office, civil rights was not high among President Kennedy's legislative priorities at the outset of the 88th Congress.[11] He barely mentioned the issue in his 1963 State of the Union address, wherein only an assertion that "the right to vote in a free American election, must not be denied to any citizen on grounds of his race or color" and a nod to the "centennial year of Emancipation" signaled any commitment at all to a civil rights legislative program.[12] Pro-civil rights members of the House and Senate meanwhile introduced the usual complement of civil rights bills, but, in the absence of rules reform and presidential support, few expected they would gain much traction.

On February 28, Kennedy rounded off a series of agenda-setting special messages to Congress with a missive on civil rights. Again invoking the hundred-year anniversary of the Emancipation Proclamation, he urged Congress to consider legislation to aid desegregating schools, protect voting rights, and extend the Civil Rights Commission for four years.[13] Though the message exceeded expectations that the president would not propose even that much,[14] its limitations quickly came under fire. New York Governor Nelson Rockefeller, who at that point seemed likely to square off against Kennedy as the Republican nominee in the 1964 election, criticized the message in a rally sponsored by the New York State branch of the NAACP. While acknowledging "a step in the right direction," he maintained that it was "two years too late" and did not come close to fulfilling either the recommendations of the Civil Rights Commission or the civil rights commitments articulated in the Democratic Party's 1960 platform.[15] Representative Emanuel Celler, a Democrat from New York who had long been at the forefront of efforts to shepherd civil rights legislation through Congress, in turn accused Rockefeller of "mak[ing] a political football of civil rights" and undermining bipartisan cooperation on an issue that could not progress without it.[16]

Shortly after this exchange, eight Republican senators introduced a package of twelve far-reaching civil rights bills, including measures to protect voting rights, accelerate school desegregation, promote fair housing and employment practices, facilitate the administration of justice, and make the Civil Rights Commission a permanent agency. In a press release announcing their action on March 28, the senators echoed Rockefeller's view that Kennedy's stance was inadequate: "We regret that the President in his Special Message on Civil Rights last month . . . did not implement the [Civil Rights] Commission's recommendations," they wrote. "The Administration's proposals . . . fall far short of the Commission's recommendations and both national party platforms." Turning Kennedy's exhortations against him, they added, "The centennial of the Emancipation Proclamation merits a more comprehensive program. If the President will not assume the leadership in getting through Congress urgently-needed civil rights measures, we in Congress must take the initiative."[17]

By coincidence, the LCCR's Executive Committee met that same day. It is the only Executive Committee meeting I could find any record of for the entirety of 1963,[18] and its proceedings suggest that civil rights lobbyists were neither optimistic about the prospects for achieving any legislation nor equipped to navigate the partisan wrangling that had surfaced. The meeting had been called to finalize the Executive Committee's response to Kennedy's February 28 message, a lengthy statement that led by expressing disappointment that the president's "legislative proposals ... fall so woefully short of meeting the needs that exist, needs that the President recognizes in his message, and needs for which legislative remedies were promised in the party platform and campaign speeches on which he was elected in 1960." It offered an expansive critique of the proposals' limitations but concluded by enumerating just three legislative priorities carried over from the LCCR's lobbying efforts in previous years: mandatory desegregation compliance plans for all school districts, authority for the attorney general to file civil injunctive suits in all civil rights cases (i.e., the Civil Rights Act of 1957's excised Part III), and a fair employment practices law.[19] These were among the bills that had been introduced prior to Kennedy's special message, and Bill Oliver, who attended the meeting on behalf of UAW President Walter P. Reuther, reported that these were identified by the Executive Committee as "three of the most imperative areas in which the Leadership Conference hope to concentrate during this session of the 88th Congress."[20]

News of the Republican senators' civil rights package complicated this prioritization, however. According to Oliver, the senators' press release came as "a surprise to the Executive Committee," not only because the lobbying community was not expecting any such initiative at that juncture, but also because the bills they introduced went so far beyond the president's program. Still, the meeting participants decided against endorsing the Republicans' package "because of the pending efforts of ... Democratic friends in the Senate" and instead agreed only to "commend these GOP Senators" for their statement.[21] Under these circumstances, there was little opportunity for the LCCR leadership to settle on a legislative plan of action, let alone rally the long roster of member organizations for coordinated activity in support of specific proposals. Joe Rauh, an attorney affiliated with several of the LCCR's core member organizations and a leading member of its Washington lobbyists group, later recalled that "the meeting broke up in disarray."[22]

Mounting protest activity and anti-civil rights violence revived efforts to secure civil rights legislation in April and May. Rather than make the case for a sweeping civil rights program, however, pro-civil rights legislators and lobbyists capitalized on the opportunity to highlight the need for legislation to protect civil rights activists. A few days after surging conflict prompted Kennedy to deploy antiriot troops to Birmingham, Alabama, a group of senators urged him to broaden the civil rights program he had proposed in February to include "legislation that would enable the Attorney General to institute or intervene in civil injunction suits . . . to safeguard by court order all the rights of U.S. citizens under the 14th Amendment." Promising bipartisan support for "supplementing the Administration's pending requests for civil rights legislation in this way," they framed their request as a means of enhancing the president's capacity to respond to civil conflict: "We are deeply cognizant of the heavy responsibilities you have been called upon to bear as Chief Executive in the trying and dangerous situation in Birmingham," they wrote, and "we do not believe that the only alternatives available to the President should be mediation or the use of federal troops."[23] Lobbyists, likewise, began drafting legislation to facilitate indemnification for those injured while attempting to exercise their civil rights but coordinated this work informally rather than under the aegis of the Leadership Conference.[24]

It eventually became clear that the Kennedy administration was preparing some sort of legislative proposal, but the substance and form it would take remained to be seen. The timeline was likewise uncertain. Though it was initially suspected that Attorney General Robert Kennedy would present the administration proposal at a House Judiciary Committee hearing during the last week of May,[25] he postponed his testimony to mid-June, a move lobbyists understood as buying time "in order to decide what new legislation they [i.e. the administration] were going to support."[26] There were some opportunities for selected organizations to weigh in on the president's plans; for example, Andy Biemiller, director of the AFL-CIO's Department of Legislation, was asked to prepare a statement on organized labor's position on civil rights legislation, and a follow-up meeting at the White House was planned for labor movement leaders.[27] However, pervasive uncertainty coupled with longstanding organizational procedures and habits that militated against proactive consensus negotiation kept the Leadership Conference from pursuing a coalition response.

The turning point came finally on June 11, when President Kennedy unveiled the administration's plans in a televised address. Reminding the public of the founders' stated commitment to equality, he announced his intention to "ask the Congress of the United States to act, to make a commitment it has not fully made in this century to the proposition that race has no place in American life or law." The legislation he had in mind would be expansive, including, among "other features" left unspecified in the June 11 speech, the integration of "all facilities which are open to the public," authorization for the Justice Department "to participate more fully in lawsuits designed to end segregation in public education," and "greater protection for the right to vote."[28]

Throughout June, President Kennedy and other top administration officials convened a series of meetings with "educators, business leaders, lawyers, women's organizations, and the like" to secure their cooperation in the president's efforts to shepherd his omnibus bill through Congress.[29] The meetings culminated on June 22 with a gathering of about thirty organizational leaders in the White House. Roy Wilkins, executive secretary of the NAACP and chairman of the Leadership Conference, met alone with Kennedy and other administration officials that morning, and he and Arnold Aronson were both in attendance at the group meeting in the afternoon. The other "big six" civil rights movement organizations—the Congress of Racial Equality (CORE), National Urban League (NUL), Southern Christian Leadership Conference (SCLC), Student Nonviolent Coordinating Committee (SNCC), and A. Philip Randolph's Brotherhood of Sleeping Car Porters—were also represented, as were the National Council of Negro Women (NCNW) and several of the LCCR's most prominent labor, Jewish, fraternal, church, civic, and professional member organizations.[30]

Though they vary in the details, most accounts of the day's events describe some jockeying among organizational leaders to take charge of the civil rights groups' efforts in support of the omnibus bill. According to the report of Boris Shishkin, an LCCR Executive Committee member who attended the White House meeting in his capacity as director of the AFL-CIO's Civil Rights Department, Wilkins made the first move by proposing that the Leadership Conference serve as the "central coordinating machinery." This, Shishkin added, "did not set too well" with several of the other principal civil rights leaders, who "each plugged his own organization."[31] Several published accounts suggest that Wilkins's proposal was in turn prompted by rumors that Walter Reuther, president of the United Automobile Workers (UAW) and director of the AFL-CIO's Industrial Union Department, planned to take charge of the legislative campaign by reorganizing the lobbying forces into a new, UAW-led "Coalition of Conscience." Had Wilkins not preempted him, Reuther presumably would have advanced this plan at a luncheon he convened for selected organizational leaders at the Statler Hotel immediately after the White House meeting. Instead, at both the White House and his own meeting, Reuther could only affirm the UAW's commitment to the president's civil rights program and promise financial support to the LCCR's efforts on its behalf.[32]

The June 22 meetings also featured disagreement over tactics. Public demonstrations and civil disobedience had become hallmarks of the southern civil rights movement by 1963 and some organizational leaders hoped to bring direct-action protest activity to bear on the national legislative operation. Plans for a late-summer march on Washington were already underway, as A. Philip Randolph had formed a committee some months earlier to resurrect his abortive World War II–era March on Washington Movement. By mid-1963, he had enlisted Dr. King's agreement to cosponsor an event they billed a "March on Washington for Jobs and Freedom."[33] Wilkins and other heads of organizations that were inclined to favor conventional lobbying over mass protest activity were skeptical, however. They had resisted Randolph's earlier overtures and now worried that the march—let alone other direct action campaigns—could derail what seemed like their best opportunity yet to achieve their legislative goals. President Kennedy, too, expressed concern about the prospect of a march on Washington; per Shishkin's report, the president "hoped it would not have the effect of defeating its purpose by giving those in Congress who are now on the fence, an excuse to vote against the program."[34] A principal focus of the meeting at the Statler Hotel, therefore, was to resolve this disagreement. Those in attendance finally agreed to support the march with the proviso that its logistics and program be carefully controlled to minimize the possibility of missteps that could alienate lukewarm supporters of the omnibus bill. They further agreed to convene Leadership Conference members and other groups' top officials and lobbyists to rally broad organizational support for both the March on Washington and the lobbying campaign.

The LCCR's leadership of the Civil Rights Act lobbying campaign was ratified at this next meeting, a robust gathering of about a hundred organizational leaders on July 2, 1963, at the Roosevelt Hotel in New York.[35] While there was some consideration of initial plans for the March on Washington, much of the discussion was devoted to the legislative situation. There was a prevailing sense that oversight of the protest and lobbying campaigns should be kept separate to allow greater flexibility in dealing with members of Congress who opposed direct action. As Dave Cohen, the ADA's legislative representative, reported, "King, who knows how to organize demonstrations effectively, will organize the Washington demonstrations, and others who know the ins and outs of Congress will concentrate on building support for civil rights legislation."[36] Amid this discussion, Reuther presented a $5,000 check from the AFL-CIO's Industrial Union Department to establish a Washington headquarters for the LCCR's coordination of the lobbying campaign. This set off a parade of organizational representatives pledging support, financial and otherwise, to the Leadership Conference. When all was said and done, more than $20,000 had been raised for the lobbying effort, and an "enlarged Leadership Conference"—that is, the fifty-two official coalition members plus a number of other organizations that would go on to join or otherwise support the LCCR's Civil Rights Act campaign in the ensuing year—was committed to working together to secure passage of the strongest civil rights bill possible.[37]

## The LCCR's Organizational Changes

The centerpiece of the LCCR's organizational changes during the summer of 1963 was the opening of a permanent office with a dedicated staff. Wilkins announced plans for a Washington office at the June 22 White House meeting as part of his proposal for the Leadership Conference to take charge of the lobbying campaign, and he and Reuther authorized initial financing from the NAACP and UAW a few days later. They secured office space in the Mills Building on the corner of Pennsylvania Avenue and 17th Street N.W. soon after the Roosevelt Hotel meeting in early July.[38] Marvin Caplan, a DC-based journalist and civil rights activist with no prior ties to the Leadership Conference, was brought on as the Washington Office director; Violet Gunther, a former national director and longtime associate of the ADA who had been involved in events leading to the LCCR's founding, was named administrative assistant; and a small secretarial staff was assembled.[39] The office was sufficiently operational to host a strategy meeting attended by more than thirty organizational representatives on July 17, and an announcement of its opening was released a week later.[40]

The new headquarters enhanced the LCCR's administrative efficiency, enabling the Leadership Conference to operate as a central hub and clearinghouse for a multifaceted lobbying campaign that mobilized an assortment of human and other resources continuously for nearly a year. It also facilitated new organizational practices that further enhanced the LCCR's coordination capacity. One such innovation was the use of the new office space for regular meetings for the Washington representatives of *all* member organizations—that is, not just those with representation on the Executive Committee or the select group of lobbyists who had been meeting in Clarence Mitchell's office since 1957. These strategy meetings were held most weeks on Wednesday afternoons throughout the year leading up to the Civil Rights Act's passage.[41] While attendance varied from week to week, there were typically thirty to forty meeting participants—though sometimes quite a few more.[42] Upward of twenty-five member organizations were represented at the typical meeting, as were several organizations that worked closely with the Leadership Conference but, for various reasons, were not formally affiliated with it.[43]

The Washington representatives meetings served several coordinating functions. First and foremost, they facilitated information sharing and division of labor among the many professional lobbyists who were working to secure the Civil Rights Act's passage. Jane O'Grady, who began attending Washington representatives meetings a few months after being hired as a legislative representative for the Amalgamated Clothing Workers union late in 1963, described this function in a recent interview. "Clarence [Mitchell] and Joe [Rauh] were on the Hill all the time," she recalled, "[and they] would at these meetings be telling us what our supporters on the Hill were saying and doing. . . . Then we'd have a sort of roll call of members of Congress and if [the Washington representative of] any group thought they had some influence on that person, they would put their hand in the air and say, 'I'll take him.'"⁴⁴ The meetings were also the first port of call for the coordinated mobilization of member groups' resources. O'Grady depicted the Washington representatives as "foot soldiers" charged with disseminating legislative and tactical updates from Mitchell and other core lobbyists who had their fingers on the pulse of the legislative process to national and branch organization officials, who would activate their grassroots networks accordingly. "We were given information about what was happening," she recounted, "and from us would go the information about the bill to our respective organizations."⁴⁵

Finally, and in a striking departure from past practice, the Washington representatives meetings became the LCCR's "principal agency for operation."⁴⁶ While the Executive Committee was still responsible for the coalition's administrative affairs,⁴⁷ and while there was still a small core group of lobbyists who remained point people for consultation and negotiation with top-level congressional and executive branch officials, decisions about the LCCR's position on the civil rights bill's contents and legislative strategy became the purview of the Washington representatives. Consensus remained a watchword for Leadership Conference officials, but the Washington representatives meetings ushered in a new understanding of what it entailed. Previously, as discussed in Chapter 3, consensus had been touted as an ideal—and, frequently, as a limiting device that enjoined against unified position taking or otherwise acting in the name of the Leadership Conference for fear of compromising member groups' autonomy. The heads of member organizations had been asked to weigh in on LCCR positions on occasion, but no routine mechanism had existed to ascertain, let alone negotiate, consensus. The inception of regular meetings that could in principle (even if never in practice) be attended by representatives of all member organizations gave rise to a more permissive view, which Aronson offered plainly in a letter to the Washington Office director of an organization he hoped to recruit to the LCCR: "Opinions expressed in the name of the [Leadership] Conference are the consensus of Washington representatives of the cooperating organizations expressed at our weekly meetings."⁴⁸

It bears emphasizing that consensus remained a high decision threshold. It was not always reached and, on those occasions when it proved elusive, the Leadership Conference did not take a position or coordinate lobbying activities in the name of the coalition.⁴⁹ But even while the Washington representatives could not always come to agreement, consensus was obtained often enough to mount a united front at key junctures in the legislative process. Indeed, O'Grady indicated that there tended to be a rubberstamp quality to the decision-making process at the Washington representatives meetings. Most groups, she sensed, "really trusted that . . . Roy Wilkins, Clarence Mitchell, and Joe Rauh were taking them down the right path . . . and were not going to interfere in something that . . . Roy, as the representative of the civil rights community, and Clarence and Joe, were proposing."[50] Furthermore, the fact that routine consensus negotiation was even attempted was itself a noteworthy step for a coalition whose leaders had previously deemed it unfeasible. In addition to its practical utility in the context of the Civil Rights Act campaign, it was reassuring for organizations that had chafed under the haphazard approach to consultation with member organizations in the LCCR's first decade. Perhaps most notably, the National Council of Jewish Women, an original member organization that had disaffiliated out of frustration with the LCCR's "informal and unstructured" approach to coordination during the 1950s, rejoined once the Leadership Conference "developed a more formal method of developing a consensus" in 1963.[51]

In addition to managing the coalition's administrative affairs and hosting the Washington representatives meetings, the LCCR's new office and staff supported the production and circulation of the *MEMO*, a numbered series of newsletters sent more or less weekly to member organizations and other supporters of the Civil Rights Act campaign. Though branded as memorandums from Arnold Aronson to the LCCR's cooperating organizations, many nonmember groups and individuals who indicated support or interest in legislative and lobbying developments joined the mailing list as the lobbying campaign wore on. About midway through the year, the LCCR added reporters from an assortment of national media outlets to the mailing list as well, "to acquaint [them] with the goals and attitudes of the Leadership Conference and to keep [them] abreast of its planning and decisions."[52] When all was said and done, Caplan wrote, "more than 3,000 groups and individuals" were receiving these communiqués.[53]

While most issues included a reminder of the next strategy meeting's date and time, the *MEMO* was not generally directed to the Washington representatives. Rather, it served to update non-Washington-based readers on emergent legislative developments and to encourage them to pressure lawmakers in accordance with the Washington representatives' decisions. In addition to action prompts, some issues highlighted exemplary activities by member organizations—for example, the Council for Christian Social Action's interfaith political action workshops as the lobbying campaign got underway (*MEMO* no. 2), the National Council of Negro Women's issuance of five hundred messages pressuring House members to sign a discharge petition when the bill was held captive by the Rules Committee (*MEMO* no. 20), and B'nai B'rith Women's "Wire for Rights" Day and the Delta Sigma Theta sorority's innovative letter-writing campaign during the long Senate filibuster (*MEMO*s no. 32 and no. 40, respectively). They also often included a packet of supplemental materials—background reports on members of key congressional committees, sample letters and telegrams to elected officials, copies of newspaper clippings, and the like—or otherwise directed readers to auxiliary resources to bolster their activity on behalf of the civil rights bill.[54]

In short, the *MEMO* was a vehicle for coordinating messaging and grassroots resource mobilization by the LCCR's diverse and diffuse coalition. In an era without teleconferencing—let alone email and social media—it became a crucial means of promulgating information from Washington to diverse constituencies nationwide and coordinating their activity in support of coalition goals. In addition to reaching those who read it directly, member and allied organizations quoted, paraphrased, and cited the *MEMO* in communications with branch chapters and grassroots members, effectively amplifying and certifying LCCR positions as their own.[55] The *MEMO* likewise promoted esprit de corps among member organizations, "keep[ing] them in touch with each other," as Caplan wrote, for the duration of the yearlong Civil Rights Act campaign.[56]

The new office and the Washington representatives meetings and distribution of the *MEMO* it supported did not fundamentally transform the Leadership Conference; its basic structure, identity, and mission were unchanged. In Darren Halpin and Carsten Daugbjerg's phrasing, these were "routine" adjustments to "strategy or technique/settings" rather than a "radical" shift in organization form.[57] These changes were nevertheless consequential for the LCCR's capacity to capitalize on its resource potential. The next section delves into some of the Leadership Conference's efforts to shape the contents and secure passage of the Civil Rights Act to illustrate how its new organizational apparatus facilitated coordination among civil rights lobbying organizations and their grassroots supporters.

## Lobbying for the Civil Rights Act of 1964

President Kennedy submitted his omnibus bill to Congress on June 19, 1963, a few days prior to his meetings with Wilkins and other organizational leaders. As the background memorandum for the LCCR's July 2 meeting at the Roosevelt Hotel acknowledged, it was "the most comprehensive [civil rights] bill ever to receive serious consideration by the Congress of the United States." Its eight titles promised a variety of civil rights reforms, including voting rights protections, desegregation of public accommodations and facilities, federal aid to desegregating school districts, a four-year extension of the Civil Rights Commission and creation of a new Community Relations Service, and measures to curb discrimination in federal government employment. It was nevertheless a "moderate and restrained" bill drafted with a view to maximizing the likelihood of passage rather than revolutionizing U.S. race relations. Civil rights lobbyists therefore eyed its introduction as a two-pronged challenge: they sought not merely to secure the president's bill—itself a monumental feat considering the track record on civil rights legislation up until that point—but also, "if at all possible," to expand and strengthen its provisions.⁵⁸

The remainder of this chapter explores how the Leadership Conference pursued these goals during the year in which Kennedy's omnibus bill wended its way through Congress. This case study is not a comprehensive account of the Civil Rights Act's passage—or, for that matter, of Leadership Conference activity on its behalf.⁵⁹ Instead, it focuses on three episodes during the bill's long legislative journey to illustrate the LCCR's newly enhanced capacity for coordination. The first section considers the five-month period during which the administration bill was in the hands of the House Judiciary Committee. It is a relatively long discussion, not merely because this was a lengthy stage of the legislative process but because of its significance to the lobbying campaign. As Ken Kollman writes in a study of interest groups' efforts to mobilize popular support for their legislative goals, the "agenda-shaping" stage of the legislative process, "when a bill is in congressional committee," is of critical importance to those seeking to shape a bill's contents, as committees are empowered to "amend, defeat, strengthen, or . . . emasculate a given bill." As a result, "intense bargaining takes place among policymakers, legislative chambers, branches of government, and of course, interest groups." Indeed, he adds, "for many interest groups . . . the agenda-shaping stage is when the real action takes place."⁶⁰ Two shorter sections describe LCCR-led initiatives to secure passage of the strengthened civil rights bill on the House and Senate floors. Kollman notes that interest groups are generally less proactive during this "debate and voting" stage of the legislative process; rather, they "begin to follow the lead of politicians, who themselves coordinate and mobilize groups of constituents . . . to convince colleagues in the government" to support the legislation they are championing.⁶¹ Though Kollman's observations are true to some extent in the case of the Civil Rights Act of 1964, supporting politicians' efforts for its enactment entailed the LCCR's development of creative lobbying techniques and sustained resource mobilization to overcome obstruction on the House and Senate floors.

## *Lobbying to Strengthen the Administration Proposal*

Shortly after Kennedy submitted his omnibus civil rights bill to Congress on June 19, 1963, Representative Celler introduced it in the House of Representatives, where it was assigned bill number H.R. 7152 and referred to the Judiciary Committee. As chairman of the Judiciary Committee, Celler assigned the bill to Subcommittee No. 5, which he chaired as well, and which would get the first opportunity for hearings and markup before voting to recommend the bill to the full Judiciary Committee. It would then take until November 20—fully five months from the bill's introduction—for the Judiciary Committee to report it for consideration by the full House.

This protracted sojourn in the House Judiciary Committee marked the first test of H.R. 7152's viability and the LCCR's best opportunity for strengthening it. "The importance of the Judiciary Committee's final product cannot be over estimated," the ADA's legislative action plan urged. "*It will be more difficult to strengthen a civil rights bill on the floor of the House than to maintain majority support for a strong committee bill.*"[62] Nevertheless, the Leadership Conference and its member groups play a negligible role in most accounts of the Civil Rights Act's transformation during this crucial agenda-shaping stage. To the extent that they make any significant appearance, it is in late September, when they are charged with inciting Celler's move to circumvent a carefully negotiated interbranch, bipartisan course of action and have his subcommittee report out a revised bill that far exceeded the administration's proposal.[63] Otherwise, they remain on the sidelines as largely passive spectators who occasionally testify at hearings or react with a comment to the press while delicate negotiations over the bill's contents were carried out by legislative and executive branch principals. A different picture emerges from the present description of the LCCR's activity during the five-month period that the bill was before the Judiciary Committee. Far from a sidelined or primarily reactive lobby, it finds sustained, proactive efforts to establish a lobbying agenda, initiate and broker plans to strengthen the administration bill, and strategically mobilize professional and grassroots forces to lobby for specific strengthening amendments.

This work began once the contents of the administration's bill became apparent in mid-June, about two weeks prior to the Roosevelt Hotel meeting and the LCCR's subsequent organizational changes. As in previous years, therefore, initial plans for the Civil Rights Act campaign were developed by core civil rights lobbyists—that is, the members of the unofficial committee of fifteen or so individuals who had been meeting under Clarence Mitchell's direction since 1957. Two memorandums from the ADA's Dave Cohen to Joe Rauh illustrate the range of decision points that weighed on their minds as legislative consideration of H.R. 7152 got underway.[64] It was roundly understood that they would seek House passage of "the strongest bill possible," but that phrase left a good deal to be determined. "Does this mean we support the Civil Rights Act of 1963 as is, plus a general Part III . . . and immediate plans for school desegregation?" Cohen mused. Doing so would enhance the administration bill with two of the three legislative priorities advocated by the Leadership Conference in the wake of Kennedy's paltry February 28 message, but other possibilities abounded. Cohen named three alternative proposals for strengthening H.R. 7152's voting rights provisions, for example, and the LCCR's most long-standing legislative priority—a permanent Fair Employment Practices Commission with robust enforcement power—was yet another option.[65] The lobbyists also understood well that the vicissitudes of the legislative process would necessitate compromise and sought to determine which elements of the administration bill they would be willing to either trade for strengthening amendments or relinquish altogether to preserve the most important provisions.

Alongside these substantive considerations was a slew of strategic questions. Subcommittee hearings were slated to begin with testimony from Attorney General Kennedy on June 26; with this in mind, Cohen wondered how lobbyists might begin pressing their case for strengthening amendments:

> Should not a meeting with Celler [as chairman of the subcommittee] be arranged by the various civil rights groups . . . [to] discuss the possibilities of going beyond the Administration bill? Even if the situation is hopeless on Celler's part, should we not go through with this meeting anyway? Rodino . . . is next in seniority. If Celler makes no commitment, should also a delegation visit him and, indeed, visit every member of that subcommittee, Democrat and Republican, after the visit with Celler? If a . . . coalition meeting is not feasible, should I feel free to go ahead and concentrate my efforts on each Congressman on that subcommittee and the full committee after them?[66]

A further concern pertained to lobbying organizations' participation in the hearings: Should each organization seek to testify individually, which would draw attention to the support of different interest group sectors for a strengthened bill and enable them to bring a wider range of arguments to bear, or would they be better served by presenting a single, joint testimony to highlight the unity of the lobbying coalition and prevent unnecessary delay in reporting out the bill? The dilemma was especially fraught in light of civil rights lobbyists' long view of the legislative process. While the near-term hurdle—getting the bill through a House subcommittee stacked with northern liberals—might not have merited such painstaking consideration on its own, the lobbyists recognized that practically all subsequent headway would require support from Midwestern and Mountain State legislators who were far less responsive to the groups that were traditionally associated with the civil rights lobby. "We must find ways to pressure the pressure groups that are strong in [those regions]," Cohen wrote.[67] He proposed integrating "church groups and others that do not normally participate in civil rights legislative actions" into the lobbying coalition, both as a means of eliciting "some sort of greater commitment" to the Civil Rights Act from those organizations and as an early signal to hesitant representatives and senators.[68]

A final concern was that of outside lobbying—and, in particular, the mobilization of pro-civil rights organizations' grassroots members in support of a stronger bill; as Cohen put it, "we must think of pressures, apart from [professional] lobbying pressures, on these Congressmen." The problem as he saw it was twofold: first, what sort of pressure would be most effective? The Leadership Conference and its members had historically relied on traditional letter-writing campaigns, but Cohen anticipated that "something more" would be necessary in this case. Second, Cohen noted that the usual reliance on mailed action prompts to mobilize grassroots support was not promising. He recognized from past experience that "the response [to this approach] is anything but good," and he and other core lobbyists understood that anything short of robust public endorsement would imperil the legislation.[69]

Core lobbyists had been mulling over these issues for nearly two weeks by the time the Leadership Conference convened the Roosevelt Hotel meeting on July 2, and their initial determinations were set forth in that meeting's background memorandum, a sixteen-page analysis of the administration bill and likely legislative opportunities and hurdles coauthored by Rauh and Frank Pohlhaus, the NAACP Washington Bureau's legal counsel. Prior coalition positions dictated a course of action in some instances. For example, in reviewing Title VII, which in the original version of H.R. 7152 would have created a Commission on Equal Employment Opportunity with statutory authority to prevent discrimination only in federal government and contract employment, Rauh and Pohlhaus emphasized that the proposed commission was "not . . . a substitute for national FEPC . . . with enforcement power." It affirmed the latter to be "one of the most necessary legislative requirements" and asserted that "the adoption of one of [the pending FEPC bills] as an amendment to the Administration's civil rights bill should be strongly supported." A less strident tone was taken in other places. Rather than lay out a full-fledged plan of action, the memorandum invited organizations to "consider what techniques to utilize and how best to work together" to achieve common goals.[70]

The LCCR's position on strengthening amendments concretized in the following weeks as the new headquarters opened and Washington representatives began meeting on Wednesday afternoons. Their initial consensus was summarized in the first issue of the *MEMO*, which instructed civil rights supporters to contact House Judiciary Committee members with letters "call[ing] for support of the president's total civil rights package *plus*" five additional provisions:

> 1. An "across the board Part III" authorizing the Attorney General to bring injunctive suits in *all* civil rights violations . . .; 2. A full FEPC with enforcement powers . . .; 3. Coverage of all places of public ac-

commodation, regardless of size . . .; 4. Recognition that sixth grade education is conclusive proof of sufficient literacy to vote in both state and federal elections . . .; and, 5. A requirement that school districts begin complying with the Supreme Court's school decisions in 1963.[71]

The order in which these five strengthening amendment proposals were listed indicated a prioritization; indeed, only the first three were still touted later on.[72] The list also illustrates how the LCCR's consensus rule tended to constrain the coalition lobbying agenda. The Part III, FEPC, and school desegregation provisions had all been adopted as Leadership Conference positions long before the Civil Rights Act campaign; essentially, they were the same three priorities for the 88th Congress the Executive Committee had identified in its response to Kennedy's February 28 message to Congress on civil rights. The public accommodations proposal was not so much a strengthening amendment as an effort to preempt any dilution of what Rauh and Pohlhaus declared to be the bill's "most important title."[73] The voting rights provision, on the other hand, was a compromise position. While Rauh and Pohlhaus's memorandum acknowledged that "there are stronger proposals in the voting field than those contained in the Administration bill," it suggested a disinclination to push for their addition to the Civil Rights Act. "Every legislative advance cannot be obtained at once," it asserted, and it reiterated that H.R. 7152's voting rights title (Title I) did already promise some improvement on existing voting rights protections.[74] SNCC's lobbyists rejected this assessment. In their view, Title I was "the key title" of the proposed legislation, and they sought much stronger protections than the administration bill afforded.[75] They argued strenuously for the Leadership Conference to adopt SNCC's position, but other Washington representatives' disagreement precluded the consensus the SNCC lobbyists sought. The proposal that was adopted instead drew on a prior LCCR position—in this case, its endorsement of a 1962 bill that would have made completion of a sixth-grade education prima facie evidence of literacy in both federal and state elections.

Once these five strengthening amendments were agreed to and promulgated to member organizations, there was little appetite for reopening the question. Even as SNCC's Washington representatives fought to keep more robust voting rights protections on the table, other lobbyists pushed back. One argued that they had "moved past the stage of deciding on such changes to the bill," another offered that it was "too late to make [SNCC's position] the Leadership Conference position," and a third mused that "the real problem [for lobbyists at this point] is not to perfect the bill but to perfect legislative support for the bill."[76] As a result, discussion at the late-July Washington representatives meetings—the only two for which detailed records of the proceedings have been preserved—was primarily devoted to figuring out how the LCCR and its member organizations would pursue their legislative objectives.

Amending H.R. 7152 to include a strong FEPC provision spurred the shift from identifying the coalition's legislative priorities to active lobbying for their achievement. In light of the prevailing wisdom that an FEPC provision would disaffect pivotal members of Congress from new civil rights legislation altogether, President Kennedy opted against including one in the administration bill. Upon submitting it to Congress, however, the president affirmed that he would support any of the standalone FEPC bills that had been introduced earlier in the session.[77] Civil rights lobbyists thus faced the delicate task of persuading otherwise supportive legislators—both those who were wary of FEPC's legislative viability and those who, as sponsors of standalone FEPC bills, had a vested interest in securing their passage regardless of the omnibus bill's success—that incorporating FEPC into H.R. 7152 was politically salable. An opportunity to begin making the case arose on July 22, when the House Education and Labor Committee favorably reported H.R. 405, a strong FEPC bill that had been introduced by Representative James Roosevelt in January and that the NAACP and a number of other lobbying organizations had supported in hearings prior to Kennedy's June 11 speech.

A member of Roosevelt's staff attended the LCCR's Washington representatives meeting on July 24 to solicit support for his plan to use the risky Calendar Wednesday procedure to bypass the Rules Committee and bring his bill directly to the House floor.[78] Several lobbyists voiced concern about this strategy, both as a first resort to secure passage of H.R. 405 on its own (it would be "unwise to use a last ditch tactic at the start," Jack Conway of the AFL-CIO's Industrial Union Department asserted) and, more important, because it would imperil H.R. 7152. As AFL-CIO legislative director Andy Biemiller maintained, "it would be a big mistake [to take extraordinary steps to expedite passage of H.R. 405] until the big bill is disposed of once and for all." Clarence Mitchell, who chaired the LCCR's legislative strategy meetings, moved to postpone a decision on the matter, assuring the Washington representatives that "at the next meeting (July 31) you will be in a position to give further views from your organization" and indicating that, in the meantime, some investigation would be made into the feasibility of incorporating Roosevelt's bill into H.R. 7152.[79] One Washington representative contacted Roosevelt right after the meeting and clarified that, although "very anxious that [H.R. 405] not get lost in the legislative shuffle," the congressman was open to incorporating its substance into the president's bill.[80] A delegation of lobbyists subsequently met with Celler, who advised them to begin securing evidence of Judiciary Committee members' willingness to consider the amendment. Biemiller, who reported on this conversation at the start of the July 31 meeting, noted that Celler was generally amenable to adding FEPC to H.R. 7152 and willing to consider the LCCR's other strengthening amendment proposals. Celler made no commitments, however, and it was clear that the lobbyists would have to convince him that their objectives were politically feasible. "We have to analyze first Judiciary and then Rules," Biemiller concluded, "and get to work."[81]

Spurred by Biemiller's report, the Washington representatives spent much of the July 31 meeting figuring out which subcommittee members to target as potential sponsors of the strengthening amendments and laying the groundwork for background reports to facilitate lobbying of all Judiciary Committee members.[82] And, recognizing that "the church is the determining force" in many pivotal districts where the LCCR's traditional reliance on NAACP chapters and labor unions would not give them much traction, they gave extensive consideration to white church organizations' participation in this phase of the lobbying campaign and established a subcommittee "to concentrate on religious matters."[83] By the time *MEMO* no. 2 went out a week later, the Washington office had compiled lists of Judiciary Committee members' religious affiliations, organizational memberships, and major campaign donors. The lists were appended to the *MEMO*, which reiterated the LCCR's five strengthening amendment priorities and urged organizations to use the attached information to "decide who in your organization or acquaintanceship can most effectively approach these men" and begin making contact with them "at once."[84]

The following weeks featured robust effort to coordinate and sustain pressure on the Judiciary Committee. It kicked off with an NAACP-sponsored Legislative Strategy Conference in early August, which brought several hundred NAACP branch leaders from some thirty states to Washington for three days of legislative briefings, lobbying, and grassroots-mobilization strategy discussions.[85] A memorandum for attendees brought them up to speed with the LCCR's strengthening amendment priorities and instructed them on precise substantive and procedural commitments to seek while lobbying their home-state representatives.[86] The LCCR's core lobbyists and other Washington representatives, meanwhile, drew on their own contacts, feedback from Legislative Strategy Conference participants, and reports from others who wrote or visited with members of the House both to hone their direct lobbying tactics and to target key grassroots constituencies for mobilization.[87] They were also in close contact with the civil rights steering committee of the Democratic Study Group (DSG), a legislative service organization of liberal Democratic members of the House of Representatives.[88] Mitchell, Rauh, Biemiller, and a few others frequently participated in DSG meetings to develop legislative strategy and were involved in the steering committee's efforts to negotiate language in the bill's public accommodations title to ensure its acceptability to both Democratic and Republican supporters. The DSG also relied on the LCCR's organizational membership network for outreach to Midwestern and Mountain State representatives and worked with LCCR officials to stimulate and coordinate religious organizations' efforts to secure their support for a strong bill.[89]

By the end of the summer, civil rights lobbyists were assured that their strengthening amendment proposals were receiving serious consideration, but they understood well that their work on this front would stand or fall with their ability to secure credible commitments from moderate Judiciary Committee members. Celler reaffirmed his openness to the possibility of incorporating H.R. 405 into Title VII and adopting other strengthening provisions, but, *MEMO* no. 5 cautioned, "he leaves the next move up to . . . Subcommittee No. 5." In turn, "although a majority of the subcommittee is on record as in favor of the [LCCR's] amendments these members are reluctant to make the additions if they feel they will not survive the full [Judiciary] Committee."[90] Aronson put a finer point on it in the following *MEMO*, which he drafted as the subcommittee began winding down its work on H.R. 7152 after a long Labor Day recess. "*It is not enough to reach out to just members of the subcommittee. All 35 members of the full House Judiciary Committee must be approached.* It is a mistake to assume the two groups are independent. The subcommittee will approve strengthening amendments *only* if its members think the full committee will accept them."[91] Well in advance of Celler's late-September gambit to force his subcommittee's approval of a full slate of strengthening amendments, therefore, LCCR officials and staff, civil rights lobbyists, and rank-and-file members of a vast array of advocacy organizations were engrossed in persuading Judiciary Committee members of the necessity and broad public support for a strengthened civil rights bill.

Their work continued into October, when the subcommittee finally voted to approve a marked-up version of H.R. 7152 that contained, among other changes, "all of the major proposals advanced by the Leadership Conference."[92] As the bill advanced to the full Judiciary Committee, the LCCR took up a new mantra: having secured "the strongest bill possible" from Subcommittee No. 5, it now urged full committee passage of that bill "without dilution and without delay."[93] At their meeting on September 30, a day before the subcommittee convened to vote and report out the bill, the Washington representatives committed the Leadership Conference to a "massive nationwide campaign" to preserve the gains enshrined in the subcommittee bill.[94] Subsequent issues of the *MEMO*, as well as communications from Washington representatives to their home organizations' executive leadership, and member organizations' mailings to branches and grassroots supporters hammered home the challenges inherent in this new phase of the legislative process. In contrast to the predominantly liberal subcommittee that had strengthened the bill, *MEMO* no. 9 cautioned, "the full Committee includes a fairly sizeable complement of members who want a moderate (i.e. weak) bill or none at all."[95] Additional difficulties surfaced as full committee consideration got underway. Some members who supported the strengthening amendments in principle took issue with their draftsmanship, precluding swift action to simply approve the subcommittee's changes.[96] "The slow progress being made on the bill," *MEMO* no. 10 reported, "is a sign of danger," especially as it had become apparent that serious consideration was being given to weakening amendments as well.[97]

If it was not clear to civil rights lobbyists before, Attorney General Kennedy's testimony on October 15 and 16 drove home the possibility that all of the subcommittee's strengthening amendments could be swept away. Among other rollbacks, Kennedy urged the Judiciary Committee to limit voting rights protections to federal elections, replace the subcommittee's expansive public accommodations coverage with the more limited listing of business types that had appeared in the administration bill, and eliminate the subcommittee bill's new Part III provision. Only the employment title, which the subcommittee had replaced in its entirety with the substance of H.R. 405, did not elicit firm objection. But even here, the attorney general urged caution. While the administration would be on board if the committee was determined to keep the subcommittee version, he noted that "there are some experienced Members of Congress who feel that the inclusion of this provision in the omnibus bill could make it more difficult to secure a rule . . . and could even jeopardize ultimate passage of the omnibus bill" and reiterated that the administration would be equally supportive of a separate FEPC bill.[98]

Clarence Mitchell's pronouncement that Attorney General Kennedy's testimony was "a sellout" is widely referenced in retrospective accounts of the Judiciary Committee's machinations.[99] But Mitchell's comment to the press was just the start of the LCCR's intensive effort to preserve its most highly prioritized strengthening amendments. At the regularly scheduled strategy meeting on October 16, the Washington representatives offered their consensus for Aronson to send the president, the attorney general, and the Judiciary Committee members a telegram in the coalition's name. In contrast to the careful phrasing used to avoid the appearance of speaking for organizations that had not explicitly endorsed LCCR positions in previous years' lobbying campaigns, the October 17 missive began with a full-throated effort to showcase the coalition's breadth and unity: "On behalf of the Leadership Conference on Civil Rights, its cooperating organizations and their millions of members," Aronson wrote, "I wish to express sharp disagreement with the Attorney General's proposals for softening the Subcommittee's Civil Rights Bill."[100] *MEMO* no. 11, which was sent on October 18—just four days after the previous issue instead of the usual week—exhorted member organizations and other supporters to flood the White House and representatives' offices with "a barrage of messages" opposing the attorney general's position. It likewise encouraged them to organize "mass delegations" to visit Judiciary Committee members in their district offices during the weekend; to urge Republican representatives to speak out against Kennedy's suggestion that undoing the subcommittee's improvements was necessary to ensure bipartisan support; and to "try to get local newspapers to run editorials in support of the Subcommittee bill." *"Messages. Telegrams. Phone Calls. Delegations to home offices. Editorials. Statements that place the issue of a strong bill above Partisanship.* This is the kind of action we need if we are to stave off attacks of those whose notion of moderation is emasculation." The *MEMO* concluded, "This kind of action on a massive basis is what we need if we are to keep a strong, comprehensive bill."[101]

The next ten days witnessed a tense flurry of activity as executive branch officials and legislative party leaders negotiated a compromise bill after their initial plan to moderate the subcommittee version with individually sponsored weakening amendments fell through. Lobbyists were excluded from these private meetings, but the LCCR's earlier efforts to bring professional lobbying and grassroots pressure to bear on cautious Judiciary Committee members had already taken root. The compromise bill the Judiciary Committee reported thus bore the imprint of the Leadership Conference's work to shape the Civil Rights Act's contents even as it moderated civil rights forces' initial gains. Though not quite as broad as the subcommittee version, its public accommodations title still offered more coverage than the administration's; though empowering the Department of Justice only to intervene rather than initiate suits, Part III stayed in the bill; and though tempered by a new requirement that fair employment complaints be adjudicated in the courts rather than by administrative action, the H.R. 405 substitute for the original Title VII remained.

## *Debate and Voting on the House Floor: January 31–February 10, 1964*

It took more than two months from the Judiciary Committee's report for H.R. 7152 to reach the House floor. President Kennedy was assassinated mere days after the committee completed its report on November 20 and, in a rousing address a week later, President Lyndon B. Johnson exhorted the members of Congress to expedite their work on the legislation in his predecessor's memory: "no memorial oration or eulogy could more eloquently honor President Kennedy's memory than the earliest possible passage of the civil rights bill for which he fought so long."[102] The Rules Committee nevertheless sat on the bill. Civil rights forces, including the Leadership Conference, attempted to secure the requisite signatures on a discharge petition to force the bill to the floor, but Howard Smith, the committee's segregationist chairman, deflected this threat when he announced that he would undertake hearings at the start of the 1964 legislative session. The committee finally approved a rule for consideration of the civil rights bill on January 30, and it was taken up on the House floor the next day.

Though of short duration—the House debated for just nine days before voting to pass H.R. 7152 on February 10—this was a critical stage in the Civil Rights Act's journey through Congress. While civil rights forces were generally optimistic that the bill would pass the House, they were less confident that it would not be diluted in the process. Indeed, more than a hundred amendments were introduced and considered, nearly all efforts by southern representatives to weaken the bill's provisions or otherwise undermine its effectiveness. It was also an unconventional phase of the lobbying campaign, and several contemporary and retrospective treatments of the Civil Rights Act's passage acknowledge—and even describe at some length—the LCCR's creative measures to keep tabs on supportive representatives, urging their attendance on the floor and observing their performance in unrecorded teller votes.[103] This section embellishes and supplements these accounts by highlighting the planning and coordination that shaped these efforts. Far from improvised capers thrown together as floor debate got underway, the unusual lobbying activities on display in February 1964 showcased the LCCR's newfound capacity to follow through on core lobbyists' collaboration with congressional allies and mobilize nationwide organizational resources for strategic collective action.

Preparation for this stage of the lobbying campaign began months prior to H.R. 7152's arrival on the House floor. While the Judiciary Committee was still haggling over the bill's contents, the DSG's civil rights steering committee began laying plans for ensuring floor attendance by friendly legislators during unrecorded votes. The LCCR's core lobbyists were on hand for these discussions and pledged to supplement the DSG whip system with their own efforts to promote floor discipline.[104] To this end, the November 11 issue of the *MEMO* opened with a question: "Can you come to Washington on a week's notice?" At that point still optimistic that the Rules Committee hurdle could be overcome in time for the House to consider the bill before the end of the 1963 session, Aronson exhorted, "we must mobilize *now* for the final push this year on a strong civil rights bill." Therefore, "*Every* group in the Leadership Conference should make immediate plans to send delegates to Washington on short notice." The *MEMO* also clarified this would not be the usual mass lobbying event: "We will need watchers, when the bill is on the House floor to keep an eye on Congressmen and to keep track of unrecorded votes. We particularly need people who know their Congressmen by sight and ... whom the members of Congress will recognize as being from his home district or state."[105]

A reminder in *MEMO* no. 21, circulated while Rules Committee hearings were still underway, reiterated the call in a fully underlined paragraph:

> *If your organization has members in particular Districts who know their congressmen well; who have special connections with them; who can speak to them and sit in the gallery and watch how they vote when the bill comes up; or who can urge them to help move the bill out of Rules; now is the time to urge them to clear their calendars and be ready to come to the Capitol. Send us their names, addresses, telephone numbers and the names of the Congressmen they will be ready to work with.*[106]

The Rules Committee finally released the bill in late January and, as preparations were made for its arrival on the House floor, *MEMO* no. 22 led with this headline: "COME TO WASHINGTON THE WEEK OF FEB 3RD. *THE HOUSE MAY PASS THE BILL!*" The *MEMO* announced that, in addition to its office in the Mills Building, the Leadership Conference would set up a command center in the Congressional Hotel to serve as "headquarters for all the delegations planning to come to Washington." Here volunteers arriving to join the lobbying effort would receive their marching orders, report back on their observations, and receive daily briefings from Mitchell and Rauh. *"Mere numbers are not enough,"* the *MEMO* emphasized, once again reminding member groups that the LCCR's effort to secure House passage of an undiluted bill would be a specialized operation. "This is not the time for mass delegations or mass demonstration. Rather it is the time to send to Washington those members and officers who know their Congressmen personally or who can impress Congressmen because of what they represent. We want men and women who can speak for your organization as they urge House members to keep the bill intact, fight off attempts to weaken it, try to strengthen it and pass it."[107]

Hundreds of organizational representatives from congressional districts across the country joined the Leadership Conference in Washington. As *MEMO*s leading up to the floor debate had anticipated, the centerpiece of their effort was a large cadre of observers—or "vultures," as they were derogated by one southern representative—who watched floor proceedings from the House gallery.[108] Each observer was assigned to an individual member or small group of congressmen and tasked with keeping a close eye on them when votes were taken. As Aronson described in the *MEMO* that circulated shortly after House passage, this was no simple task:

> Since the House met as the Committee of the Whole House, there were no roll call votes on amendments. In these circumstances, votes are done by voice, where Representatives simply shout "aye" or "no"; by "division,"

where they stand up and are counted by the Committee chairman; or by "teller vote," where they march up the center aisle and are tapped on the shoulder by tellers as they pass, to determine if they are for or against an amendment.[109]

House rules prohibit reading and writing in the galleries, which meant that those monitoring the "rapid and chaotic movement" entailed by these voting procedures could not make their own written record.[110] Therefore, the LCCR observers operated as "mental tellers" who would commit their observations to memory until they could return to the Congressional Hotel headquarters to deliver their report.[111]

In addition to tracking representatives' votes, LCCR forces took pains to ensure that supportive members of Congress were present to cast them in the first place, an effort coordinated by Jane O'Grady and Peggy Roach, novice Washington representatives for the Amalgamated Clothing Workers and the National Council of Catholic Women, respectively.[112] "Clarence Mitchell insisted that all of us [Washington representatives] participate, from the oldest to the youngest," O'Grady recalled.

> He knew that [Roach and I] weren't skilled or had much in the way of contacts on Capitol Hill, and that's when he . . . zeroed in on the two of us and said we should set up this roving squad . . . in the House of Representatives, which at the time was a kind of freewheeling body with people wandering around all the time. Having the bill on the floor with amendments and getting votes on them truly did involve being sure people showed up. So Clarence said, "Why don't you take on the responsibility of trying to corral this crowd when there are votes going on?"

O'Grady and Roach organized a second group of volunteers who have come to be known as "O'Grady's raiders." As O'Grady described, she and Roach "established a system of putting people in friendly [representatives'] offices. When the bells went off that there was going to be a vote, we would go down that corridor where these offices were . . . and just check in to see where the member of Congress was. Was he going to the floor? Was he off to lunch or whatever? There were no cell phones; it was all just legwork."[113] This was an unconventional approach, to be sure. "Some of the press people thought it was funny," O'Grady recalled, and her AFL-CIO associates "thought it was ridiculous." But, she added, "it did work." "Not once did fewer than 400 [representatives] answer a quorum call," the *New York Times* reported as House debate was winding down, and it credited the "civil rights groups, labor groups, [and] religious affiliates" keeping tabs on attendance for giving those friendly to the civil rights cause "compelling reasons to be on hand."[114]

## *Debate and Voting in the Senate: March 9–June 10, 1964*

By necessity, the lobbying operation in the Senate was conducted differently. In addition its longer duration—in contrast to just nine days of House floor debate, a protracted filibuster kept H.R. 7152 before the Senate for several months—the Senate was understood from the start to be a more challenging venue. Rauh and Pohlhaus's memorandum for the lobbying campaign's kickoff meeting on July 2, 1963, anticipated several challenges once the bill reached the Senate, from a Judiciary Committee that would be far less amenable than the one Celler chaired in the House to the likelihood of a prolonged filibuster in light of the Senate's principle of unlimited debate and high threshold for cloture.[115] The institutional climate likewise required a different approach. As O'Grady explained, "The Senate is a bit of an august body. You don't quite tell senators to go to the floor and vote."[116]

The LCCR nevertheless orchestrated a vigorous offensive in support of its new objective of achieving Senate passage of the House-passed bill. Unlike the "gallery vultures" and "O'Grady's raiders," these efforts have received scant coverage in most accounts of the Senate's handling of H.R. 7152, which tend to focus on behind-the-scenes meetings the bill's floor managers convened to hone legislative strategy. Selected lobbyists, including Mitchell, Rauh, and Biemiller, attended many of these meetings, and their efforts to shape key senators' approach to securing the Civil Rights Act receive due consideration. Overlooked by this backroom focus, however, are the array of initiatives the Leadership Conference undertook to keep pressure on weary senators as the filibuster dragged on into the summer; indeed, as this section suggests, these efforts were perhaps the most variegated and sustained demonstration of the LCCR's new capacity for coordinated resource mobilization.

Leadership Conference officials and staff laid the groundwork for this work in the latter half of February 1964 as the Senate prepared to take up the House-passed civil rights bill. *MEMO* no. 25, which was circulated the same day that H.R. 7152 was delivered to the Senate, asserted that "it would be a terrible mistake for any of us to be so cheered by the success in the House that we feel the battle is over." Rather, Aronson cautioned, "the most critical and dangerous phase . . . starts *now*." The prospect of a lengthy filibuster, which had been on the minds of civil rights supporters since President Kennedy first submitted his bill to Congress, was now imminent. "Though the great debate is still a week or so away," the *MEMO* urged, "it is surely not too early for us to begin our efforts to win Senate support for the House-passed bill." It prompted supporters to begin contacting their home-state senators with three directives: "1. support the bill as passed by the House; 2. vote down all weakening amendments; and 3. vote down any motion to lay the bill aside."[117] As they had in the past, core lobbyists solicited feedback on these initial contacts as a means of fine-tuning their preliminary nose count of senators' positions and of developing direct lobbying plans. And, anticipating ambivalence from Midwestern and Mountain State legislators, the Leadership Conference created a Committee on Church Representation—essentially a subcommittee of religious organizations' Washington representatives—to coordinate church groups' efforts to shore up support for the bill.[118]

Debate, and the inevitable filibuster, finally began on March 9. While there was no need for "mental tellers" and a corridor patrol cadre would have been ill-advised, the Washington representatives did see value in keeping the Senate galleries manned with "civil rights advocates" and drew up a schedule of shifts to ensure that some were present even "after 4 o'clock and into the night," when professional lobbyists were less likely to be on hand. "Our presence in the gallery helps and encourages" pro–civil rights senators, Violet Gunther reminded the Washington representatives in a memorandum urging them to sign up for a night shift,[119] a sentiment O'Grady echoed as she recalled her work during the long filibuster: "The Senators love to see a crowd of people who are in their corner . . . so we filled up the chairs a lot, I guess you might say."[120] Olya Margolin, the NCJW's Washington representative, took charge of this "Senate Gallery Project" at the end of March and began developing a more "orderly program" for gallery watching activities after 4 P.M. Though she reported initial frustration with getting organizations to follow through on their pledges to produce members for the evening shifts, by mid-April she had begun recruiting additional volunteers from local colleges and universities, secured space for 3:45 P.M. briefings at a church near the Capitol building, and, with support from the LCCR office staff, produced badges to make the gallery fillers more readily identifiable.[121]

As initial enthusiasm ebbed and it became clear that they would need to maintain a full-force offensive for some time, LCCR officials convened an "emergency strategy meeting on Senate Civil Rights developments" in lieu of a Washington representatives meeting on April 1. "Need participation of top leaders [of] all organizations cooperating with Leadership Conference to make important decisions," Wilkins's telegram urged.[122] The event was significant in part because it drew in individuals and groups other than the Washington representatives who were already well integrated into lobbying campaign operations. Well over half of the LCCR's member organizations were represented, including at least thirteen that had never participated and another eight whose Washington representatives had attended fewer than five weekly strategy meetings.[123] While many Washington representatives were in attendance, most of the participants were top executives and other organizational officials from outside Washington who did not usually see Leadership Conference operations firsthand. In addition to highlighting the critical nature of the legislative situation, therefore, the emergency meeting helped generate new energy and ideas for the coalition's efforts to build support for cloture.

An important initiative that grew out of the April 1 meeting was the coordination of visits by delegations from each state to meet with their senators on Capitol Hill. To maximize their effect, special care was to be given to the composition of each state's delegation. "The emphasis is not to be upon numbers," Aronson stressed, but on forming delegations of "representative spokesmen" from a range of interest groups and religious congregations to highlight the breadth of support for an undiluted bill. Moreover, unlike the mass lobbying events the LCCR had staged in previous years, which brought hundreds of activists from across the country to lobby their representatives simultaneously at one crucial juncture in the legislative process, these delegations would come to Washington in waves. As the *MEMO* described, the idea was to "bring in state delegations throughout the length of the debate . . . one or two at a time . . . on Mondays, Fridays, and Saturdays."[124] This arrangement would mitigate the problem of peaking too soon in what was shaping up to be an uncommonly long struggle to break the filibuster, but it was a logistically complex operation made possible by the new Washington office and staff whose workflow for the next two months expanded to include a variety of delegation-related tasks: keeping track of and promulgating the delegation schedule as it developed, identifying and communicating with local coordinators for each state delegation, preparing briefing materials and hosting meetings for delegates as they arrived in Washington, collecting reports on their interactions with senators as they departed, and transmitting information from the reports to the appropriate professional lobbyists.[125]

Once this project was underway, LCCR staff used the *MEMO* to keep a steady stream of citizen-lobbyists pouring into the Capitol for weeks after the initial state delegations announcement. "Delegations continue to come to Washington from all over the country," *MEMO* no. 38 announced in mid-May, for example, and described the two most recent state visits:

> *From Kentucky*, a group of community leaders, headed by Hal Thurmond of Hopkinsville, former president of the Associated Industries of Kentucky, came in to meet with Republican Senators Thruston B. Morton and John Sherman Cooper . . . *Massachusetts* sent a delegation of citizens representing more than 30 statewide organizations

and a busload of students from Amherst and Mount Holyoke Colleges. The group numbered more than 100 and its members met with their Senators, Edward M. Kennedy and Leverett Saltonstall.

The *MEMO* also reported on a visit by Alpha Kappa Alpha sorority members from seventeen states and announced that delegates from Indiana, Kansas, and Wyoming would arrive the following week. "If you have members in these states ready to come to the capital," it directed member groups, "tell them to get in touch with the *coordinator*."[126] The next issue of the *MEMO* similarly heralded upcoming visits from "North[,] South and Midwest" and challenged readers: "Why not join a delegation or start organizing one of your own?"[127]

More generally, and even more than in previous stages of the legislative process, the *MEMO* became a vital means for engaging groups in the work of the Leadership Conference and sustaining their active support for H.R. 7152 until cloture was finally achieved in June. In addition to the usual legislative updates and talking points for letters to senators, issue after issue was replete with vivid accounts of creative initiatives by LCCR members and others, invitations to participate in ongoing LCCR activities, and inventive suggestions for keeping pressure on the Senate and raising media and public awareness. The *MEMO* was also the principal vehicle for promulgating the "Quorum Box Score." This new feature was introduced in *MEMO* no. 32, which explained the procedural necessity of having at least fifty-one senators on hand at all times and announced that the Leadership Conference would keep a running tally of senators' attendance at quorum calls. It also instructed readers on how to deploy this information, which would be updated and attached to each *MEMO* for the duration of the filibuster: "If your Senator has been present, congratulate him. . . . If your Senator has been missing calls consistently, you might say you have been disappointed to notice this; that you are sure he recognizes the importance of being present for them and that you hope he will make the [quorum] calls from now on." It also encouraged organizational branches to take the further step of "try[ing] to get your local newspaper to reprint your Senators' score . . . as one way to alert the public—and the Senators—to the importance of the procedure."[128] A near miss when only thirty-nine senators were present for a quorum call the first weekend in April prompted Aronson to lead with this concern in the next issue. "ARE YOU URGING SENATORS TO ANSWER QUORUM CALLS?" the main headline asked. After reciting Senator Hubert Humphrey's assertion that "the only way we can lose . . . is not to have a quorum when we need it," the *MEMO* reminded groups of the Box Score's purpose: "Have your members check it for their Senators' names. If their Senators have been missing calls, a restrained, well-reasoned reminder—no, thousands of reminders—telling them we expect them to be on hand to answer 'Present!' when their names are called, are very much needed."[129]

Cloture was invoked finally on June 10—"V-Day for Civil Rights," *MEMO* no. 41 trumpeted—marking the culmination of three months of intensive lobbying in pursuit of that outcome.[130] Several weeks of work still remained to ensure that the bill stayed intact as the Senate completed its consideration and the House prepared to vote on the Senate-passed version, and the Leadership Conference continued to lead lobbying efforts through these final stages of the legislative process. But the struggle to break the filibuster stands out for its test of the LCCR's newfound coordination capacity. Perhaps more than any other phase of its campaign to strengthen and enact the Civil Rights Act, the months-long push for Senate passage of H.R. 7152 demonstrated how new organizational capabilities enabled the Leadership Conference to mobilize its diverse membership resources on a sustained basis.

## Conclusion

President Johnson signed the Civil Rights Act into law On July 2, 1964, exactly a year after the Leadership Conference formally committed itself to fortifying its coalition operations in pursuit of a bill that would exceed the Kennedy administration's initial omnibus proposal. As this chapter has shown, the ensuing lobbying campaign was quite different from those mounted during the LCCR's first decade. It demonstrated an unprecedented degree of coordination among member and allied groups in developing and advancing coalition goals, and it was sustained for a full year. This, in turn, was facilitated by new organizational apparatus—in particular, a staffed Washington, DC, office, regular strategy meetings for the Washington representatives of all member groups, and publication of the *MEMO* to promulgate coalition positions and coordinate resource mobilization.

The LCCR's contrasting experiences in 1956–1957 and 1963–1964 illustrate the important role interest group coalitions' own organizational features play in shaping their coordination capacity. Both were high-profile policymaking episodes culminating in the achievement of momentous civil rights legislation. But, as Chapter 3 recounts, the Leadership Conference was not organizationally poised to marshal broad participation by its member groups in coalition efforts to prevent dilution—let alone enhance the scope—of the bills that became the Civil Rights Act of 1957. In contrast, the July 1963 opening of the Mills Building office and inception of weekly Washington representatives meetings and *MEMO* circulation set the stage for an impressively coordinated campaign that engaged the full diversity of the LCCR's membership base in a variety of lobbying activities to strengthen the bill's contents while it was under House Judiciary Committee consideration and secure its undiluted passage in subsequent stages of the legislative process.

Even with its new organizational features in place, the LCCR remained "most informal," Caplan wrote in August 1964. As had been the case since its founding, the coalition's organizational structure and operating procedures remained uncodified and there were no requirements for member groups' participation. Echoing Aronson's missive two years earlier, Caplan continued, "There is no constitution and there are no bylaws. There are no set dues."[131] It bears emphasizing, moreover, that the organizational changes the Leadership Conference implemented in the year leading up to the Civil Rights Act's passage were intended and designed to facilitate this particular campaign—that is, to coordinate and mobilize an array of civil rights lobbying forces in support of the singular objective of securing the strongest omnibus civil rights bill possible after H.R. 7152 was introduced. Once the Civil Rights Act was law, this raison d'être was no longer germane, but the LCCR's new organizational arrangements persisted, as did its expanding roster of member organizations and an esprit de corps among their Washington representatives, who had worked closely together for longer than anyone had envisioned at the campaign's inception. "By the time it was all over," Jane O'Grady reminisced, "it was such a band of brothers. We had all bonded together through this ordeal."[132] How this new organizational apparatus fared in an increasingly complex and trying policy-making milieu is the subject of the next chapter.

# 5

# The Leadership Conference Plans to Continue

The twenty-first-century Leadership Conference is a far cry from the "permanent ad hoc body" of its first decade and even from the more robust operation it developed during the campaign for the Civil Rights Act of 1964.[1] It has a new name—the Leadership Conference on Civil and Human Rights—adopted in 2010 to signal the breadth of its ideological vision. There are more than two hundred member organizations, bringing the coalition to more than four times its original size, and a professional staff of some sixty individuals with specialized roles. Eleven task forces tackle a range of issues—including traditional concerns like employment discrimination and voting rights and those that were far from the early LCCR's radar, such as health care, immigration, and media and telecommunications.[2]

This chapter explores how the groundwork for the contemporary Leadership Conference took shape in the wake of the Civil Rights Act's passage. It does not trace the LCCR's organizational development through the present; rather, the focus is on the two-and-a-half-year period from the summer of 1964 through January 1967, when the Leadership Conference adopted its first-ever by-laws, finally codifying—and to some extent modifying—its organizational structure and operating procedures in light of emergent pressures on the nearly twenty-year-old coalition. The post–Civil Rights Act milieu presented both opportunities and challenges for the Leadership Conference. The LCCR's impressive showing in 1963–1964 left little question as to its primacy as the lobbying arm of the civil rights movement, and the mechanisms it had introduced to coordinate lobbying for the Civil Rights

Act endowed the coalition with an organizational apparatus and esprit de corps that left it relatively well equipped to pursue further gains. But—and in contrast to the aftermath of the Civil Rights Act of 1957, which had been diluted in ways that effectively dictated the LCCR's legislative objectives for the next six years—the matter of which civil rights goals to pursue after the Civil Rights Act of 1964 was far from straightforward. Nor was it clear how the Leadership Conference would or should respond to the pressures of a changing membership base, financial and other resource strains, an increasingly inhospitable political environment, and a civil rights movement that was increasingly diffuse and conflict-ridden.

The chapter begins by identifying the aftermath of the Civil Rights Act's passage as a unique juncture in the LCCR's organizational development. Focusing in particular on the way in which coalition officials and lobbyists grappled with the problem of charting a forward course in the wake of unprecedented policy success, it documents the LCCR's transformation from a lobbying coalition that mobilized periodically on an ad hoc basis to one that maintains a constantly active multi-issue lobbying agenda. The second and third sections describe two principal sources of strain on the Leadership Conference in the post–Civil Rights Act context: a web of organizational growing pains that developed and festered as the coalition adapted to a new milieu and challenges posed by mounting conflict within the broader civil rights movement during the mid- to late 1960s. Both sets of challenges beckoned Leadership Conference officials to revisit long-standing assumptions about the utility of their informal coalition management style. The chapter's final section recounts their decision to finally break with this traditional approach with the adoption of the LCCR's first-ever by-laws in January 1967.

## The Civil Rights Lobbying Agenda after the Civil Rights Act of 1964

The question of the LCCR's continuation had rarely if ever been broached during its first decade. This is not to suggest that great pains were taken to ensure the coalition's persistence during the 1950s and early 1960s; paradoxically, perhaps, the early LCCR's rudimentary organizational structure and ad hoc lobbying campaigns meant that little routine maintenance was needed to keep it afloat. Once the decision to maintain the Leadership Conference as a permanent lobbying coalition was made in February 1953, it was assumed that it would persist as long as coalition leaders saw fit to use it as a vehicle for interorganizational collaboration, and neither internal nor external developments gave reason to doubt or debate the merits of its existence. In contrast, the final weeks of the Civil Rights Act campaign invited numerous inquiries about the coalition's post-passage plans: Would the LCCR stay together now that the legislative purpose to which it had rededicated itself the previous summer was achieved? If so, what would it work on? And would it continue to function as it had during the Civil Rights Act campaign, with a dedicated staff and office in Washington, or would it revert to the barebones, voluntary operation that had been its dubious hallmark for most of its history?

Despite ubiquitous questions about the LCCR's future, there seems to have been little urgency to determine what its next steps would be. Page after page of correspondence from Leadership Conference officials and staff as the Civil Rights Act campaign came to a close offer variations on the same theme: the LCCR would continue to exist, but no decisions had been made regarding how it would operate or what it would work on. The future of the Leadership Conference "is a bit hazy at the moment—or rather the form in which it will continue is hazy," Caplan wrote to the head of one member organization. "The one certain thing," he added, "is that the Conference will go on."[3] Aronson likewise noted that "there is a strong disposition . . . to keep the Conference functioning. At this moment I am unable to say how this will be done, but I am convinced it will."[4] This sense was formally ratified at a meeting of the Washington representatives, the assemblage of organizational lobbyists who had been gathering weekly to discuss legislative strategy in the year leading up to the Civil Rights Act's passage. According to *MEMO* no. 44—billed as the "last *MEMO*—in this series, anyway" in its header—maintaining the LCCR "was the unanimous view of the Washington representatives," and so it would continue. But that was all they had decided. "The exact form [the post–Civil Rights Act Leadership Conference would take] is not certain yet," the *MEMO* added, and it noted that, with the impending demolition of the Mills Building, even the physical location of its headquarters was uncertain.[5]

It further appears that had Leadership Conference officials had their druthers, the post–Civil Rights Act coalition would have attended primarily to enforcement of the Civil Rights Act rather than pursue new legislative conquests. A few days before President Lyndon B. Johnson signed the bill into law, Caplan wrote, "implementation and enforcement . . . are the great tasks now and it is our hope that organizations within the Leadership Conference will bend their energy to this work."[6] Similarly, even as it described an uncertain future for the LCCR, *MEMO* no. 44 led with the headline "The Bill Is Law. The Task of Enforcement Begins" and asserted that "the Conference . . . is going on to the work of education and implementation."[7] A few weeks later, Caplan assured the director of the American Baptist Convention's Division of Christian Social Concern that "the Leadership Conference as an organization will continue" and that "our efforts will be directed toward educating the general public and developing techincs [*sic*] for enforcing the present civil rights law."[8] Some communications suggested that the LCCR would also pursue new legislative enactments—for example, form letters thanking heads of member organizations for their Washington representatives' participation in the Civil Rights Act campaign noted that "the Leadership Conference . . . is going to go on, working for enforcement of the law *and for new legislation*"—but offered no indication as to desired provisions or even the general focus of such laws.[9]

The failure to articulate new legislative priorities is especially striking since 1964 was a presidential election year. The Leadership Conference had historically capitalized on these quadrennial opportunities to solicit civil rights commitments from the Democratic and Republican Parties. Indeed, its very first campaign, back when "Leadership Conference on Civil Rights" was still the name of an event and not yet a permanent coalition of lobbying organizations, aimed to secure strong civil rights planks in the major parties' 1952 platforms. In both 1956 and 1960, Leadership Conference officials began laying the groundwork for coordinated efforts to influence the parties' positions on civil rights well in advance of the summertime conventions. They were particularly effective in 1960, when both parties adopted civil rights planks that, Aronson averred, were "by all odds the strongest in history."[10] In contrast, the timing of the Civil Rights Act's passage made it virtually impossible for the Leadership Conference to mount an intensive effort to shape the parties' civil rights platform planks in 1964. In early May—the point at which the LCCR Executive Committee had met to finalize its draft platform plank proposal for circulation to member organizations four years earlier—the Senate was in the thick of a prolonged filibuster, which the Leadership Conference confronted with a multifaceted campaign that kept its staff's hands full overseeing a range of direct and outside lobbying activities, tabulating quorum box scores, and hosting a steady stream of citizen lobbyist delegations until cloture was finally obtained in mid-June. Moreover, while greater administrative capacity might have enabled the Leadership Conference to divide its attention between the ongoing Senate battle and a new campaign to influence the party platforms, it would not have mitigated the more fundamental problem of having to identify future policy goals when the status quo was still in flux. With the fate and final contents of the Civil Rights Act still uncertain mere weeks before the Republican National Convention, specifying—let alone securing nearly ninety organizations' consensus on—a new four-year plan would have been an exercise in futility.[11]

Leadership Conference officials nevertheless prepared to resume operations as they had run during the Civil Rights Act campaign. They quickly secured new office space near Capitol Hill and retained Caplan as its director, a position he would hold until his retirement in 1981.[12] A mid-August issue of the *MEMO*, which Aronson resurrected to update member organizations on the Mississippi Freedom Democratic Party's challenge to the seating of the all-white Mississippi delegation to the Democratic National Convention, indicated that Washington representatives would convene "early in September" to "make plans for a future program."[13] The meeting was not held until late in November, however, and, in the interim, LCCR staff worked primarily on tying up loose ends from the Civil Rights Act campaign and getting the coalition's implementation and enforcement efforts off the ground. They took on just one new legislative issue when, in the wake of the Supreme Court's holding that state legislative districts must encompass roughly equal population shares, members of Congress introduced a slew of bills to nullify, delay, or otherwise undermine the court's rulings.[14] In addition to circulating issue no. 46 of the *MEMO* to explain the situation and provide a list of action prompts "for groups interested in doing something about this,"[15] Leadership Conference officials convened the Washington representatives for the first time in nearly two months since their final Civil Rights Act campaign meeting for a "special emergency session" to identify a coalition position and discuss legislative strategy.[16] A few days later, the Leadership Conference released a statement on behalf of thirty organizations, about a third of the coalition's membership at that time. "It would be ironic," the statement observed, for the Congress that had just passed the Civil Rights Act to now curb voting rights, and it called on legislators to "resist . . . hasty attempts to hamper the courts" and "vote down legislation that can place new obstacles in the way of those Americans working to establish full constitutional rights for all citizens."[17]

A closer look at this brief foray into the reapportionment issue suggests that the Leadership Conference seemed to be settling into pre-1963 habits despite maintaining the organizational apparatus it had developed for the Civil Rights Act campaign. As had so often been the case during the 1950s and early 1960s, the LCCR's response to the reapportionment controversy was long in coming. The Supreme Court rendered the "one man, one vote" decisions on June 15, 1964, and the two principal legislative efforts to undermine them—the Tuck Bill (H.R. 11926) in the House and a rider to a foreign aid bill that Senator Everett Dirksen introduced to delay implementation and buy time for the next Congress to consider a constitutional amendment to void the court's rulings—were introduced within the next few weeks. Jack Pemberton, executive director of the ACLU, approached Aronson about having the Leadership Conference mobilize opposition shortly thereafter and drafted what would become *MEMO* no. 46 before July 20.[18] It was not circulated to member organizations until August 19, however, by which time some groups had already been acting on their own.[19] The House passed the Tuck Bill that same day, as a postscript to the *MEMO* prominently announced: "*FLASH: JUST AS WE WERE PREPARING TO MAIL THIS MEMO, THE HOUSE PASSED THE TUCK BILL. THIS MAKES IT ALL THE MORE URGENT TO CONCENTRATE ON THE SENATE.*"[20] But this was also the eve of the Democratic

National Convention, and so the Washington representatives did not meet until August 31, nearly two weeks later. It became clear at that point that not enough was known about member groups' stances on the issue to develop a corporate position; consequently, the statement that was released on September 3 presented a message to senators from the endorsing organizations rather than the coalition view of the Leadership Conference. Though it was apparent that reapportionment would remain salient in national politics, moreover, there seems to have been little appetite to negotiate a consensus position or have the Leadership Conference take the lead on this issue.[21]

The situation changed drastically in 1965. A five-month effort to secure passage of the Voting Rights Act was the LCCR's signature campaign that year, but other issues simultaneously and subsequently joined its lobbying agenda. The reapportionment issue resurfaced when a movement to amend the Constitution took off just as the Voting Rights Act effort was getting underway. For a few months, the National Committee for Fair Representation, an ad hoc coalition organized by the ACLU, coordinated lobbying against the proposed amendment, but its leaders eventually opted to function solely as an informational clearinghouse, and reapportionment was officially added to the LCCR's lobbying agenda in June.[22] The Voting Rights Act became law on August 6 and, just days later, the Washington representatives convened to discuss the possibility of initiating a campaign to raise the minimum wage. An August 19 issue of the *MEMO* announced that the Leadership Conference would take on both minimum wage and home rule for Washington, DC, as new focal issues.[23] These were joined by the end of the year by a new initiative to draft a personal security bill to protect civil rights workers and support pending legislation to strengthen the Civil Rights Act's employment title (Title VII). Finally, implementation and enforcement of existing civil rights legislation, which Leadership Conference officials had established as a priority when the Civil Rights Act was passed and took off in earnest once the dust from the 1964 election settled, remained an ongoing coalition focus.

From this point forward, the Leadership Conference would always maintain an active, multi-issue lobbying agenda. Tables 5.1 and 5.2 illustrate the emergence of this new normal by tracking coverage of the LCCR's enforcement and legislative work in the *MEMO*.[24] Nearly all forty-four *MEMO*s issued during the Civil Rights Act campaign were single-mindedly focused on that one piece of legislation. In contrast, seventeen of the twenty-eight *MEMO*s sent in 1965 dealt with at least two issues. This stemmed, in part, from a flurry of activity at the start of the year, as the Leadership Conference simultaneously mounted its usual push for rules reform at the start of the new Congress and stepped up its work on Civil Rights Act enforcement even before the Voting Rights Act campaign got underway. But it grew especially

TABLE 5.1   ISSUE COVERAGE IN THE *MEMO*, 1965

| MEMO Date | No. | Lobbying agencies for enforcement of existing laws | Lobbying Congress for congressional rules reform and new legislation ||||||||
|---|---|---|---|---|---|---|---|---|---|---|
| | | | Rules reform | Voting rights | State leg. districts | Min. wage | Home rule | Personal security | Amend Title VII | Other |
| 1/9/1965 | 52 | | ✓ | ✓ | | | | | | |
| 1/18/1965 | 53 | ✓ | | ✓ | | | | | | |
| 2/2/1965 | 54 | ✓ | | ✓ | | | | | | |
| 3/8/1965 | 55 | ✓ | | ✓ | | | | | | |
| 3/24/1965 | 56 | | | ✓ | | | | | | |
| 3/27/1965 | 57 | | | ✓ | | | | | | |
| 4/14/1965 | 58 | | | ✓ | | | | | | |
| 4/23/1965 | 59 | ✓ | | ✓ | | | | | | |
| 4/29/1965 | 60 | | | ✓ | | | | | | |
| 5/6/1965 | 61 | | | ✓ | | | | | | |
| 5/17/1965 | 62 | ✓ | | ✓ | | | | | | |
| 5/24/1965 | 63 | ✓ | | ✓ | | | | | | |
| 5/31/1965 | 64 | ✓ | | ✓ | | | | | | |
| 6/14/1965 | 65 | | | ✓ | | | | | | |
| 6/24/1965 | 66 | ✓ | | ✓ | ✓ | | | ✓ | | |
| 7/1/1965 | 67 | | | ✓ | ✓ | | | | | |
| 7/12/1965 | 68 | | | ✓ | | | | | | |
| 7/23/1969 | 69 | | | ✓ | ✓ | | | ✓ | | |
| 8/2/1965 | 70 | | | ✓ | ✓ | | | | | |
| 8/10/1965 | 71 | | ✓ | ✓ | | | | | | |
| 8/17/1965 | 72 | | | | | ✓ | ✓ | | | |
| 8/26/1965 | 73 | | | | | | ✓ | | | |
| 9/15/1965 | 74 | | | | | | | | | ✓ |
| 9/21/1965 | 75 | | | | | | ✓ | | | |
| 9/29/1965 | 76 | | | | | ✓ | | | | |
| 10/15/1965 | 77 | | | | | ✓ | ✓ | | ✓ | |
| 11/24/1965 | 78 | ✓ | | | | ✓ | ✓ | ✓ | | ✓ |
| 12/10/1965 | 79 | ✓ | | | | | ✓ | | | |

*Source:* Part I, Box 38, Folder 3, LCCR Records, Manuscript Division, Library of Congress, Washington, DC.

TABLE 5.2   ISSUE COVERAGE IN THE *MEMO*, 1966

| *MEMO* | | Lobbying Congress for new legislation | | | | | | | |
|---|---|---|---|---|---|---|---|---|---|
| Date | No. | Lobbying agencies for enforcement of existing laws | Min. wage | Home rule | Personal security | Amend Title VII | Housing | CRA 1966 | Other |
| 1/25/1966 | 80 |   | ✓ | ✓ | ✓ |   | ✓ |   |   |
| 2/11/1966 | 81 |   | ✓ |   |   |   |   |   |   |
| 2/21/1966 | 82 |   | ✓ |   |   |   |   |   |   |
| 3/21/1966 | 83 | ✓ | ✓ |   |   |   |   |   |   |
| 4/12/1966 | 84 |   | ✓ |   |   |   |   |   | ✓ |
| 5/3/1966  | 85 | ✓ | ✓ |   |   | ✓ |   | ✓ | ✓ |
| 5/11/1966 | 86 | ✓ |   |   |   | ✓ |   | ✓ |   |
| 6/7/1966  | 87 |   | ✓ |   |   |   |   | ✓ |   |
| 7/5/1966  | 88 | ✓ |   |   |   |   |   | ✓ |   |
| 7/15/1966 | 89 | ✓ | ✓ | ✓ |   |   |   | ✓ |   |
| 8/16/1966 | 90 |   |   |   |   |   |   | ✓ |   |
| 8/22/1966 | 91 |   | ✓ |   |   |   |   | ✓ |   |
| 9/5/1966  | 92 |   | ✓ | ✓ |   |   |   | ✓ |   |
| 9/22/1966 | 93 |   | ✓ | ✓ |   |   |   | ✓ |   |
| 10/4/1966 | 94 |   |   | ✓ |   |   |   |   | ✓ |
| 10/11/1966| 95 |   |   |   |   |   |   |   | ✓ |
| 10/26/1966| 96 | ✓ |   | ✓ |   |   |   |   | ✓ |

*Source:* Part I, Box 38, Folder 4, LCCR Records, Manuscript Division, Library of Congress, Washington, DC; Part IX, Box 135, Folder 3, NAACP Records, Manuscript Division, Library of Congress, Washington, DC.

apparent during the late summer and fall, as a growing variety of civil rights issues took their place on the lobbying agenda.

The pattern continued in 1966, as Table 5.2 shows. While the array of issues was not identical, the seventeen *MEMO*s circulated that year paint a similar picture.[25] At the start of the year, the LCCR announced ambitious plans for the second session of the 89th Congress. For the first time in its history, the Leadership Conference was drafting its own legislation: a personal security bill that Congress would consider alongside an alternative that the Department of Justice was preparing. In addition, the LCCR would continue lobbying for two bills it had taken up after the Voting Rights Act's passage:

the minimum wage bill, which was "expected to come up in the House in the very near future," and a bill to establish an elected mayor and city council in Washington, which, Aronson wrote, was "still a very live possibility."[26] In late April, the Johnson administration submitted an omnibus bill containing personal security, fair housing, and school desegregation provisions, to Congress; this Civil Rights Act of 1966 became a focal point of civil rights lobbying until it succumbed to Senate filibuster in September. But throughout the nearly five months during which the Civil Rights Act of 1966 was pending, the Leadership Conference carried on with its efforts to raise the minimum wage, secure home rule for Washington, DC, and promote vigorous enforcement of the Civil Rights Act of 1964.

## Organizational Growing Pains

Despite valiant efforts to coordinate and mobilize support for a broad array of new civil rights legislation, 1966 was a disappointing year for the Leadership Conference. The Civil Rights Act of 1966, minimum wage, and home rule bills all died by mid-October and, adding insult to injury, civil rights forces were blindsided by a series of efforts to defund and otherwise stymie civil rights enforcement programs in the final weeks of the legislative session.[27] "The events in Congress these past two weeks," *MEMO* no. 95 lamented, "amount to an incredible retreat from the kind of whole-hearted support for full equality that led to the enactment of the major civil rights laws of the past nine years."[28] It was also an organizationally taxing year. A variety of internal challenges accompanied the LCCR's adaptation to the post–Civil Rights Act milieu and came to a head in 1966, prompting Leadership Conference officials to take stock and contemplate changes to coalition operations as 1967 approached.

One readily apparent development was an unprecedented and rapid increase in the number of groups affiliated with the Leadership Conference during the mid-1960s. After practically no change in size in the decade following the LCCR's founding, the coalition roster swelled from fifty-two member organizations on the eve of the Civil Rights Act campaign to eighty-six when the Civil Rights Act was enacted in July 1964 and eighty-nine by the end of that year. This growth continued at a slower pace in the ensuing months but then accelerated in the wake of the Voting Rights Act's passage, as Figure 5.1 shows.[29] By the end of 1966, the Leadership Conference had more than doubled from its original size to 113 members.

The composition of the LCCR's membership shifted as it grew, as Figures 5.2 and 5.3 summarize. In both graphs, member organizations are sorted according to a classification scheme Aronson drew up in 1969, which placed each of the LCCR's members at the time into one of ten categories: labor,

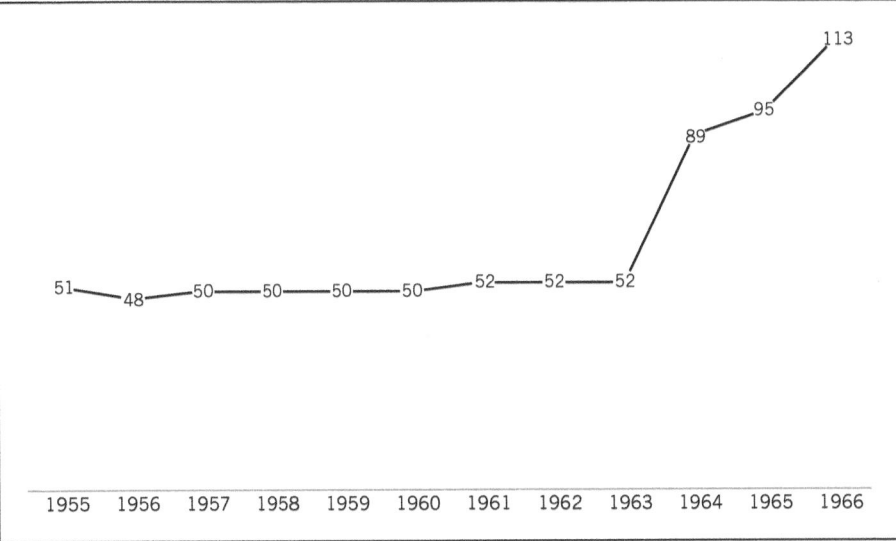

Figure 5.1  LCCR membership, 1955–1966.

Catholic, Protestant, Jewish, fraternities and sororities, professional, civic, civil rights, Negro churches, and miscellaneous. By his own admission, Aronson's typology was "somewhat arbitrary," reflecting his gut sense of how to classify groups rather than considered deliberation over either the categories themselves or the placement of individual groups within them.[30] Nevertheless—or perhaps precisely because it captures the way in which Leadership Conference officials were accustomed to thinking about the makeup of their coalition—Aronson's categories permit a first cut at assessing the compositional changes that were underway.

All ten sectors grew in absolute terms as the LCCR's membership roster expanded during the mid-1960s, as Figure 5.2 illustrates. They did all not grow at the same rate, however, leading to a gradual reconfiguration of the coalition's membership base. As Figure 5.3 shows, labor and Jewish organizations accounted for nearly half of the total membership from the LCCR's founding up through the eve of the Civil Rights Act campaign. By 1966, however, their combined membership share had dropped to about a third. An influx of Catholic and Protestant organizations, which had been recruited to help shore up support from Midwestern and Mountain State legislators in 1963–1964, made up a good part of the difference, but other new entrants into the coalition contributed as well.

The growth of the miscellaneous sector merits special consideration—and, indeed, suggests that long-standing assumptions about who composed the Leadership Conference were becoming outdated even as Aronson still relied

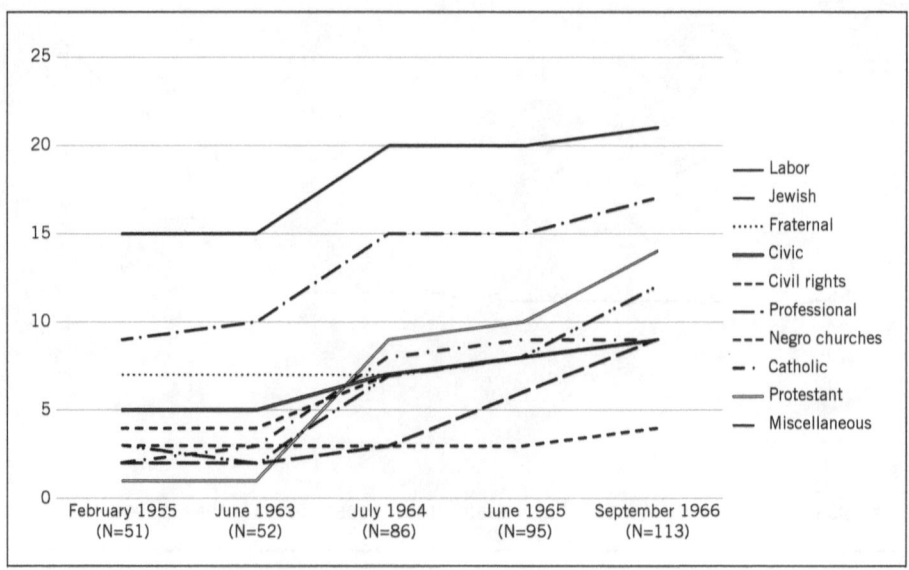

**Figure 5.2** LCCR membership by sector, 1955–1966.

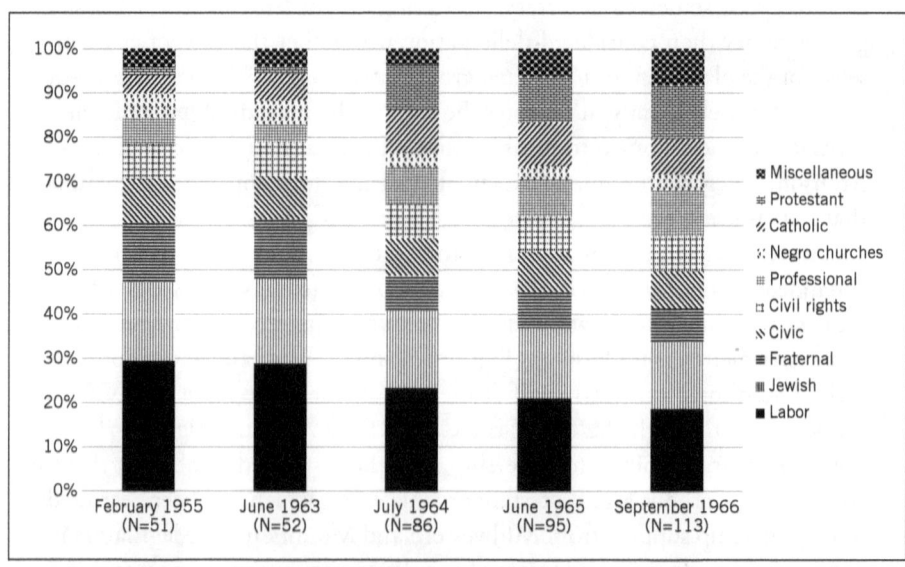

**Figure 5.3** LCCR membership by sector as a share of total membership, 1955–1966.

on them to inform his classification. On its face, this growth was not extraordinary. Just two groups, the American Veterans Committee and Japanese American Citizens League (JACL), populated this catchall category for the LCCR's first decade. By the end of 1966, there were nine miscellaneous organizations, accounting for about 8 percent of the total LCCR membership, on par with several other coalition sectors. Still, it indicated a growing ensemble of member groups representing new civil rights constituencies—or, rather, constituencies whose civil rights interests had not traditionally been addressed by the civil rights lobby. Whereas the JACL had been the lone organization representing a non-black, non-Jewish ethnic minority group in the Leadership Conference for many years, for example, it was now joined by two Latino organizations. Among other miscellaneous newcomers were the National Farmers Union, National Sharecroppers Fund, and National Council on Agricultural Life and Labor, whose shared focus on rural poverty and other farmworker challenges introduced new concerns to a lobbying coalition that had long been dominated by groups that took special interest in urban labor issues.[31]

Aronson's typology also masks an emergent solidarity among women's groups within the Leadership Conference. Many of these organizations were long-standing coalition members and were included in the 1969 list. But rather than envision them as a distinct sector, these frequently intersectional organizations were distributed across the nine non-miscellaneous categories. For example, the National Council of Jewish Women, B'nai B'rith Women, and Hadassah were grouped with the AJC, ADL, and NCRAC as simply Jewish organizations; the National Council of Negro Women was counted with the NAACP, CORE, SCLC, and SNCC as a civil rights group; YWCA was a civic organization; and the National Association of College Women was placed in the professional category. Even while they were not yet perceived as a cohesive set of groups, however, these and other women's organizations came increasingly into collaboration during the Civil Rights Act campaign. Some one hundred prominent women, including several leaders and Washington representatives of LCCR member groups, attended a White House meeting in July 1963 to discuss ways in which they might mobilize public support for the legislation. One by-product of this meeting was the creation of a new coalition, the National Women's Committee for Civil Rights, which served as a sort of women's auxiliary to the lobbying effort led by the LCCR.[32] The Women's Committee disbanded at the end of 1964 but turned its mailing list and cash balance over to the Leadership Conference, and Yvonne Price, who had served as its administrative secretary, became the administrative assistant of the LCCR's Washington office.[33] Within the next few years, old organizations revitalized their programs and new organizations formed as an incipient feminist movement took shape. While it would be some time before women's issues became a mainstay of the Leadership Conference agenda, a first portent came at end of 1966, when the newly formed National Organization for Women (NOW) tendered its application to join the Leadership Conference. NOW's application letter, which LCCR leaders did not act on for several months, signaled a desire to harness the LCCR's coordination capacity to the cause of women's rights: "Since we are aware that vital issues affecting equal employment opportunity for women . . . will require action and the mobilization of public opinion during the coming session of Congress, we wish to begin working with the Leadership Conference as soon as possible."[34]

As this discussion suggests, the changing composition of the LCCR coalition brought new issues to the fore, contributing to the development of the permanent, multi-issue lobbying agenda described earlier in this chapter. Indeed, the decision to adopt minimum wage as a Leadership Conference priority was made at the behest of A. Philip Randolph, the venerable labor and civil rights leader who had just cofounded the A. Philip Randolph Institute, a new LCCR member organization dedicated to the pursuit of economic opportunity for the black working poor. In a letter drafted just after the Voting Rights Act campaign concluded, Randolph asked Clarence Mitchell to put the issue before the Washington representatives. "While I am aware that we must . . . give time and energy to the implementation of the new act," he wrote, "I feel we must also give most careful consideration to the next major step of our struggle for equality." For Randolph—and in line with his institute's theory of change—this next step should address economic concerns; in his words, "the progress we have made at the constitutional and political levels must now be undergirded firmly by economic stability in the Negro community if we are to exercise and expand freedom." Therefore, he continued, "I . . . urge that you immediately call a meeting of the members of the Leadership Conference to consider a major campaign to support legislation now before Congress to increase the minimum wage and to extend coverage of the Fair Labor Standards Act."[35]

The Washington representatives did agree to make minimum wage a Leadership Conference issue, but it raised questions as to how member organizations' suggestions for new lobbying campaigns would be vetted and, for that matter, what properly fell under the rubric of civil rights. Defining the scope of civil rights had not been much of a concern in the early years of the Leadership Conference. While Executive Committee members had disagreed about the inclusion of DC home rule and statehood for Alaska and Hawaii as civil rights issues in the LCCR's party platform plank proposal in 1956, a narrow understanding of civil rights as what by the mid-1950s had become a standard package of bills targeting overt discrimination based on race, religion, and national origin generally prevailed. The early LCCR's operating procedures and track record also militated against organizations bringing new issues to the table. Prior to the inception of the Washington representatives meetings in 1963, there was no forum for member organizations to shape the coalition's lobbying agenda and, without strong evidence of the LCCR's effectiveness, it was not clear that any benefit would accrue from finding a way to do so. With the rise of the Washington representatives meetings during the Civil Rights Act campaign, however, the Leadership Conference became a more participatory organization with member groups more empowered to weigh in on coalition affairs. Back-to-back successes coordinating lobbying for the Civil and Voting Rights Acts, moreover, made the Leadership Conference an appealing vehicle for advancing member organizations' other goals.

The Washington representatives were generally enthusiastic about embracing new issues at first, as evidenced by the rapid expansion of the LCCR's lobbying agenda after the Voting Rights Act's passage. But the operating procedures that had been so effective for coordinating the LCCR's work in pursuit of a single legislative objective in 1963–1964 now strained to accommodate the needs of a lobbying coalition whose attention was increasingly divided. Leadership Conference officials mitigated this to some extent by creating ad hoc committees and subcommittees and eventually separated the coalition's efforts to work with federal agencies on Civil Rights Act enforcement from its legislative lobbying by creating a Committee on Compliance and Enforcement in the spring of 1966.[36] Still, the Leadership Conference was neither accustomed nor equipped to juggle so many legislative balls at once. After news that the 1965 bill to strengthen Title VII would be deferred to the next session of Congress, an AJC lobbyist reported that "the Leadership Conference groups have so many other priorities . . . that they are not unhappy about this postponement, as they do not have time and manpower to spend on it anyway."[37]

There was also some restiveness about the degree to which Washington representatives meetings were sufficiently participatory. Roy Millenson, an AJC lobbyist whose involvement in the LCCR's legislative efforts predated the Civil Rights Act campaign by at least four years, offered this observation:

> I am not alone among the Conference's participants who are beginning to have a feeling of disquiet with respect to our meeting procedures, the actual discussion allowed and the arriving at a "consensus" which seems to be preordained. . . . The virtue of the Leadership Conference is not that it adopts right-sounding resolutions but that it is a sophisticated body which can effectively achieve in a constructive way our mutual goals. Without this full participation of all concerned, the effectiveness of the Leadership Conference in the final analysis becomes quite limited.[38]

The head of a sorority that had joined the LCCR during the Civil Rights Act campaign voiced similar concerns, suggesting that the meetings would not be worth her Washington representatives' time if the "meetings . . . [are] so noticeably 'cut and dry' that volunteers feel—'why give up time when one cannot participate but has to listen all the time.' . . . [The representatives designated in the letter will] offer to participate actively in the program if this is the procedure of the meetings. If it is only to import your report, we will not require their attendance at each meeting."[39]

Financial strain compounded these organizational challenges. Prior to the Civil Rights Act campaign, the Leadership Conference had subsisted on a shoestring budget—that is, to the extent that it had maintained a budget at all, as opposed to relying on periodic donations of funding and in-kind contributions from a handful of member organizations to support short-term projects. With no independent headquarters or staff, there were no fixed costs that needed to be financed on a routine basis. This state of affairs changed dramatically when the Leadership Conference opened its Washington office in July 1963. As described in Chapter 4, the LCCR was showered with an unprecedented infusion of financial donations at the inception of the Civil Rights Act campaign; by one estimate, more than $20,000 was raised in a single day.[40] With occasional prodding from coalition officials, donations ranging from $10 to $10,000 from both LCCR members and nonmember allied groups continued to flow in, financing the Washington office and its staff, which operated at a cost of about $750 per week throughout the campaign, as well as special expenses incurred at key junctures in the legislative process.[41] All told, nearly $60,000 had been raised from voluntary contributions by the time the Leadership Conference moved out of its Mills Building office and began seeking new accommodations at the end of July 1964.[42]

This funding stream all but dried up as the Civil Rights Act campaign came to a close. As Aronson wrote, "there has been a relaxation of mood following the successful enactment of the Civil Rights Act of 1964. A loss in the sense of crisis and, as a result we are left with a number of bills to settle."[43] Keeping the Leadership Conference financially solvent in the after passage of the Civil Rights Act was not simply a matter of paying off expenses from the 1963–1964 campaign, moreover. The year-long effort to strengthen and secure the Civil Rights Act had entrenched the LCCR's new operating procedures, which relied on an independent headquarters—and, in turn, on a continuous stream of funding to maintain it. The LCCR's commitment to working on an ongoing basis for enforcement of the new legislation likewise meant that reverting to the previous decade's model of ratcheting up barely existent coalition operations to support periodic bursts of activity was no longer tenable.

For the next two years, Leadership Conference officials worked to make ends meet without resorting to making coalition membership contingent on monetary contribution. In addition to their usual reliance on periodic appeals to heads of member organizations for donations, they experimented with new fundraising possibilities. As the Voting Rights Act campaign got underway in March 1965, for example, they sought to defray some operating costs by encouraging supporters to contribute to the LCCR as individuals. "How about Becoming a *MEMO* Subscriber?" the final section of *MEMO* no. 56 began, and, after noting that producing and circulating the *MEMO* was among the LCCR's "principal expenses," with "postage alone" running about $3.00 a year per recipient, it offered this appeal:

> Our costs are high, our bank balance low, and the demands on our resources never greater than they are now, when we are in the midst of a campaign for new civil rights legislation. Won't you help? We would greatly appreciate it if each reader would send us a "subscription"—whatever amount he or she can afford to keep the MEMO coming in the crucial weeks ahead.[44]

The call for *MEMO* subscriptions was reissued at the start of 1966. After detailing ambitious plans for pursuing new legislation to curb discrimination in the justice system, establish home rule for Washington, DC, raise the minimum wage, and promote fair housing, *MEMO* no. 80 reminded supporters that "the Leadership Conference makes no general appeals for funds to the readers of the MEMO" and assured them that "with a new session of Congress before us and the increased pace of our activities we will send you free MEMOs almost every week and numerous other mailings designed to help civil rights workers." But the cost of circulating the *MEMO* need not fall entirely to the Leadership Conference: "*You* can help us meet our increased expenses," the *MEMO* continued. "It costs us about $3 a year in postage to send you the MEMO. Won't you treat that as a subscription and send us at least that much? Larger amounts are, of course, always welcome!!"[45]

Ultimately, however, long-standing reluctance to burden cash-strapped groups with mandatory dues gave way to a new feeling that sustaining an effective civil rights lobbying coalition would require financial support from all of its member organizations. A series of letters to groups that had never made a contribution articulated this emerging sensibility. The first, sent late in 1965, described a "desperate" financial situation on the eve of the 1966 session of Congress. "While the Conference levies no fixed amount," it implored, "it is only if *every group* gives *something* that this office can survive."[46] Five months later, a similar missive framed the request for contribution in terms of member organizations' responsibility to the coalition. "The Leadership Conference has never established a fixed schedule of membership dues in recognition of the fact that our constituent organizations have their own financial problems, and that they vary considerably in the extent of their financial resources," it posited, "but membership in the Conference carries with it an obligation to participate in the financing as well as in the program of our common enterprise."[47] By the end of the year, the tone grew strident and, for the first time, suggested that remittance of an annual contribution was a matter of coalition policy. "In the process of closing our books for 1966," it began, "we are sorry to find that _____ has not made its annual dues contribution." After reminding recipients of the LCCR's reliance on such contributions, it added, "we expect each organization to recognize the obligations of its participation in the Conference and contribute each year as much as it is able. We cannot survive without your help. For that reason we ask you to please make your annual contribution now and help us end 1966 without a deficit."[48]

These appeals yielded some fruit, as some twenty organizations made their first-ever financial contribution to the Leadership Conference in 1966. About half had joined the coalition sometime prior to that year and would have received the messages quoted in the last paragraph; others were new to the coalition and would have received a welcome letter informing them that "the Conference office is supported entirely by *annual* voluntary contributions from our cooperating groups."[49] But nearly twenty other groups still made no contribution and at least ten that had donated at least once during the Civil and Voting Rights Act campaigns did not give again in 1966.[50] In contrast to 1964 and 1965, moreover, there was no signature legislative victory in 1966 that could be touted to generate fund-raising momentum in 1967, a year that was shaping up to be just as busy and frustrating as the previous one.

## Challenges from a Changing Civil Rights Movement

The internal challenges the Leadership Conference faced in the post–Civil Rights Act era were exacerbated by mounting conflict between moderate and militant forces within the civil rights movement.[51] The mid-1960s was a turning point in the movement's development—a turning point driven in part by policy achievements like the Civil Rights Act of 1964, which invited violent backlash and highlighted the limitations of legislative civil rights reform even as they introduced monumental change.[52] The movement's organizational center of gravity shifted as civil rights activists grappled with prior assumptions about how to achieve meaningful change in the new context and reconsidered their relationships with liberal allies. The four prominent organizations that had orchestrated the vast majority of civil rights movement activity during the early 1960s—NAACP, SCLC, CORE, and SNCC—were now joined by a growing array of upstart groups.[53] "It is our feeling that the focus and thrust of the civil rights movement has shifted since the March on Washington in 1963," SNCC chairman John Lewis wrote in March 1965; in SNCC's view, the assemblage of decidedly mainstream organizational leaders who had headlined that event and were being recalled to coordinate the triumphant finale of the Selma-to-Montgomery marches for voting rights were "no longer representative."[54] Among and within the "big four," meanwhile, conflict over ends and means grew increasingly heated. Tensions that had churned beneath the surface in the early 1960s came to the fore during the campaign for the Voting Rights Act of 1965 and finally boiled over in June 1966, when SCLC, CORE, and SNCC leaders butted heads over practically every decision they made in the course of a fraught collaborative effort to sustain the Meredith March against Fear. It was at this juncture that "black power" became a rallying cry for some civil rights workers, who increasingly found the principles of nonviolence that had inspired activists a few years earlier untenable—and a troubling specter to others, who feared the new mantra would imperil the movement.[55]

For its part, the Leadership Conference was predisposed to moderation. It was a lobbying outfit wedded to conventional institutional approaches to influencing policy makers, after all, and its officials and most influential member groups were of a decidedly integrationist bent. But the LCCR's membership coalition encompassed civil rights organizations with a range of orientations, including a few that were at the vanguard of the civil rights movement's radicalizing edge. SNCC in particular was a persistent source of tension, and its disruptive role within the coalition intensified as its priorities diverged from those of its more traditional counterparts and a new leadership cadre redirected the group's energies into increasingly militant directions.[56] Still, the Leadership Conference's confrontation with a changing civil rights movement was not simply a matter of dealing with one difficult member; rather, it struggled more generally to assert and define its role as the consortial lobbying arm of a social movement that was straining in different directions.

Early signs of these challenges emerged in 1963, when SNCC's lobbyists faced off repeatedly with other Washington representatives at legislative strategy meetings. Due in part to the vicious hostility young civil rights workers faced on the ground in southern communities, SNCC's vision of how to strengthen the bill that would become the Civil Rights Act—and, indeed, its preference for replacing that bill with one that promised greater voting rights and civil rights worker protections—were at odds with most other LCCR members' inclinations.[57] For the most part, though, the Leadership Conference maintained a clear line of demarcation between its lobbying work and the more public-facing activities of the broader civil rights movement, which shielded it from intramovement conflict for the duration of the Civil Rights Act campaign.[58] As Chapter 4 recounts, organizational leaders resolved early on to separate the LCCR's management of the lobbying campaign from the March on Washington planning committee to facilitate lobbyists' work with legislators who opposed direct action as a matter of principle. Furthermore, while many, if not most, groups affiliated with the Leadership Conference participated in the march (and, indeed, the ten march leaders were all heads of LCCR member organizations), others—most prominently the AFL-CIO—withheld their support.[59] While Washington representatives received updates on plans for the march at their first few meetings, they did not take part in its planning nor was Leadership Conference staff involved in the arrangements. As Caplan wrote to a student seeking information about the LCCR's relationship to other civil rights groups, "our office . . . had almost nothing to do with the August 28th March."[60] The July 1963 decision to keep the Leadership Conference focused strictly on lobbying was maintained throughout the ensuing Civil Rights Act campaign. In response to a November 1963 query about the possibility of another march, for example, Aronson wrote, "we serve only as a liaison office . . . and do not ourselves plan direct actions such as the 'March on Washington.'"[61] He also declined a request for the Leadership Conference to take a stand on CORE activists' plans to stage a civil disobedience campaign at the 1964 New York World's Fair. "There is . . . a wide range of viewpoints among the 85 organizations cooperating in the Leadership Conference," he wrote, and "attempting to get them all to agree on a single position on 'stall-ins' and . . . [other] tactics of this sort, would be a difficult and unrewarding task." He concluded with a general statement of LCCR policy: "We have found that the only way to maintain unity within the Conference is to keep our groups concentrated on one issue: bringing national support for a strong civil rights bill, and getting it passed by Congress."[62]

This stance began to soften midway through 1964 as the campaign for the Civil Rights Act wound down and, especially, in the aimless months after the act's passage. Two events that summer nudged the Leadership Conference toward greater involvement in civil rights movement affairs—or, at least, toward a keener appreciation for the linked fates of its legislative work and the extra-institutional civil rights movement activities that technically fell outside its purview. The first was the disappearance of James Chaney, Andrew Goodman, and Mickey Schwerner, three college students who had just arrived in Mississippi to participate as civil rights workers in SNCC's Freedom Summer project in late June. Shortly after the news broke, the Leadership Conference circulated an unnumbered "Special Emergency" issue of the *MEMO*. Headlined "Mississippi Disappearances Should Be Protested," it informed readers that the "NAACP . . . has resolved to protest the incident before the White House and the Justice Department." No action would be taken in the LCCR's name, but the *MEMO* exhorted member organizations to follow the NAACP's lead. "We call this to your attention because we feel your organization may also want to express its indignation," it suggested, and offered these instructions: "wires should be sent to the Attorney General . . . to the President and to members of Congress, urging an all-out effort to solve a possible crime that could make a mockery of the years of work they and millions of us have put into the passage of the civil rights bill."[63]

The second incident came nearly two months later, as civil rights workers affiliated with the newly formed Mississippi Freedom Democratic Party (MFDP) prepared to challenge the seating of the all-white regular Mississippi Democratic Party's delegation at the upcoming Democratic National Convention. About two weeks before the convention, LCCR officials resurrected the *MEMO*, which had ceased circulation at the close of the Civil Rights Act campaign in July, and produced issue no. 45 to apprise member organizations of these developments. "While the Leadership Conference has not taken a formal consensus of its constituent organizations on the question of the seating of the Mississippi delegation," it announced, "so many Conference organizations have indicated support of the Freedom group . . . that we are sending out this Memorandum for the information and guidance of those organizations who have a concern in this matter."[64] But even as LCCR officials were encouraging member groups to notify Democratic National Convention delegates and credential committee members of their support for the MFDP, emergent political conditions rendered the challenge increasingly problematic. Alarmed by the Republicans' nomination of Barry Goldwater and a spate of racial violence in northern cities in the weeks leading up to the convention, President Johnson left no stone unturned in his efforts to undermine the MFDP initiative and enlisted Hubert Humphrey, his presumptive vice presidential nominee and a long-standing congressional ally of the Leadership Conference, to work out a compromise to keep the challenge from reaching the convention floor. Johnson's move fomented discomfort and discord among liberal interest group leaders, who, still basking in the afterglow of their productive work with Johnson and Humphrey to secure the Civil Rights Act, now had to choose between their relationship with these powerful policy makers and their commitment to the civil rights movement and the democratic cause. Caught in the middle were the MFDP delegates themselves, but also their attorney, Joe Rauh—a prominent figure within the Leadership Conference and general counsel for the UAW, whose president, Walter Reuther, came down forcefully in favor of the Johnson-Humphrey compromise.[65]

As others have recounted,[66] Johnson succeeded at cutting the convention challenge off at the knees. Pressure on the delegates from ostensible allies in the liberal establishment, moderate civil rights movement leaders, and even a handful of members of the MFDP itself further strained relations among civil rights and allied organizational leaders. These tensions grew as the MFDP's challenge to traditional Democratic Party politics in Mississippi continued after the convention. Rauh no longer represented the group, whose next project was to challenge the seating of Mississippi's elected representatives to Congress—an effort he and other leading attorneys and lobbyists within the Leadership Conference deemed both politically and legally unsound. Nevertheless, the LCCR was all but forced to address the issue when Bill Higgs, one of SNCC's lobbyists, sought endorsement of the MFDP's plans at a Washington representatives meeting on December 15. The report of Bill Oliver, a lobbyist for the UAW, paints a raucous picture:

> One of the unfortunate developments during the meeting . . . was an appeal from the Mississippi Democratic Freedom [sic] Party . . . by Attorney Higgs, who persisted in trying to get the Leadership Conference on Civil Rights to endorse the anticipated action which they will take on the opening day of Congress. . . . Despite the fact that the Leadership Conference made it crystal clear that it could not support or endorse this move . . . without first obtaining the approval of the numerous organizations affiliated with the Conference, the people from Mississippi were rather insistent that at least some concensus [sic] be taken. . . . Higgs made a motion to appeal the decision [of] the Chair [i.e., Clarence Mitchell] when a discussion of the matter was ruled out of order. The Chair was upheld but towards the end of the meeting the Mississippi people again raised this issue and Jake Clayman [a lobbyist for the AFL-CIO's Industrial Union Department] then recommended that there be an informal discussion of the matter after the meeting . . . was adjourned. Such informal discussions did take place but the Leadership Conference did not take any official action for or against the contemplated action of the Mississippi Freedom Party on January 4 in the House of Representatives.[67]

Mitchell sought to head off the possibility of a recurrence at the next meeting with an opening announcement that "there will be an opportunity to discuss the MFDP Challenge at the conclusion of the agenda," which focused on plans for working with the Johnson administration on Civil Rights Act enforcement and the prospects for congressional rules reform.[68] Still, Oliver reported "four and a half hours of heated debate" as Washington representatives hashed over the issue.[69]

While controversy over the congressional challenge abated in the weeks following the opening of the 89th Congress, conflict between Mississippi civil rights activists and moderate forces within both the movement and the LCCR resurfaced on February 27, 1965, when a memorandum was sent to "All Participating Groups in the American Civil Rights Movement," including the Leadership Conference and all its members, on behalf of four civil rights leaders: James Farmer (CORE), James Forman (SNCC), Martin Luther King Jr. (SCLC), and Lawrence Guyot (MFDP). Introducing a longer memorandum containing a statement of the MFDP's position on voting rights legislation, it exhorted other organizations to adopt the MFDP stance. Appealing to Farmer, Forman, King, and Guyot's authority as leaders of "the organizations most actively working on voter registration in the South," the memorandum asserted, "we see it as the duty and responsibility of the Civil Rights Movement to militate against any manoever [sic] that would dissipate our energies by the tokenism of still another fraudulently ineffectual piece of legislation."[70]

King subsequently circulated a second memorandum to "clarify and supplement" the February 27 missive, which, he averred, "does not accurately reveal either the manner in which I feel so important a debate should take place nor . . . fully represent the spirit and position of the SCLC." King walked back the original memorandum's barely veiled criticism of the Civil Rights Act, which he declared to be "a tremendously positive achievement" despite the limitations of its voting rights protections, and credited its passage to the LCCR: "it could only have been accomplished by the unity of more than 80 groups within the Leadership Conference working together in mutual trust and confidence." King also rejected the February 27 memorandum's suggestion that the MFDP statement should carry the day and called for the Leadership Conference to take the lead in negotiating a consensus position. "We all knew that the voting section of the 1964 Act would prove ineffectual and that additional legislation would be necessary," he reminded the lobbyists. He asserted that "it is most important for the Civil Rights movement to support the strongest possible legislation." But the contents of such legislation were not, in his view, preordained; rather, "we must all strive to bring about a unified position of the Leadership Conference and then working through the Conference carry that position to fruition. In any event, wherever disagreements exist they should be worked out fully, debated and resolved, within the framework of the Leadership Conference."[71] It is highly probable—perhaps even inevitable—that the Leadership Conference would have assumed control of the Voting Rights Act lobbying campaign without King's blessing. In contrast to June 1963, when there was credible jockeying among organizational leaders to take charge of the lobbying effort for the Kennedy administration's omnibus civil rights bill, the LCCR's capacity for coordinating an effective lobbying campaign was well established when President Johnson submitted his administration's voting rights proposal to Congress in March 1965. Nevertheless, King's missive was likely instrumental in minimizing disruption to an intensive campaign to strengthen and secure passage of the Voting Rights Act during the next five months.

The MFDP controversy cropped up again soon after the Voting Rights Act's passage, however, as the House Administration Committee completed its report on the congressional seating challenge in mid-September and four member organizations—SCLC, SNCC, CORE, and the National Council of Churches' Commission on Religion and Race—requested that the Washington representatives convene to "formulate a Leadership Conference position" in advance of the widely anticipated dismissal of the challenge.[72] Some eighty-five individuals attended the September 14 meeting, including many of the usual attendees but also a substantial contingent from the MFDP and several prominent civil rights movement leaders, including the heads of SNCC and CORE, as well as Dr. King himself.[73] Others, according to Mitchell's biographer, "were pointedly absent."[74] As usual, there is no official record and I have found only a partial set of NCJW lobbyist Olya Margolin's notes on the meeting's proceedings. Her notes suggest far less discord than Oliver had observed at the December 1964 meetings, and the participants ultimately agreed to adopt a statement opposing dismissal on procedural grounds. But this was the limit of their consensus; should the House vote against dismissal and consider alternative courses of action, one participant pointed out, "we . . . have no agreement."[75]

Meanwhile, SNCC's relationship with the Leadership Conference grew increasingly strained. A statement announcing SNCC's opposition to the Vietnam War in January 1966 set off a frenzy of concern by Johnson administration officials and others in the liberal establishment.[76] SNCC sought to clarify and justify its opposition to the war in a memorandum to the LCCR, but moderate civil rights leaders—including Wilkins—publicly denounced its stand.[77] Tension between SNCC and LCCR leadership increased two months later, when Higgs revealed information about internal Leadership Conference proceedings while testifying on behalf of the Washington Human Rights Project at a Senate subcommittee hearing on the Johnson administration's plan to move the Community Relations Service to the Department of Justice. The Human Rights Project was not an LCCR member, but Higgs was also SNCC's Washington representative and, in that capacity, had been actively engaged in the LCCR since 1963. In December 1965, he joined a small ad hoc committee within the Leadership Conference to study the president's civil rights reorganization plan.⁷⁸ It was the work of this committee and the proceedings of a subsequent Washington representatives meeting that Higgs recounted, at length and in detail, to the Senate subcommittee in March.⁷⁹ Upon learning of Higgs's remarks, Wilkins complained to John Lewis, SNCC's chairman: "Mr. Higgs, without consulting anyone in the Leadership Conference, chose to make public a matter that was still under discussion in closed meetings." This, Wilkins contended, was a grave offense against the Leadership Conference. "Confidentiality . . . is essential to the conduct of Conference business. The representatives of our various organizations come together and discuss matters of crucial importance to the civil rights movement with the understanding that what they say will remain private until a concensus [sic] is reached and there is a basis for formal announcement. What Mr. Higgs did strikes directly at that understanding."⁸⁰

The situation was further complicated when a new organization, Associated Community Teams (ACT), requested to join the Leadership Conference and designated Higgs as one of its Washington representatives.⁸¹ ACT's founder, Julius Hobson, balked at Wilkins's request for information about its "program and activities, particularly in relation to efforts to secure the enactment of federal civil rights legislation" and insisted that he would comply only if Wilkins could demonstrate that the same was requested of all prospective member organizations.⁸² This correspondence was recounted in a lengthy memorandum recommending rejection of ACT's membership appeal on the grounds that it was "so atypical of the organizations in the Leadership Conference that both we and they would be best served if they were not part of the conference."⁸³ Among other concerns, the memorandum contrasted the LCCR's "principal purpose" of "attempt[ing] to correct grave injustices in American life through legislative means" to ACT's self-description as "not a civil rights organization in the classical sense but a revolutionary one . . . believing in the abolition of those institutions which inherently foster oppression and exploitation."⁸⁴ While this was not the first time the Leadership Conference turned down a membership application, Wilkins's tense exchange with Hobson and the broader context of ACT's formation within the changing civil rights movement heightened LCCR officials' sense that steps should be taken to prevent a future recurrence.

## The 1967 By-Laws

The risks posed by the challenges described in the last two sections were painfully apparent by the end of 1966, motivating Leadership Conference officials to finally reconsider their long-standing reliance on uncodified traditions and ad hoc management decisions and to adopt a more formal approach to administering the nearly twenty-year-old coalition. A late-December telegram from Wilkins to heads and Washington representatives of LCCR member organizations signaled their intentions:

> Most urgent you attend special meeting of participating organizations in Washington January Eleven . . . to plan course on rights legislation in 90th Congress including crucial fight to amend Senate filibuster rule *plus revisions of Leadership Conference structure to meet new needs.*[85]

A reminder circulated prior to the January 11 event reiterated its significance. It "promises to be one of the most important meetings of our entire 17 years," Wilkins noted, and he identified two agenda items: discussion of the LCCR's ongoing campaign for filibuster reform and "consideration and action on a set of bylaws governing the scope of the Leadership Conference." A draft of the proposed by-laws was attached to the memorandum, which exhorted meeting attendees to "review it in advance" in preparation for its "consideration and adoption."[86] The by-laws were adopted with just a few modifications and took effect immediately, marking the first time in Leadership Conference history that the coalition's organizational structure and operational procedures were codified. As described in the next few paragraphs, the brief document—it is not quite three pages long—formalized many arrangements that were already in place but also introduced some changes to address challenges that had been mounting since the Civil Rights Act's passage.[87]

The by-laws opened with a statement of purpose, identifying the Leadership Conference as a "voluntary, non-partisan association of autonomous national organizations seeking to advance civil rights for all Americans through government action at the national level" and defining civil rights broadly to encompass initiatives such as the previous two years' minimum wage campaigns: "by civil rights we mean not only the establishment and enforcement of rights in law, but also the realization of social and economic conditions in which alone the fulfillment of these rights is possible." It subsequently identified three "principles and commitments," clearly positioning the Leadership Conference among the moderate organizations of an increasingly polarized civil rights movement:

> A. We are committed to an integrated, democratic, plural society, in which every individual is accorded equal rights, equal opportunities and equal justice without regard to race, sex, religion or ethnic origin; and in which every group is accorded an equal opportunity to enter fully into the general life of the society with mutual acceptance and regard for differences.

B. We believe this goal can and must be achieved through peaceful, democratic means within the American political system.

C. The responsibility for achieving our goals is shared by all Americans who believe in justice and equality. Accordingly, there can be no distinctions based on race, sex, religion or ethnic origin among those engaged in the common effort to achieve them.[88]

In turn, and in addition to long-standing requirements that member organizations be "national in scope" and maintain "an ongoing civil rights program," they would henceforth be required to "share the principles and purposes" articulated in the statement of purpose. Likely in reaction to the controversy over ACT's application for LCCR membership, a full section of the by-laws spelled out the documentation organizations must provide to be considered for membership. And, in what was perhaps the biggest change from past practice, membership in the Leadership Conference would now carry a price tag. "Participation in the decision-making processes of the Conference carries with it an equal responsibility to participate in the financing of the common enterprise," the by-laws asserted. "Each participating organization is expected to make an annual financial contribution commensurate with its means and resources."

In addition to establishing membership guidelines, the by-laws sketched out an organizational framework for the coalition. A National Board, consisting of one representative from each member organization, would be the LCCR's "highest governing body . . . and ultimate source of policy authority." It would be empowered to approve new membership applications and elect coalition officers and it, alone, would have the authority to amend the by-laws. In contrast to other governing entities stipulated in the by-laws, the National Board—not to mention its supreme status—was an innovation. Over the years, the heads of member organizations had occasionally been invited for special meetings to discuss the LCCR's lobbying plans and were often asked to endorse public-facing statements; until 1967, however, this collective had never been given a name or accorded any decision-making authority within the coalition.

While the National Board would meet annually to establish the upcoming year's lobbying agenda, vote on new membership applications, and conduct other business,[89] four officers—a chairman, a secretary, a legislative chairman, and a general counsel—would bear the day-to-day responsibility for administering the Leadership Conference. All four positions already existed; the first two had been established and held by Roy Wilkins and Arnold Aronson since the LCCR's founding, while the others had emerged organically by the mid-1960s and were filled by Clarence Mitchell and Joe Rauh. The by-laws introduced new limitations on their tenure, however, as all four would now be subject to election by the National Board for three-year terms.

There would also be three permanent committees, with the proviso that "the Chairman shall be authorized to appoint such additional standing or ad hoc committee as he deems necessary to further the purpose of the Conference." The first was an Executive Committee "consist[ing] of the officers, the chairmen of all standing committees and not more than fifteen additional members representative of organizations comprising the Conference." Essentially resurrecting the Executive Committee that had governed the LCCR during its first decade, this committee, whose members would be subject to approval by the National Board, would "exercise all the power and prerogatives of the National Board in the interim between Board meetings." The second was a Legislative Committee, which formalized the long-standing tradition of maintaining a venue for Washington-based lobbyists to develop and collaborate on legislative strategy. In contrast to careful specification of the Executive Committee's membership, however, the by-laws did not spell out whether participation in the Legislative Committee would be selective, as had been the case for Clarence Mitchell's core lobbyists' rendezvous from 1957 through the first half of 1963, or be open to Washington representatives of all Leadership Conference members, as had been practiced since the campaign for the Civil Rights Act of 1964.[90] The third preserved the new Committee on Compliance and Enforcement's status as a constitutional standing committee, solidifying the LCCR's commitment to both lobbying for new legislation and promoting scrupulous implementation of existing civil rights laws.

Finally, two brief sections near the end of the by-laws addressed the interconnected matters of the consensus decision rule, member organizations' autonomy, and the LCCR's position-taking authority. The first reiterated the LCCR's core commitment to member autonomy: "Participating organizations retain their autonomy and distinct identities and are the sole arbiters of their own positions, policies and programs. Policies and recommendations arrived at by consensus of the Conference are not binding upon the participating organizations." As Chapter 3 highlights, this basic principle had governed LCCR activity since the early 1950s; its reiteration in the by-laws now formalized what coalition officials understood as a necessary stipulation all along. The second section laid the ground rules for public position taking by the LCCR: "When there is a consensus in the National Board or in the Executive Committee, a public statement may be issued or a public action taken in the name of the Conference, provided, however, that the names of participating organizations shall not be listed in such statement or action without express authorization." With this, the Leadership Conference reaffirmed the primacy of the National Board, shifting the authority to identify coalition positions from the Washington representatives to this more august governing body.

## Conclusion

The adoption of the 1967 by-laws marked a new stage in the LCCR's organizational development. This governing document was not revolutionary, to be sure; as the foregoing discussion suggests, it formalized far more than it innovated. Nor did it fully solve the challenges the Leadership Conference confronted during the mid-1960s. SNCC disaffiliated from the coalition soon after the January 11 meeting,[91] eliminating a palpable source of conflict, but other concerns—for example, which issues to prioritize within an expanding civil rights advocacy field, how to advance the interests of the coalition without compromising the autonomy of its members, and how to achieve financial solvency—were perennial. Nevertheless, the shift from the ad hoc operating style Aronson had touted as essential to coalition maintenance in 1962 to the more formal approach he and other Leadership Conference officials embraced in 1967 signaled a new understanding of what it would take for the lobbying coalition to thrive in the waning years of the Second Reconstruction.

The developments that precipitated this shift shed light on the situational nature of interest group coalitions' coordination capacity. That is, the organizational procedures that facilitate coalition decision making and concerted action by member groups in one policy-making context may be less conducive as circumstances change. In this case, practices that were well suited to the situation for which they had been developed—a sustained campaign focused on a single, highly salient legislative objective—grew less effective in an environment marked by mounting issue complexity, interorganizational conflict, and oppositional backlash. Policy success can sometimes be a boon to advocacy groups' momentum. This was arguably the case for the Leadership Conference after passage of the Civil Rights Act of 1957, which helped focus civil rights lobbyists who had previously struggled to coalesce around legislative priorities.[92] In this instance, however, passage of the Civil Rights Act of 1964 created a sort of vacuum in the civil rights policy agenda, which tested the Leadership Conference's capacity to navigate a new—and increasingly hostile—policy context. The LCCR's growing and progressively more diverse membership roster exacerbated the challenge, contributing to pressure to expand the coalition's traditional range of issue priorities even as its financial and human resources were increasingly strapped. As a result, even while the Leadership Conference could claim to represent a larger and more variegated array of constituencies than ever before, its capacity to coordinate their civil rights lobbying efforts was compromised.

Within this context, the move to draft and adopt the 1967 by-laws represents Leadership Conference officials' first recourse to an organizational solution—that is, to adjust the coalition's governance structures and operating procedures as a means of ensuring its viability and enhancing its capacity for policy work. Even with relatively modest operational changes, this marked a fundamental shift from a long-standing informal approach to coalition management to one that not only formalized the LCCR's organizational apparatus, but also set costly requirements for member organizations. The next and final chapter explores the implications for the study of interest group coalitions more generally and reflects on the Leadership Conference's role in civil rights policy development.

# Conclusion

## *To Speak for Millions*

Some months into the LCCR's campaign to strengthen and secure passage of the Civil Rights Act of 1964, Marvin Caplan described the lobbying coalition's work to the president of a prospective member organization. "Our sole goal is unity," he wrote. "We believe that by speaking as one voice on the subject of civil rights or by agreeing to advance the same position when we speak as individual groups, we greatly enhance our effectiveness. In this way, the Conference is able to speak for millions."[1] As this book as shown—and as Caplan surely understood well—neither speaking as one voice on the subject of civil rights nor agreeing to advance the same position when speaking as individual groups came naturally to the organizations that composed the Leadership Conference. Coordination did not flow automatically from their shared commitment to securing federal civil rights legislation or formal membership in a lobbying coalition; rather, it was an occasional product of coalition leaders' efforts to ascertain points of consensus and encourage allied organizations to mobilize grassroots and professional lobbying resources in unison.

Caplan joined the Leadership Conference staff just as the decade-old coalition was developing the organizational capacity to carry out these tasks on a robust and routine basis. Prior to his hire in July 1963, the LCCR's operational structure and practices offered few means of negotiating consensus among its fifty or so member organizations or harnessing their resources in support of coalition goals. While a smaller core of about fifteen organizational lobbyists did collaborate more consistently, it was difficult to produce the sort of unity Caplan described. In contrast, the Washington office he was hired to direct and other organizational innovations implemented that summer facilitated unprecedented coordination. "Speaking as one voice" and "agreeing to advance the same position" remained a challenge, to be sure. But a dedicated headquarters and staff, regular meetings for member organizations' Washington representatives, and new communication mechanisms helped the Leadership Conference confront that challenge over the course of the year it took to enact the Civil Rights Act of 1964. After the Civil Rights Act's passage, this organizational apparatus continued to yield fruit. In addition to supporting a vigorous lobbying campaign for the Voting Rights Act in the spring and summer of 1965, it facilitated a broadening of the civil rights lobbying agenda even as emergent pressures drove LCCR leaders to reconsider long-standing coalition maintenance practices.

This final chapter reflects on the LCCR's historical experience to tease out implications for interest group coalitions more broadly and our understanding of the role advocacy groups played in the Second Reconstruction. Rather than draw definitive conclusions from one distinctive coalition operating during a unique historical moment, it discusses how this case might prompt researchers to broaden investigations into the conditions that facilitate coordination among lobbying coalition partners and what it suggests about interest group coalitions' interactions with changing political circumstances.

## Lessons for Interest Group Coalitions

This book's account of the LCCR's organizational development highlights the centrality of coordination to interest group coalitions' policy work. Rather than focus on the ways in which coordination may be costly to member groups, it explores how—that is, the mechanisms and practices through which—coalition leaders facilitate organizations' coalescence around substantive and strategic decisions and encourage sustained, concerted resource mobilization in support of coalition goals. From this standpoint, coordination is a product of painstaking, iterative efforts to bring the priorities and activities of disparate groups into alignment—efforts that are in turn constrained by a coalition's own organizational limitations.

Thinking about coordination in this way complements previous research on interest group coalitions' role in the policy process. In line with prior studies, it proceeds from the intuition that coalitions enhance groups' influence to the extent that they amplify signals to cautious policy makers about the extent of support for controversial reforms. It likewise accepts that diverse membership can augment coalition signals by demonstrating that support extends beyond those most obviously affected and broadening the array of resources that might be deployed in lobbying efforts.[2] But delving into the mechanics of the processes through which interest group coalitions produce and broadcast signals to policy makers problematizes this relationship. Strong signals of broad support for coalition positions do not materialize spontaneously from the fact of coalition; in fact, diversity can complicate the determination of what exactly a coalition's position is and otherwise hinder collaboration, yielding mixed signals that deter policy makers from acting in its favor.

Those who created and ran lobbying coalitions during the long postwar era perceived this trade-off and sensed that well-conceived efforts to coordinate groups' civil rights work were essential both to overcoming the tendency for diversity to undermine coalition unity and to tapping into its potential for conveying strong signals of broad support for their policy goals. As Chapter 2 describes, NAACP leaders sought organizational solutions to the problem of "increasingly conflicting" drives for civil rights legislation during the late 1940s.[3] The decision to hold a two-day leadership conference on civil rights in lieu of a grassroots convention in February 1952 reflected organizational officials' fear that insufficient planning time to ensure ample participation would risk implying that support for making civil rights an election-year issue was not truly widespread. These concerns persisted as the LCCR began operating as a permanent lobbying coalition during the 1950s and 1960s. As the vignette at the start of this chapter suggests, unity was a hard-fought end rather than a starting assumption for Leadership Conference officials. They appreciated and trumpeted the potential inherent in their variegated roster of "upward of fifty national religious, labor, civic, fraternal and veterans organizations."[4] But they also struggled—with varying degrees of success—to rally these fifty-plus member groups to endorse coalition positions and devote resources to LCCR initiatives.

The contrasting experiences recounted in Chapters 3 and 4 point to an organizational explanation for the conditions that facilitate or hinder coordination within diverse interest group coalitions. Put simply, the organizational structures and procedures used to administer coalitions can make it relatively easy or difficult to discern member organizations' consensus on policy and strategic considerations and encourage them to mobilize grassroots and professional lobbying resources accordingly. Though intuitive, this is a new direction for research on interest group coalitions' role in policy making. To the limited extent that scholars have sought to account for variation in diverse interest group coalitions' success, they have tended to home in on environmental factors—that is, on external conditions in the political milieus within which coalitions operate that yield more or less favorable circumstances for eliciting collective action from coalition partners.[5] But this book's account of the LCCR's first decade suggests that coalition leaders are not always equipped to capitalize on opportune political conditions and that investigation into the organizational qualities that enable them to do so should be a priority for future research.

Methodologically, studying the implications of interest group coalitions' internal structure and operating procedures entails a shift in the level of analysis from individual member groups to coalitions as organizational entities unto themselves. It likewise necessitates what Wiebke Marie Junk has called a "behavioral" or "organizational" approach rather than a "preference similarity" approach to defining interest group coalitions.[6] Only alliances of groups in an explicitly cooperative relationship—whether for an ad hoc, issue-specific purpose or on an enduring, formal basis, as in the case of the LCCR— stand to benefit from coalitional mechanisms that facilitate coordination; in contrast, it does not make sense to apply organizational analysis to a "camp" or "side" of groups that lobby for the same policy outcome without collaborating. Finally, it calls for gathering and analyzing information on the ways in which coalitions operate, which is admittedly not without challenges. In making an analogous case for greater attention to organizational form at the individual group level, Darren Halpin acknowledges that such "finer judgments about qualitative variation" can be onerous, especially in large-n studies.[7] Junk similarly notes that the requisite data "are far from easily available."[8] She suggests that automated analysis of "traces" of coalition signaling—joint statements, cosigned legal briefs, and the like—offer a "promising" solution,[9] but these artifacts provide evidence only of the outcome of coordination, not of the organizational processes that support or hinder it.

This book's focus on the policy-work implications of the LCCR's developmental career also addresses a tension between interest group coalitions' survival and advocacy goals.[10] Sociological research in this vein tends to home in on the conditions that enable coalitions to endure and recommends that coalitions embrace organizational practices that downplay conflict, minimize demands on member groups, and otherwise deter them from disaffiliating.[11] This is consistent with LCCR leaders' initial instincts, as Chapter 3 recounts. As they saw it, relatively informal coalition management was best suited to maintaining a long, diverse roster of member organizations, which they valued for its potential to convey broad-based support for civil rights reform. But the chapter also shows that this minimalist approach impeded coordination when opportunities for collaborative lobbying arose. Will Hathaway and David Meyer anticipate that lobbying coalitions can engage members in collective action more easily when political conditions are conducive—that is, "when the issue is salient . . . and when there is a growing movement uniting groups."[12] But this was not the case for the Leadership Conference during its first decade. Despite bright opportunities heralded by surging civil rights movement activity, the *Brown v. Board of Education* ruling, and legislative and executive branch actors' renewed interest in civil rights legislation, the Leadership Conference struggled without the organizational means to negotiate a coalition agenda and solicit member groups' participation in its work.

Chapter 5 also complicates Hathaway and Meyer's depiction of lobbying coalitions' post-peak trajectory. There was some demobilization after the exhilarating campaign for the Civil Rights Act of 1964, to be sure; as the chapter recounts, a fundraising strategy that relied solely on member groups' voluntary contributions grew increasingly untenable as the civil rights movement's heyday faded. But, at the same time, longtime members brought new issues to the lobbying agenda and new groups sought to join the coalition precisely because they appreciated that the post–Civil Rights Act Leadership Conference had the organizational wherewithal to mount an impressive lobbying campaign. Unlike the Coalition for Arms Control in Hathaway and Meyer's study, moreover, the Leadership Conference did not resist formalization when changing political conditions simultaneously heralded the need for continuous mobilization and intensified ideological conflict among coalition members. Instead, the very same officials who had previously favored the sort of ad hoc arrangement embraced by the Coalition for Arms Control took a different course in 1967 when they moved to sustain their coalition by codifying its mission and operations, vesting decision-making authority in central governing bodies, and mandating for the first time in LCCR history that all member groups contribute financially. These outcomes call for further research into the relationship between interest group coalitions' purposive and organizational goals and coalition leaders' efforts to prioritize and reconcile them. In line with its larger argument that coordination capacity derives from coalitions' organizational form, this book's account of the LCCR's developmental trajectory suggests that a coalition's existing capabilities might shape its leaders' perception of how to balance organizational survival and policy objectives and, in turn, their decisions about how to adapt its operations to suit changing political conditions.

It bears reiterating, finally, that *The Civil Rights Lobby* does not seek to explain the Second Reconstruction's policy outcomes. Its focus, rather, is on the organizational conditions that facilitate or hinder coordination; from this standpoint, an interest group coalition is successful to the extent that it manages to engage diverse coalition partners in concerted lobbying activity even if no policy changes ensue. Still, the LCCR's experience offers some direction for conceptualizing success in research on interest groups' policy influence. The pre-1967 Leadership Conference rarely anticipated, let alone experienced, what political scientists call "preference attainment"—that is, the achievement of its policy goals, or at least achievement of some degree of greater correspondence between its goals and policy outputs.[13] For all its salience, federal civil rights legislation was enacted very rarely during the 1950s and 1960s, and not at all before that in the twentieth century. While civil rights lobbyists did of course advocate for passage of substantive legislation throughout this period, much of their work was directed toward nonpolicy objectives that they hoped would make the eventual realization of their policy goals more likely—for example, changing the House and Senate's procedural rules and shaping political parties' platform commitments. In this challenging context, incremental progress that fell short of actual policy enactments was also valued insofar as it generated momentum, reset expectations for what could be achieved in subsequent congresses, and provided learning experiences for organizational lobbyists and their congressional allies. And, when the stars did finally align to produce legislative civil rights reform, preferences about the content of that legislation were not fixed; instead, the LCCR and its member organizations' policy goals were developed and refined in response to emergent legislative developments.

Focusing on enacted policy as the sole standard for success obscures this complex reality, which is not unique to the mid-twentieth-century civil rights context.[14] A more promising approach might heed Kenneth Andrews and Bob Edwards's call for "measurement [of advocacy groups' influence] across different dimensions of the policy process." Andrews and Edwards identify five such dimensions, only the third of which, "achieving favorable policies," relates to preference attainment concerns. The other four dimensions—"agenda setting," increasing "access to decision-making arenas," "monitoring and shaping implementation," and "shifting the long-term priorities and resources of political institutions"—help capture the broader range of advocacy objectives interest groups and lobbying coalitions pursue.[15] More generally, the LCCR's Second Reconstruction–era experience suggests that lobbyists' influence and success in the policy realm are nuanced and situational. In addition to accounting for the multifaceted nature of interest groups' goals, therefore, research on the impact of lobbying should be attentive to this contextual concern and exercise due caution when assessing the determinants of policy influence.

## The Leadership Conference and American Political Development

Much as the LCCR's experience is instructive for research on interest group coalitions generally, *The Civil Rights Lobby*'s foremost goal in telling its story is to shed new light on the politics of the Second Reconstruction and the role nongovernmental organizations played in the development of the civil rights state. This final section teases out its lessons for students of American political development by returning to two contributions highlighted in the introduction: this book's focus on lobbying as a civil rights movement activity that goes largely unremarked upon in prior research on the Second Reconstruction; and its emphasis on the coalitional dynamics of civil rights lobbying in the long postwar era.

In both scholarly and popular treatments, the Second Reconstruction is a political spectacle in which protesters and public officials are the dramatis personae. The role of the former—civil rights movement leaders and rank-and-file participants in the campaigns they orchestrated—was to motivate reform through high-profile, extra-institutional collective action that drew attention to the horrors of Jim Crow, reframed the desirability and urgency of civil rights in the public mind, and raised the stakes for economic and political elites who previously saw it unfit to intervene.[16] As the ultimate target of this unconventional political activity, public officials—presidents, attorneys general, and key members of Congress in particular—responded increasingly heroically to confront entrenched segregationist forces in the House and Senate and enact long-awaited reform. Once motivated to act, moreover, public officials did so more or less as they saw fit. Ongoing or emergent protest activity may have encouraged them to keep at it, but the contents of the legislation they pursued and the tactics they used to secure it are depicted as the product of unimpeded interbranch and partisan maneuver.

At the most basic level, casting a sustained spotlight on the LCCR challenges the traditional dichotomy between protest and politics—that is, between the actions of civil rights movement actors whose boycotts, sit-ins, and marches inspired from outside the Beltway and those of institutional actors whose legislative and administrative maneuvers transformed protesters' dreams into policy outcomes in the halls of power. As the civil rights movement's lobbying arm, the Leadership Conference bridged the protest and institutional spheres. Its member organizations' lobbyists brought social movement demands directly into the legislative process by drafting model legislation, testifying at hearings, facilitating contact between constituents and representatives, collaborating with lawmakers to develop legislative strategy, and otherwise drawing on their institutional relationships and expertise to urge friendly policy makers to champion their cause and encourage hesitant legislators to come around to support their position. Through these institutionally embedded activities, they pressed not only for civil rights legislation to be passed with alacrity, but for its contents to reflect civil rights organizations' priorities and preferences despite the legislative process's tendency toward dilution.

It is noteworthy that these activities were carried out simultaneously with the protest events that marked the civil rights movement's heyday, belying the conventional view that a turn to institutionally embedded advocacy is an occasional end-stage development in social movements' life cycles. "The residue of protest activity is frequently a symbolic policy response that defuses the immediate pressure," Kay Lehman Schlozman wrote in an analysis of women's rights interest groups during the late twentieth century. "To realize and consolidate substantive political benefits usually requires the kind of coordinated effort and sustained vigilance and follow-through that are difficult to achieve in a decentralized political movement." Lobbying-oriented interest groups, from this standpoint, are an "organizational legacy of social movements" rather than an essential component of ascendant movements themselves.[17] Scholarship on the African American experience similarly sees a mid-1960s shift "from protest to politics," a phrase March on Washington organizer Bayard Rustin used to capture his observation of "direct-action techniques" being "subordinated to strategies calling for the building of community institutions or power bases" after the Civil Rights Act's passage.[18] This periodization is echoed in contemporary research on Black politics. Though more often invoked in the context of post–Voting Rights Act electoral and legislative behavior,[19] the notion that protest gave way to conventional institutional politics after the mid-1960s also appears in accounts of the organizational sector. In a recent study of congressional committees' responsiveness to lobbying by minority group organizations (including the Leadership Conference), for example, Michael Minta writes, "these organizations are best known for using marches, boycotts, and litigation to break the system of racial oppression. . . . *In the post-civil rights movement era, however,* they spend most of their time advocating for the rights of marginalized groups directly with federal government officials."[20]

*The Civil Rights Lobby* challenges scholars to reconsider this periodization. Rather than the residual outgrowth of a spent social movement or a marker of newfound efficacy once policy reforms granting institutional access were attained, the LCCR, its member groups' Washington offices and legislative affairs personnel, and the lobbying activities they pursued were part and parcel of the Second Reconstruction landscape. In fact, as Chapter 2 demonstrates, organized civil rights lobbying by a variegated interest group sector *preceded* the civil rights movement's signature protest campaigns. Much as Chapter 3 shows that the LCCR lacked robust coordination mechanisms throughout the 1950s, a core civil rights lobby was nevertheless already a fixture of the federal policy-making scene when Montgomery Bus Boycott began in 1955. The NAACP's Washington Bureau was well established by that time, as were the Washington offices of several other groups that lobbied actively for civil rights legislation throughout the postwar era; Clarence Mitchell and others who had cut their teeth in the FEPC before transitioning to civil rights and labor advocacy were increasingly seasoned lobbying professionals with impressive institutional knowhow and connections; and the Leadership Conference itself was coming into its own as the principal vehicle for coordination among the most active civil rights lobbyists, even if it was not yet well-equipped to realize the potential of its extensive membership roster. As Chapters 3 and 4 highlight, moreover, policy makers actively sought organizational lobbyists' input and participation in the legislative process. President Kennedy's meetings with Roy Wilkins and other lobbying organization leaders after his decision to advance an omnibus civil rights bill in June 1963 is a prominent example, but evidence suggests that such outreach was longstanding practice—as, for example, when Representative James Roosevelt solicited lobbyists' assistance with his efforts to facilitate civil rights bills' progress through the legislative process in 1956.

Appreciating this timeline complicates the conventional attribution of roles to social movement and policy-making actors. Civil rights movement leaders and participants did inspire and motivate policy makers through protest activity, to be sure; but civil rights lobbyists were concurrently on hand—and institutionally situated—to encourage legislative follow-through and push lawmakers to embrace the strongest possible reform provisions. This squares with research on interest groups that envisions lobbying as legislative subsidy provision. Legislators, in this view, are not merely stimulated by mobilized reform-seekers to enact new legislation, but rely on them throughout the legislative process for information about the benefits and drawbacks of policy alternatives and assistance in marshaling the support of less-invested colleagues.[21] Historically oriented research on social movement and policy reform trajectories tends not to account for this sort of relationship between public officials and social movement organizations, but this book suggests some utility in doing so. In addition to providing a fuller sense of the strategies civil rights movement organizations used to advance their goals, it sheds light on the forces that shaped federal policy makers' legislative interventions and clarifies how nongovernmental action contributed to the Second Reconstruction's policy outcomes.

Finally, in theorizing lobbyists' role in the Second Reconstruction, *The Civil Rights Lobby* underscores the coalitional nature of their efforts to influence federal civil rights policy making in the long postwar era. Its focus on interest groups' collaboration in pursuit of shared legislative objectives—and on the Leadership Conference's ascendance chiefly as a vehicle for coordination among a diverse network of pro-civil rights lobbying organizations—distinguishes this book from prior accounts of how nongovernmental organizations participated in the development of the civil rights state, including both those that investigate groups' unilateral work to shape policy priorities and outcomes and those that identify alliances between civil rights and other interest group sectors on the basis of groups' support for each other's issue concerns rather than active cooperation.[22] This book's contribution is partly descriptive; that is, it helps round out our understanding of Second Reconstruction–era politics by delving into a feature of the civil rights movement's organizational landscape that is typically glossed over. But zeroing in on how groups worked together to lobby for civil rights legislation also sheds new explanatory light on policy development and democratic interest representation.

Throughout the period under consideration in this book, the Leadership Conference made decisions about which civil rights issues to include on the coalition's lobbying agenda, which pending bills and strengthening amendments to prioritize, and how to pursue its substantive objectives according to the consensus of its member organizations. While coalition leaders' understanding of what securing this level of agreement entailed shifted with the organizational changes they implemented during the mid-1960s, the consensus requirement still limited the range of issues they took on and otherwise yielded a lobbying agenda suited to the common-denominator tastes of diverse groups with disparate preferences beyond their general agreement that Congress should enact civil rights legislation. Chapters 4 and 5 highlight ways in which this stance frustrated radical civil rights organizations like SNCC, whose policy aims were frequently out of step with other member organizations' sensibilities. But even moderate groups frequently disagreed about means and ends, and coalition priorities and positions—or, at times, the failure to adopt a coalition stance—reflected the vagaries of the coordination process.

To the extent that interest group coalitions enhance the prospects for the representation of marginalized and underresourced groups,[23] the LCCR's experience suggests that the procedures coalitions use to develop lobbying agendas and rally member organizations to support them can be quite consequential. While many legislative proposals were promoted by civil rights advocates during the 1950s and 1960s, only a select few benefited from intensive coalition lobbying. In many instances, organizations were left to their own devices when deliberation failed to produce a consensus or was deemed too arduous to undertake in light of organizational limitations, time constraints, or known disagreement. In others, a sort of path dependence shaped coalition priorities; once a position was agreed to, it received precedence over competing possibilities at subsequent agenda-setting junctures. Counterfactual scenarios are notoriously difficult to evaluate, but these findings raise intriguing questions about plausible roads not taken: What if LCCR members had managed to rally around a concrete lobbying agenda during the mid-1950s, for example? Or what if some issue other than FEPC—say, enforcement of school desegregation or fair housing—had been prioritized during the lobbying campaign for the Civil Rights Act of 1964, or if SNCC's lobbyists' efforts to prioritize strengthening amendments to the Civil Rights Act's voting rights title had carried the day? While it is impossible to know how these alternative coordination outcomes might have altered the course of civil rights policy development, considering these counterfactual outcomes highlights the importance of the cooperative work civil rights and allied organizations undertook to join lobbying forces and "speak for millions" during the Second Reconstruction.

# Appendix

*Methodological Note, Interviews, and Archival Collections*

Reconstructing the antecedents and organizational development of the Leadership Conference on Civil Rights entails extensive archival research. While I was able to interview two individuals who participated as relatively young lobbyists in the LCCR's Washington representatives meetings during the mid-1960s, nearly all the actors who were involved in the creation and management of the Leadership Conference in its early years are deceased.

This task is complicated by a sprawling documentary record. The LCCR's own organizational records, an extensive collection housed at the Manuscript Division of the Library of Congress, offers an important starting point for this work, but this collection has at least two limitations. The first is the bias that is to be expected of any collection. While official coalition communications are often illuminating, they tend to overrepresent the perceptions and viewpoints of certain actors and, in some cases, offer a sanitized account of intracoalitional dynamics. The second pertains to the organizational history of the Leadership Conference in particular. As I recount in chapters 3 and 4, the Leadership Conference did not maintain its own headquarters or professional staff until July 1963; rather, those responsible for its operations handled coalition affairs alongside other work in their home organization offices. As a result, the collection's pre-1964 coverage is limited and haphazard. To compensate for these limitations, I have supplemented examination of the LCCR Records with those of several member organizations, as well as the papers of selected coalition officials, organizational officials, and lobbyists, and policy makers.

## TABLE A.1  INTERVIEWS

| | |
|---|---|
| Rabbi Richard G. Hirsch | Telephone interview by author, January 19, 2017. |
| Jane O'Grady | Personal interview by author, Washington, DC, March 15, 2019. |

## TABLE A.2  ARCHIVAL COLLECTIONS

| | |
|---|---|
| ADA Records | Americans for Democratic Action Records, Wisconsin Historical Society, Madison. |
| AFL-CIO CRD Records | Records of the AFL-CIO Civil Rights Department, George Meany Memorial AFL-CIO Archive, University of Maryland, College Park. |
| AJC Records | American Jewish Committee Records—Alphabetical Files (for pre-1962 records); American Jewish Committee Records—Washington Representative (1962–1968), both at YIVO Institute for Jewish Research, Center for Jewish History, New York. |
| DSG Records | Democratic Study Group Records, Manuscript Division, Library of Congress, Washington, DC. |
| Hedgeman Papers | Anna Arnold Hedgeman Papers, Manuscript Division, Library of Congress, Washington, DC. |
| Humphrey Papers | Papers of Hubert H. Humphrey, Minnesota Historical Society, St. Paul. |
| LCCR Records | Leadership Conference on Civil Rights Records, Manuscript Division, Library of Congress, Washington, DC. |
| Masaoka Papers | Papers of Mike M. Masaoka, J. Willard Marriott Library, University of Utah, Salt Lake City. |
| Meany Papers | Papers of George Meany, George Meany Memorial AFL-CIO Archive, University of Maryland, College Park. |
| NAACP Records | National Association of Colored People Records, Manuscript Division, Library of Congress, Washington, DC. |
| NCJW Records | National Council of Jewish Women Records—Washington, DC Office, Manuscript Division, Library of Congress, Washington, DC. |
| NCRAC Records | National Jewish Community Relations Advisory Committee Records, American Jewish Historical Society, Center for Jewish History, New York. |
| Rauh Papers | Papers of Joseph L. Rauh Jr., Manuscript Division, Library of Congress, Washington, DC. |
| Roy L. Reuther Papers | UAW Political Action Department, Roy Reuther Files, Walter P. Reuther Library, Wayne State University, Detroit, MI. |

TABLE A.2   ARCHIVAL COLLECTIONS (*Continued*)

| | |
|---|---|
| **Walter P. Reuther Papers** | UAW President's Office, Walter P. Reuther Records, Walter P. Reuther Library, Wayne State University, Detroit, MI. |
| **Roosevelt Papers** | Papers of James Roosevelt, Franklin D. Roosevelt Presidential Library and Museum, Hyde Park, NY. |
| **Sifton Papers** | Paul Field Sifton and Claire Sifton Papers, Manuscript Division, Library of Congress, Washington, DC. |
| **WHCF** | White House Central Files, Lyndon B. Johnson Presidential Library, Austin, TX. |
| **Wilkins Papers** | Papers of Roy Wilkins, Manuscript Division, Library of Congress, Washington, DC. |

# Notes

### ACKNOWLEDGMENTS

1. See July 1959 correspondence among Carl A. Auerbach, Joseph L. Rauh, and Herbert Garfinkel, Box 25, Folder 2, Rauh Papers, and records of the ad hoc Library Committee the LCCR established in 1973, Part I, Box 125, Folder 9, LCCR Records.
2. Minutes of the General Board Meeting of the Leadership Conference on Civil Rights, January 29, 1973, Part VI, Box A36, Folder 4, NAACP Records.

### INTRODUCTION

1. William J. Clinton, "Remarks on Presenting the Presidential Medal of Freedom," January 15, 1998, American Presidency Project, https://www.presidency.ucsb.edu/node/225767.
2. Matt Grossmann, *The Not-So-Special Interests: Interest Groups, Public Representation, and American Governance* (Stanford, CA: Stanford University Press, 2012), 3.
3. See, among others, Richard Johnson, *The End of the Second Reconstruction* (Cambridge, U.K.: Polity, 2020); Manning Marable, *Race, Reform, and Rebellion: The Second Reconstruction in Black America, 1945–1990* (Jackson: University Press of Mississippi, 1991); Richard M. Valelly, *The Two Reconstructions: The Struggle for Black Enfranchisement* (Chicago: University of Chicago Press, 2004); and C. Vann Woodward, *The Strange Career of Jim Crow* (New York: Oxford University Press, 1955).
4. Vanessa Holloway, *Black Rights in the Reconstruction Era* (Lanham, MD: Hamilton, 2018).
5. Megan Ming Francis, "The Strange Fruit of American Political Development," *Politics, Groups, and Identities* 6, no. 1 (2018): 130.
6. Megan Ming Francis, *Civil Rights and the Making of the Modern American State* (New York: Cambridge University Press, 2014), 7.

7. Vanessa Burrows and Barbara Burney, "Creating Equal Health Opportunity: How the Medical Civil Rights Movement and the Johnson Administration Desegregated U.S. Hospitals," *Journal of American History* 105, no. 4 (March 2019): 911.

8. Chloe N. Thurston, *At the Boundaries of Homeownership: Credit, Discrimination, and the American State* (New York: Cambridge University Press, 2018), 19.

9. As defined by Desmond King and Robert C. Lieberman, the civil rights state refers to "the restructuring of American state institutions and agencies to act as enforcers of rights and as desegregators instead of agents of racial inequality and segregation" ("The American State," in *The Oxford Handbook of American Political Development*, ed. Richard Valelly, Suzanne Mettler, and Robert C. Lieberman [Oxford: Oxford University Press, 2016], 246).

10. Letter from John A. Morsell to Richard B. Hertz, May 21, 1959, Part III, Box A205, Folder 4, NAACP Records.

## CHAPTER 1

1. Jane O'Grady, interview with author, Washington, DC, March 15, 2019.

2. Donald R. Matthews, *U.S. Senators and Their World* (Chapel Hill: University of North Carolina Press, 1960), 187.

3. Donald R. Hall, *Cooperative Lobbying—the Power of Pressure* (Tucson: University of Arizona Press, 1969), xi.

4. Kay Lehman Schlozman and John T. Tierney, "More of the Same: Washington Pressure Group Activity in a Decade of Change," *Journal of Politics* 45, no. 2 (May 1983), 361; see also their *Organized Interests and American Democracy* (Boston: Harper Collins, 1986), 306, where they note that "the organization and structure of Congress no longer permit even the most resourceful organized interests to press a policy issue singlehandedly."

5. See, e.g., Frank R. Baumgartner et al., *Lobbying and Policy Change: Who Wins, Who Loses, and Why* (Chicago: University of Chicago Press, 2009), 180.

6. Michael T. Heaney, "Brokering Health Policy: Coalitions, Parties, and Interest Group Influence," *Journal of Health Politics, Policy, and Law* 31, no. 5 (October 2006), 889; Marcel Hanegraaff and Andrea Pritoni, "United in Fear: Interest Group Coalition Formation as a Weapon of the Weak?" *European Union Politics* 20, no. 2 (June 2019): 199.

7. The classic statement of the inegalitarian nature of the U.S. interest group system include E. E. Schattschneider, *The Semisovereign People: A Realist's View of Democracy in America* (New York: Holt, Rinehart; and Winston, 1960). More recently, see, e.g., Lee Drutman, *The Business of America Is Lobbying: How Corporations Became Politicized and Politics Became More Corporate* (New York: Oxford University Press, 2015); Martin Gilens and Benjamin I. Page, "Testing Theories of American Politics: Elites, Interest Groups, and Average Citizens," *Perspectives on Politics* 12, no. 3 (September 2014): 564–581; Kay Lehman Schlozman, "Who Sings in the Heavenly Chorus?: The Shape of the Organized Interest System," in *The Oxford Handbook of American Political Parties and Interest Groups*, ed. L. Sandy Maisel and Jeffrey M. Berry (Oxford: Oxford University Press, 2010).

8. Dara Z. Strolovitch, *Affirmative Advocacy: Race, Class, and Gender in Interest Group Politics* (Chicago: University of Chicago Press, 2007), 203.

9. Robin Phinney, *Strange Bedfellows: Interest Group Coalitions, Diverse Partners, and Influence in American Social Policy* (New York: Cambridge University Press, 2017), 2–9.

10. Wiebke Marie Junk, "Co-operation as Currency: How Active Coalitions Affect Lobbying Success," *Journal of European Public Policy* 27, no. 6 (2020): 16. Emphasis added.

11. E.g., Jan Beyers and Iskander de Bruycker, "Lobbying Makes (Strange) Bedfellows: Explaining the Formation and Composition of Lobbying Coalitions in EU Politics," *Political Studies* 66, no. 4 (November 2018): 959–984; Janet M. Box-Steffensmeier and Dino P. Christenson, "Comparing Membership Interest Group Networks across Space and Time, Size, Issue and Industry," *Network Science* 3, no. 1 (2015): 78–97; Hanegraaff and Pritoni, "United in Fear," Marie Hojnacki, "Interest Groups' Decisions to Join Alliances or Work Alone," *American Journal of Political Science* 41, no. 1 (January 1997): 61–87; Thomas T. Holyoke, "Interest Group Competition and Coalition Formation," *American Journal of Political Science* 53, no. 2 (April 2009): 260–275; Kevin W. Hula, *Lobbying Together: Interest Group Coalitions in Legislative Politics* (Washington, DC: Georgetown University Press, 1999); Christine Mahoney, "Networking vs. Allying: The Decision of Interest Groups to Join Coalitions in the US and the EU," *Journal of European Public Policy* 14, no. 3 (2007): 366–383; Adam J. Newmark and Anthony J. Nownes, "Lobbying Conflict, Competition, and Working in Coalitions," *Social Science Quarterly* 100, no. 4 (June 2019): 1284–1296; Laila Sorurbakhsh, "Interest Group Coalitions and Lobbying Environments: Toward a New Theoretical Perspective," *Interest Groups and Advocacy* 5, no. 3 (October 2016): 200–223.

12. E.g., William P. Browne, "Organized Interests and their Issue Niches: A Search for Pluralism in the Policy Domain," *Journal of Politics* 52, no. 2 (May 1990): 477–509; Loree Byker and Ardith Maney, "Consumer Groups and Coalition Politics on Capitol Hill," in *Interest Group Politics*, 4th ed., ed. Allan J. Cigler and Burdett A. Loomis (Washington, DC: CQ, 1995); Michael T. Heaney and Philip Leifeld, "Contributions by Interest Groups to Lobbying Coalitions," *Journal of Politics* 80, no. 2 (April 2018): 494–509; Marie Hojnacki, "Organized Interests' Advocacy Behavior in Alliances," *Political Research Quarterly* 51, no. 4 (December 1998): 437–459; Hula, *Lobbying Together*.

13. E.g., Heaney, "Brokering Health Policy," and Michael T. Heaney and Geoffrey M. Lorenz, "Coalition Portfolios and Interest Group Influence over the Policy Process," *Interest Groups and Advocacy* 2, no. 3 (October 2013): 251–277.

14. E.g., Wiebke Marie Junk, "When Diversity Works: The Effects of Coalition Composition on the Success of Lobbying Coalitions," *American Journal of Political Science* 63, no. 3 (July 2019): 660–674; Junk, "Co-operation as Currency"; Geoffrey Miles Lorenz, "Prioritized Interests: Diverse Lobbying Coalitions and Congressional Committee Agenda-Setting," *Journal of Politics* 82, no. 1 (January 2020): 225–240; David Nelson and Susan Webb Yackee, "Lobbying Coalitions and Government Policy Change: An Analysis of Federal Agency Rulemaking," *Journal of Politics* 74, no. 2 (April 2012): 339–353; Phinney, *Strange Bedfellows*.

15. E.g., Hanegraaff and Pritoni, "United in Fear," 200–201; Junk, "Cooperation as Currency," 3–4.

16. A number of scholars have developed formal signaling models to theorize interest groups' role in the legislative process; see, e.g., Scott Ainsworth, "Regulating Lobbyists and Interest Group Influence," *Journal of Politics* 55, no. 1 (February 1993): 41–56; David Austen-Smith and John Wright, "Competitive Lobbying for a Legislator's Vote," *Social Choice and Welfare* 9 (1992): 229–257; Sebastian Koehler, *Lobbying, Political Uncertainty and Policy Outcomes* (Cham, Switz.: Palgrave Macmillan, 2019);

Ken Kollman, *Outside Lobbying: Public Opinion and Interest Group Strategies* (Princeton, NJ: Princeton University Press, 1998); and Keith E. Schnakenberg, "Informational Lobbying and Legislative Voting," *American Journal of Political Science* 61, no. 1 (January 2017): 129–145. Studies of interest group coalition influence that rely explicitly on this literature include Junk, "When Diversity Works"; Lorenz, "Prioritized Interests"; Nelson and Yackee, "Lobbying Coalitions"; and Phinney, *Strange Bedfellows*.

17. Janet M. Box-Steffensmeier, Dino P. Christenson, and Alison W. Craig, "Cue-Taking in Congress: Interest Group Signals from Dear Colleague Letters," *American Journal of Political Science* 63, no. 1 (January 2019): 163–180; Richard L. Hall and Alan V. Deardorff, "Lobbying as Legislative Subsidy," *American Political Science Review* 100, no. 1 (February 2006): 69–84.

18. Nelson and Yackee, "Lobbying Coalitions," 342; emphasis added.

19. See, e.g., Baumgartner et al., *Lobbying and Policy Change*, 223.

20. In addition to Nelson and Yackee, "Lobbying Coalitions," see Phinney, *Strange Bedfellows*, and Lorenz, "Prioritized Interests."

21. Nelson and Yackee, "Lobbying Coalitions," 342.

22. Phinney, *Strange Bedfellows*, 26–28.

23. Ibid., 25.

24. Baumgartner et al., *Lobbying and Policy Change*, 204.

25. Ibid., 222–223.

26. Darren R. Halpin, *The Organization of Political Interest Groups: Designing Advocacy* (London: Routledge, 2014), 176.

27. Halpin, *Organization of Political Interest Groups*, 190. Emphasis in original.

28. Nelson and Yackee, "Lobbying Coalitions," 349. Wiebke Marie Junk and Anne Rasmussen similarly show that unified issue framing by advocates on one side of the issue is a significant determinant of lobbying success; see their "Framing by the Flock: Collective Issue Definition and Advocacy Success," *Comparative Political Studies* 52, no. 4 (March 2019): 483–513.

29. The concept of tagging along is drawn from Hula's conceptualization of interest group coalitions' structure as consisting of three concentric circles: an inner circle of core members, who "are notable for their willingness to expend high levels of resources to promote overall legislative victory," a middle ring of "players," whose relatively "narrow focus and expertise are used primarily in shaping the coalition's agenda and honing the coalition's position on the points that are relevant to them," and a peripheral set of "tag-alongs," or groups that "have neither a compelling commitment to the legislation in question nor a willingness to expend significant efforts to achieve the eventual policy goal that serves as the focus of the coalition" (Hula, *Lobbying Together*, 39–48). Other studies of member organizations' disparate contributions to the coalitions they belong to include Hojnacki, "Organized Interests' Advocacy," and Heaney and Leifeld, "Contributions by Interest Groups."

30. See, e.g., Beyers and de Bruycker, "Lobbying"; Hojnacki, "Interest Groups' Decisions"; Hula, *Lobbying Together*; and Junk, "When Diversity Works."

31. In this vein, Junk, "When Diversity Works," makes a compelling case for more careful attention to the trade-offs of diversity for interest group coalitions and, in particular, to its tendency to heighten cooperation costs.

32. D. Hall, *Cooperative Lobbying*, 185.

33. A recent study by Junk finds that issue salience mediates the relationship between interest group coalitions' diversity and achievement of their desired policy

outcomes (Junk, "When Diversity Works"). Evidence from organizational records suggests that, at least for some of the LCCR's member groups, the Civil Rights Act's prominence did displace some focus on other legislative priorities; see, e.g., Report of Washington JACL Representative to 18th Biennial National Convention of Japanese American Citizens League, June 29, 1964, Box 65, Folders 19–20, Masaoka Papers.

34. The distinction between ad hoc interest group coalitions and those that co-operate long-term is long-standing; see, e.g., D. Hall, *Cooperative Lobbying*, xvii. More recently, see Mahoney, "Networking vs. Allying."

35. Halpin, *Organization of Political Interest Groups*, 194.

36. Darrin Halpin and Carsten Daugbjerg, "Identity as Constraint and Resource in Interest Group Evolution: A Case of Radical Organizational Change," *British Journal of Politics and International Relations* 17, no. 1 (February 2015): 31–48.

37. McGee Young, *Developing Interests: Organizational Change and the Politics of Advocacy* (Lawrence: University Press of Kansas, 2010), 3.

38. Young, *Developing Interests*, 10.

39. Young, *Developing Interests*. "Familiar scripts" is from Elisabeth Clemens, *The People's Lobby: Organizational Innovation and the Rise of Interest Group Politics in the United States* (Chicago: University of Chicago Press, 1997), 12.

40. Junk, "When Diversity Works."

41. While I am hardly the first to insist on defining interest group coalitions in this way (see, e.g., Christine Mahoney and Frank L. Baumgartner, "Partners in Advocacy: Lobbyists and Government Officials in Washington," *Journal of Politics* 77, no. 1 [January 2015], 206), there is some ambivalence in the literature, and several studies explicitly adopt a more permissive definition that encompasses uncoordinated assemblages of interest groups that lobby on the same side of an issue; see, e.g., Matt Grossman and Casey B. K. Dominguez, "Party Coalitions and Interest Group Networks," *American Politics Research* 37, no. 5 (September 2009): 767–800, and Lorenz, "Prioritized Interests." Junk argues similarly that "selection of an approach [to defining interest group coalitions] should go hand in hand with the theoretical expectations on how coalitions enhance lobbying access or success" (Wiebke Marie Junk, "Synergies in Lobbying? Conceptualising and Measuring Lobbying Coalitions to Study Interest Group Strategies, Access, and Influence," *Interest Groups and Advocacy* 9, no. 1 [March 2020], 33).

42. E.g., Dennis Chong, *Collective Action and the Civil Rights Movement* (Chicago: University of Chicago Press, 1991); Joseph E. Luders, *The Civil Rights Movement and the Logic of Social Change* (Cambridge: Cambridge University Press, 2010); Doug McAdam, *Political Process and the Development of Black Insurgency 1930–1970* (Chicago: University of Chicago Press, 1982); and Doug McAdam, Sidney Tarrow, and Charles Tilly, *Dynamics of Contention* (Cambridge: Cambridge University Press, 2001).

## CHAPTER 2

1. Joseph B. Robison, "Organizations Promoting Civil Rights and Liberties," *Annals of the American Academy of Political and Social Science* 275, no. 1 (May 1951), 22. Robison's use of *peripheral* differs substantially from contemporary political scientists' designation of interest group coalition members that are relatively inactive in coalition affairs as peripheral; see especially Kevin W. Hula, *Lobbying Together: Interest Group Coalitions in Legislative Politics* (Washington, DC: Georgetown University Press, 1999), 46–48.

2. Robison, "Organizations," 22.
3. Ibid., 23.
4. Eric Schickler, *Racial Realignment: The Transformation of American Liberalism, 1932–1965* (Princeton, NJ: Princeton University Press, 2016), 97. See also Christopher Baylor, *First to the Party: The Group Origins of Party Transformation* (Philadelphia: University of Pennsylvania Press, 2018), 44–48, where this coalition is mentioned in passing.
5. See, generally, Schickler, *Racial Realignment*, chapter 4.
6. Schickler, *Racial Realignment*, 93–94.
7. Robison, "Organizations," 22.
8. "Preference similarity" is the term Wiebke Marie Junk uses to distinguish approaches to interest group coalition definition that include "a positional 'camp' or 'side' of all advocates actively promoting the same policy position" from those that entail at least some modicum of explicit cooperation in support of shared policy goals (Junk, "Synergies in Lobbying? Conceptualising and Measuring Lobbying Coalitions to Study Interest Group Strategies, Access, and Influence," *Interest Groups and Advocacy* 9, no. 1 (March 2020), 24.
9. Philip A. Klinkner, *The Unsteady March: The Rise and Decline of Racial Equality in America* (Chicago and London: University of Chicago Press, 1999); Robert P. Saldin, *War, the American State, and Politics since 1898* (New York: Cambridge University Press, 2010).
10. In addition to Klinkner, *Unsteady March*, and Saldin, *War*, see Richard M. Dalfiume, "The 'Forgotten Years' of the Negro Revolution," *Journal of American History* 55, no. 1 (June 1968): 90–106, and Azza Salama Layton, *International Politics and Civil Rights Policies in the United States, 1941–1960* (Cambridge: Cambridge University Press, 2000). The classic contemporaneous source is Gunnar Myrdal's *An American Dilemma: The Negro Problem and American Democracy* (New York: Harper, 1944).
11. Mary L. Dudziak, *Cold War Civil Rights: Race and the Image of American Democracy* (Princeton, NJ: Princeton University Press, 2000). See also Layton, *International Politics*, and John David Skrentny, "The Effect of the Cold War on African-American Civil Rights: America and the World Audience, 1945–1968," *Theory and Society* 27, no. 2 (April 1998): 237–285.
12. Steven White, "Civil Rights, World War II, and U.S. Public Opinion," *Studies in American Political Development* 30, no. 1 (April 2016): 38–61.
13. Christopher S. Parker, *Fighting for Democracy: Black Veterans and the Struggle against White Supremacy in the Postwar South* (Princeton, NJ: Princeton University Press, 2009); Charles M. Payne, *I've Got the Light of Freedom: The Organizing Tradition and the Mississippi Freedom Struggle* (Berkeley: University of California Press, 1996), chapter 2.
14. Paul Frymer, *Uneasy Alliances: Race and Party Competition in America* (Princeton, NJ: Princeton University Press, 1999), 95.
15. Kevin M. Schultz, "The FEPC and the Legacy of the Labor-Based Civil Rights Movement of the 1940s," *Labor History* 49, no. 1 (2008), 74–75.
16. Anthony S. Chen, *The Fifth Freedom: Jobs, Politics, and Civil Rights in the United States, 1941–1972* (Princeton, NJ: Princeton University Press, 2009), 45. This resonates with Kay Lehman Schlozman's observation that "organizations of all kinds take advantage of the expertise gained from working for the federal government by hiring through what is commonly referred to as the 'revolving door'" (Schlozman, "Representing Women in Washington: Sisterhood and Pressure Politics," in *Women, Politics, and Change*, ed. Louise A. Tilly and Patricia Gurin (New York: Russell Sage Foundation, 1990), 354.

17. Ibid.

18. Andrew Edmund Kersten, *Race, Jobs, and the War: The FEPC in the Midwest, 1941–46* (Urbana: University of Illinois Press, 2000), 59. Hula similarly observes that interest groups that forge coalitions are often "linked through the career paths of their staff members" (Hula, *Lobbying Together*, 55).

19. The SCLC was founded in 1957 and SNCC in 1960. Both joined the Leadership Conference during the 1960s.

20. Robison, "Organizations," 20.

21. While the NAACP's use of litigation is well known, less attention has been paid to its legislative lobbying activities. Two correctives include Gilbert Ware, "Lobbying as a Means of Protest: The NAACP as an Agent of Equality," *Journal of Negro Education* 33, no. 2 (Spring 1964): 103–110, and, much more recently, Megan Ming Francis, *Civil Rights and the Making of the Modern American State* (New York: Cambridge University Press, 2014).

22. While the Urban League did participate in some postwar civil rights coalition activity, it did not join the Leadership Conference until 1963; see Arnold Aronson's December 21, 1962, letter to Tilford Dudley, which begins: "the National Urban League just advised me that it wishes to become affiliated with the Leadership Conference . . . a development that we have been working on for some time." See Part I, Box 1, Folder 4, LCCR Records. Whitney Young, who became the Urban League's Executive Director in 1961, is typically credited with its embrace of a broader range of strategies, including participation in both protest and lobbying initiatives.

23. On the NCNW's creation and prior lobbying activities by Black women's groups, see Deborah Gray White, *Too Heavy a Load: Black Women in Defense of Themselves, 1894–1994* (New York: W. W. Norton, 1999), and Jacquelyn Dowd Hall, *Revolt against Chivalry: Jesse Daniel Ames and the Women's Campaign against Lynching* (New York: Columbia University Press, 1979). That it can be taken for granted that NCNW was active in lobbying is the premise of Rebecca Tuuri's argument that the organization also engaged in direct-action civil rights movement activity in *Strategic Sisterhood: The National Council of Negro Women in the Black Freedom Struggle* (Chapel Hill: University of North Carolina Press, 2018).

24. See, e.g., Vanessa Burrows and Barbara Burney, "Creating Equal Health Opportunity: How the Medical Civil Rights Movement and the Johnson Administration Desegregated U.S. Hospitals," *Journal of American History* 105, no. 4 (March 2019): 885–911; Vanessa Northington Gamble, *Making a Place for Ourselves: The Black Hospital Movement, 1920–1945* (New York: Oxford University Press, 1995); and P. Preston Reynolds, "Dr. Louis T. Wright and the NAACP: Pioneers in Hospital Racial Integration," *American Journal of Public Health* 90, no. 6 (June 2000): 883–892.

25. Robert L. Harris Jr., "Lobbying Congress for Civil Rights: The American Council on Human Rights, 1948–1963," in *African American Fraternities and Sororities: The Legacy and the Vision*, ed. Tamara L. Brown, Gregory S. Parks, and Clarenda M. Phillips (Lexington: University Press of Kentucky, 2005), 211–230.

26. Beth Tompkins Bates, "A New Crowd Challenges the Agenda of the Old Guard in the NAACP, 1933–1941," *American Historical Review* 102, no. 2 (April 1997): 340–377; August Meier and John H. Bracey Jr., "The NAACP as Reform Movement, 1909–1965: 'To Reach the Conscience of America,'" *Journal of Southern History* 59, no. 1 (February 1993): 3–30.

27. "Statement of Purpose," n.d. (1943), Part II, Box H8, Folder 18, NAACP Records.

28. Meier and Bracey, "NAACP," 52.

29. Robison also mentions three Native American organizations, but they were not active in the era's civil rights lobbying coalitions. They, along with organizations representing other racial and ethnic minority groups (e.g., Latinos), would not join the Leadership Conference until the late 1960s.

30. Cheryl Lynn Greenberg, *Troubling the Waters: Black-Jewish Relations in the American Century* (Princeton, NJ: Princeton University Press, 2010), 116.

31. On NCRAC's origins, see Selma G. Hirsh, "Jewish Community Relations," *American Jewish Year Book* 54 (1953): 162–177.

32. Jerome A. Chanes, "Who Does What? Jewish Advocacy and Jewish 'Interest,'" in *Jews and American Politics*, ed. Sandy Maisel and Ira N. Forman (Lanham, MD: Rowman and Littlefield, 2004), 100.

33. Stuart Svonkin, *Jews against Prejudice: American Jews and the Fight for Civil Liberties* (New York: Columbia University Press, 1997), 18.

34. Greenberg, *Troubling the Waters*, 96–97.

35. This was not without controversy after the JACL's cooperation with the federal government in the early stages of the Japanese internment and, more generally, to intergenerational tension between first-generation Japanese immigrants to the United States (who were by law ineligible for U.S. citizenship) and the second generation of U.S.-born (and therefore U.S. citizen) Japanese Americans, the latter of which were the driving force behind JACL. On these tensions, see, e.g., Stephanie Bangarth, *Voices Raised in Protest: Defending North American Citizens of Japanese Ancestry, 1942–49* (Vancouver, BC: University of British Columbia Press, 2008), 120–124; Paul R. Spickard, "The Nisei Assume Power: The Japanese Citizens League, 1941–1942," *Pacific Historical Review* 52, no. 2 (May 1983): 147–174; and Ellen D. Wu, *The Color of Success: Asian Americans and the Origins of the Model Minority* (Princeton, NJ: Princeton University Press, 2014), chapter 3.

36. The JACL was founded in Seattle and originally headquartered in San Francisco, but it moved to Salt Lake City in 1942, as the evacuation of Japanese Americans from the West Coast was underway. See Bill Hosokawa, *JACL in Quest of Justice* (New York: Morrow, 1982), 156.

37. Mike M. Masaoka to National Board Members et al., April 22, 1944, Box 64, Folders 27–33, Masaoka Papers. This sentiment is reiterated in Masaoka's reports as JACL's Washington representative during the mid-1960s; see Box 65, Folders 19–21, Masaoka Papers.

38. Masaoka to National Board Members et al., April 22, 1944.

39. Washington Office, Japanese American Citizens League, "First Interim Report," August 11, 1947, Box 65, Folder 2, Masaoka Papers.

40. Paul Frymer, *Black and Blue: African Americans, the Labor Movement, and the Decline of the Democratic Party* (Princeton, NJ: Princeton University Press, 2008), 47.

41. In addition to Frymer, *Black and Blue*, see, e.g., Philip S. Foner, *Organized Labor and the Black Worker, 1619–1973* (New York: International, 1974); Paul D. Moreno, *Black Americans and Organized Labor: A New History* (Baton Rouge: Louisiana State University Press, 2008); and David R. Roediger, *The Wages of Whiteness: Race and the Making of the American Working Class* (London: Verso, 1991).

42. On the extent and limitations of the early CIO's racial progressivism, see Michael Goldfield, "Race and the CIO: The Possibilities for Racial Egalitarianism during the 1930s and 1940s," *International Labor and Working-Class History* 44 (Fall 1993): 1–32; and Robert H. Zieger, *The CIO, 1935–1955* (Chapel Hill: University of North Carolina Press, 1995), 84–85.

43. Baylor, *First to the Party*, chapters 2–5; Schickler, *Racial Realignment*, 52–68.

44. Schickler, *Racial Realignment*, 67. On the UAW in particular, see Kevin Boyle, *The UAW and the Heyday of American Liberalism 1945–1968* (Ithaca, NY: Cornell University Press, 1995), 46–47.

45. Louis C. Kesselman, *The Social Politics of FEPC: A Study in Reform Pressure Movements* (Chapel Hill: University of North Carolina Press, 1948), 145–151; Moreno, *Black Americans*, 206–207. See also Clarence Mitchell to Roy Wilkins, January 13, 1947, Part II, Box A258, Folder 5, NAACP Records.

46. Samuel Walker, *In Defense of American Liberties: A History of the ACLU* (Carbondale: Southern Illinois University Press, 1990), 60.

47. Because of its initial cooperation with the federal government, JACL was reluctant to join the ACLU in bringing test cases of the internment's constitutionality; according to Bangarth, the JACL maintained that it "'unalterably opposed' test cases" in April 1942 and began softening its position only a few months later. Nevertheless, even in 1943, "the ACLU still lacked full JACL support." See Bangarth, *Voices Raised*, 124 and 137. Masaoka singled out Roger Baldwin, the ACLU's executive director, for helping him find his footing in the report on his move to Washington. Masaoka to National Board Members et al., April 22, 1944.

48. Walker, *In Defense*, 162–166.

49. Among other places, the ADA's role in the Democratic Party's adoption of a strong civil rights platform plank in 1948 is recounted in Clifton Brock, *Americans for Democratic Action: Its Role in National Politics* (Washington, DC: Public Affairs Press, 1962), 95–99.

50. See, e.g., the UDA's undated "Projects for Minority Rights and Civil Liberties Committee," Series I, Box 10, Folder 3, ADA Records, which includes "cooperate with the NAACP" as an item in a typed list of project ideas. Handwritten marginal notes identify potential liaison organizations working in the issue areas associated with other listed projects.

51. Robison, "Organizations," 22.

52. Findlay notes that "on racial matters . . . the National Council of Churches did little more than follow or keep abreast of its constituents" until 1963 (James F. Findlay Jr., *Church People in the Struggle: The National Council of Churches and the Black Freedom Movement, 1950–1970* (Oxford: Oxford University Press, 1993), 6. The Catholic organization that would be most central to the LCCR's lobbying efforts—namely, the National Catholic Council for Interracial Justice—was not established until the late 1950s (Paul T. Murray, "From the Sidelines to the Frontlines: Mathew Ahmann Leads American Catholics into the Civil Rights Movement," *Journal of the Illinois State Historical Society* 107, no. 1 [Spring 2014]: 77–115).

53. Findlay, *Church People*, 14.

54. On the rise of the interracialist Catholic movement, see, e.g., Karen Joy Johnson, "Another Long Civil Rights Movement: How Catholic Interracialists Used the Resources of Their Faith to Tear Down Racial Hierarchies," *American Catholic Studies* 126,

no. 4 (Winter 2015): 1–27; John T. McGreevy, *Parish Boundaries: The Catholic Encounter with Race in the Twentieth-Century Urban North* (Chicago: University of Chicago Press, 2016); and Murray, "From the Sidelines."

55. Steven F. Lawson, *Black Ballots: Voting Rights in the South, 1944–1969* (New York: Columbia University Press, 1976), 145; Schultz, "FEPC."

56. Lawson, *Black Ballots*, 61–62.

57. Lawson, *Black Ballots*, 82–84. On the development of the Truman administration's civil rights agenda, see, e.g., Richard Gergel, *Unexampled Courage: The Blinding of Sgt. Isaac Woodard and the Awakening of President Harry S. Truman and Judge J. Waties Waring* (New York: Sarah Crichton, 2019); William E. Juhnke, "President Truman's Committee on Civil Rights: The Interaction of Politics, Protest, and Presidential Advisory Commission," *Presidential Studies Quarterly* 19, no. 3 (Summer 1989): 593–610; and Harvard Sitkoff, "Harry Truman and the Election of 1948: The Coming of Age of Civil Rights in American Politics," *Journal of Southern History* 37, no. 4 (November 1971): 597–616.

58. A. Philip Randolph to Walter White, September 28, 1943, Part II, Box A258, Folder 3, NAACP Records.

59. An October 10, 1945, press release states that the NCPFEPC had "70 collaborating organizations" (Box 1, Folder 3, Hedgeman Papers). A partial list of "national cooperating organizations" printed on the back of the NCPFEPC's letterhead stationery in 1948 names seventy-six groups; see reverse side of A. Philip Randolph to Members of the Board and All Cooperating Organizations, February 17, 1948, Series V, Box 25, Folder 5, ADA Records.

60. Schultz, "FEPC," 79–81. On Hedgeman's role in the NCPFEPC and her resignation, see Jennifer Scanlon, *Until There Is Justice: The Life of Anna Arnold Hedgeman* (New York: Oxford University Press, 2016). Schultz and Scanlon offer disparate accounts of the aftermath of Hedgeman's resignation. For Schultz, the fallout of her departure led to Randolph's sidelining and, as a result of organizational changes made by those who moved to fill in the vacuum, "the National Council truly became the most expansive advocacy group in the civil rights struggle" (Schultz, "FEPC," 81). Scanlon, however, maintains that Hedgeman's resignation "was the beginning of the end of the Council," a conclusion that is well borne out by archival records of the organization's ongoing financial insolvency, personnel turnover, and general disarray (Scanlon, *Until There Is Justice*, 107).

61. Minutes of a Meeting of the National Board of Directors, National Council for a Permanent FEPC, August 2, 1946. Part II, Box A258, Folder 4, NAACP Records. Hedgeman's resignation was not without controversy. The AFL's Boris Shishkin resigned from the NCPFEPC's Executive Committee upon learning of it and a letter from Allen Knight Chalmers to Walter White suggests that "a faction" of those in attendance "went after" Hedgeman at the meeting at which she resigned. Shishkin's August 12, 1946, letter to Randolph and Allan Knight Chalmers and Chalmers's August 5, 1946, letter to White are both in Part II, Box A258, Folder 4, NAACP Records.

62. On the latter concern, see the August 2 National Board of Directors meeting minutes and Milo Manley to Max Delson, September 12, 1946, Box 24, Folder 4, Wilkins Papers.

63. Roy Wilkins to Lester B. Granger, March 20, 1947, Part II, Box A258, Folder 5, NAACP Records.

64. For a frank overview of the NCPFEPC's persistent troubles, see Elmer W. Henderson to Roy Wilkins, January 7, 1948, Part II, Box A259, Folder 2, NAACP Records.

65. Paul Sifton to "Ben," August 4, 1947, Box 28, Folder 1, Sifton Papers.

66. A particularly troubling source of debt was back pay owed to Hedgeman and other former staff members who resigned or were terminated in 1946. See Roy Wilkins to Sidney Wilkinson, June 6, 1947, and other relevant correspondence in Part II, Box A258, Folder 6, NAACP Records.

67. See, e.g., Allan Knight Chalmers to Administrative Committee of the NAACP on FEPC Participation, October 25, 1946, and October–November 1946 memoranda between Roy Wilkins and Walter White, all in Part II, Box A258, Folder 4, NAACP Records; Clarence Mitchell to Roy Wilkins, February 18, 1948, Part II, Box A259, Folder 2, NAACP Records.

68. Juhnke, "President Truman's Committee."

69. "Tentative Program of Possible Procedure against Mob Violence," n.d. [August 1946], Box 94, Folder 7, AJC Records.

70. Alfred L. Bernheim to Dr. John Slawson, August 8, 1946, Box 94, Folder 7, AJC Records.

71. Ibid.

72. For example, Graham's statement that the LCCR had "twenty [member] organizations in 1949" seems to rest on this assumption (Hugh Davis Graham, *The Civil Rights Era: Origins and Development of National Policy, 1960–1972* [New York: Oxford University Press, 1990], 19).

73. White's invitation emphasized the top-level nature of the meeting and highlighted the prominence of the invitees (Walter White's letters to various recipients, December 9, 1948, Part II, Box A183, Folder 6, NAACP Records).

74. Ibid.

75. Walter White to Messrs. Carter, Marshall, Moon, and Wilkins, January 27, 1949, Part II, Box A183, Folder 6, NAACP Records.

76. Ibid. White's memo suggests the executive committee would include "top level representatives" from the following organizations: NAACP, CIO, ADA ("because of its contacts"), AFL ("if it can be induced to go along"), the American Veterans Committee, the Federal Council of Churches, and "at least one Jewish and one Catholic agency."

77. On the JCCR's new organizational structure, see NAACP press release, February 5, 1949, Series V, Box 14, Folder 1, ADA Records, and Violet Megrath to Jonathan B. Bingham, February 9, 1949, Series V, Box 5, Folder 2, ADA Records. Organizations represented on the Executive Committee were NAACP, ADA, CIO, AFL, NCNW, NCRAC, the AME Church, the National Newspaper Publishers Association, and the National Catholic Welfare Conference. The list is in Part II, Box A183, Folder 6, NAACP Records.

78. Isaiah Minkoff to NCRAC Membership, June 13, 1949, Box 77, Folder 12, NCRAC Records.

79. Ibid. The ADL's Herman Edelsberg, who was one of the NCRAC representatives at the meeting, offered a similar report in a column headlined "FEPC First" in the National Civil Liberties Clearing House's Legislative Bulletin, June 15, 1949, Series V, Box 5, Folder 2, ADA Records.

80. Minkoff reported on three subsequent meetings in his July 21 and September 23, 1949, memoranda to NCRAC membership (Box 27, Folder 2, NCRAC Records).

81. "Some fifty" is the estimate in a January 12, 1950, letter from Violet Gunther (ADA), Lewis G. Hines (AFL), George L. P. Weaver (CIO), and Elmer W. Henderson (American Council on Human Rights) to members of Congress, informing them of the

upcoming event. The letter estimates that "more than two thousand delegates" were expected; Series II, Box 30, Folder 1, ADA Records. Roy Wilkins, in a January 12, 1950, letter to Dave Niles, an administrative assistant to President Truman, noted that fifty-five organizations were cosponsoring the mobilization and that "between 1,500 and 2,000 delegates" would attend (Box 21, Folder 1, Wilkins Papers). A memo written two days after the event indicates that "over 4,000" people participated, which is also the figure given by Robison, "Organizations Promoting," 23; see Theodore Leskes to Dr. John Slawson, January 19, 1950, Box 117, Folder 10, AJC Records. A March 8, 1950, memo from Roy Wilkins and Arnold Aronson reported that "4,218 regularly accredited delegates attended the Washington conference" but did not give a final number of sponsoring organizations (Box 117, Folder 10, AJC Records). A copy of the event program is in Series II, Box 30, Folder 1, ADA Records.

82. Schickler, *Racial Realignment*, 94, for example, states simply that the NECRM "turned into the Leadership Conference on Civil Rights." In contrast, Schultz "FEPC," 84–86, goes into some depth tracing the process I recount here, though with some differences in detail and emphasis.

83. Roy Wilkins to James M. Hinton, September 30, 1949, Part II, Box A193, Folder 9, NAACP Records; NAACP Press Release, October 6, 1949, Part II, Box A193, Folder 8, NAACP Records. As quoted in Wilkins's letter, the campaign was "not only [to] activize [sic] our local branches, but . . . also . . . [to] mobilize the support of other groups on the local, state and national levels—the trade unions, churches, fraternal organizations, civic, business and professional associations."

84. Isaiah Minkoff to NCRAC Membership, September 29, 1949, Box 27, Folder 2, NCRAC Records.

85. Sanford Bolz to Will Maslow, September 9, 1949, Box 27, Folder 2, NCRAC Records. An August 23, 1949, letter from Wilkins to George L.-P. Weaver, director of the CIO's Committee to Abolish Racial Discrimination, suggests that Wilkins was planning to pitch this possibility some weeks prior to this meeting; see Part II, Box A259, Folder 4, NAACP Records.

86. Minutes of Wilkins's October 11 meeting with his staff and the Civil Rights Committee meeting he convened on October 14–15 are in Part II, Box A192, Folder 9, NAACP Records. A copy of his October 26, 1949, letter to organizational leaders is in Box 94, Folder 7, AJC Records.

87. Roy Wilkins to Hugh Baillie, December 1, 1949, Series V, Box 7, Folder 1, ADA Records.

88. Memoranda from David Danzig to Dr. Slawson and Al Bernheim, December 5, 1949, both in Box 117, Folder 10, AJC Records. The latter concern persisted through the mobilization and was expressed in feedback on the event to the NAACP; see draft letter from John Slawson to Alfred Baker Lewis, February 3, 1950, Box 117, Folder 10, AJC Records.

89. Nathan Weisman to Ted Leskes, January 10, 1950; Wm. S. Cohen to Louis S. Breier, January 11, 1950; and Louis S. Breier to William S. Cohen, January 12, 1950, all in Box 117, Folder 10, AJC Records.

90. Robison, "Organizations," 23.

91. A. Philip Randolph and Roy Wilkins, January 20, 1950, Box 117, Folder 10, AJC Records.

92. See, e.g., Roy Wilkins's early February 1950 correspondence with and about National Negro Publishers Association Washington correspondent Louis Lautier in Part II, Box A193, Folder 5, NAACP Records.

93. John Gunther to Violet M. Gunther, January 25, 1950, Series V, Box 7, Folder 1, ADA Records.

94. The thirty-one organizations are listed in the statement approved at the conference and attached to the memorandum from Walter White to participants in the Civil Rights Conference in Washington, May 31, 1951, Series V, Box 7, Folder 2, ADA Records.

95. Roy Wilkins to Walter White, June 11, 1951, Box 3, Folder 2, Wilkins Papers.

96. Walter White to Roy Wilkins, June 13, 1951, Box 3, Folder 2, Wilkins Papers.

97. Walter White to Dr. John Slawson, November 13, 1951, Box 94, Folder 7, AJC Records. The 76 figure is from White's telegram to J. Finley Wilson, December 12, 1951, Part II, Box A352, Folder 3, NAACP Records.

98. Violet Gunther et al. to Walter White, December 7, 1951, Part II, Box A352, Folder 3, NAACP Records. The organizations represented in the joint letter were (in the order of their signatures): ADA, AFL, AJCon, ADL, Brotherhood of Sleeping Car Porters, Catholic Interracial Council, CIO, Jewish Labor Committee, Jewish Veterans Committee, NCRAC, and UAW.

99. In this respect, White's November 13 letter contrasts with Wilkins's invitation to participate in the 1950 mobilization, which had asked organizations to "consent to be a sponsoring body" and immediately appoint a representative to participate in event planning (Roy Wilkins to Arnold Aronson, October 26, 1949, Box 94, Folder 7, AJC Records).

100. Violet Gunther et al. to Walter White, December 7, 1951. A telegram expressing similar sentiments was sent to White by J. Finley Wilson, Grand Exalted Ruler of the International Benevolent Protective Order of the Elks of the World, Part II, Box A352, Folder 3, NAACP Records.

101. Minutes of the Board of Directors meeting, December 12, 1951, Part II, Box A352, Folder 3, NAACP Records.

102. Ibid. While the vote tally is not reported, one board member asked to be recorded as having opposed the motion.

103. A list of attendees and their home organizations is in the meeting minutes: "Summary Minutes of Preliminary Meeting on Civil Rights Mobilization," December 14, 1951, Part II, Box A352, Folder 6, NAACP Records.

104. Ibid.

105. Bernard Trager, "Report on Leadership Conference," undated draft (likely mid-March 1952), Part I, Box 123, Folder 3, LCCR Records.

106. The "Summary Minutes of Preliminary Meeting on Civil Rights Mobilization," December 14, 1951, refer to it alternatively as a "limited mobilization," "leadership gathering," and "leadership conference."

107. Arnold Aronson to Steering Committee, December 17, 1951, Part II, Box A352, Folder 3, NAACP Records. Emphasis added.

108. Precise attendance and financial figures are difficult to ascertain. A budget document dated March 7, 1952, shows a balance of $2,706.94, but an attached note suggests expenses were still being paid and organizational donations were still coming in. An undated list of organizational contributions shows donations from twenty-one organizations; for both documents, see Box 85, Folder 14, AJC Records. At a Steering Committee

meeting on March 12, 1952, Wilkins reported a "net cash balance of $2,842.09" and "782 actual registrants and approximately 50–100 additional delegates" to the conference (Part II, Box A352, Folder 6, NAACP Records). A press release issued prior to the Republican and Democratic national conventions stated that 946 delegates were in attendance (Series II, Box 30, Folder 2, ADA Records). On the logistical challenges, see Wilkins's letter to Edwin J. Lukas, March 3, 1952, Box 85, Folder 14, AJC Records.

109. "Resolution adopted by 1952 Leadership Conference on Civil Rights," February 18, 1952, Series V, Box 7, Folder 2, ADA Records.

110. Manheim Shapiro to area directors, July 10, 1952, Box 85, Folder 14, AJC Records. A copy of the LCCR's plank is attached to Shapiro's memo.

111. Summary of Steering Committee meeting, November 12, 1952, Part II, Box A352, Folder 6, NAACP Records.

112. Minutes of Steering Committee Meeting, February 10, 1953, Part I, Box 123, Folder 4, LCCR Records.

113. Ibid.

114. Ibid. The minutes do not identify who offered these arguments but name nine of the twenty-one individuals present at the meeting as having "voiced sharp disagreement" with Mitchell's concern: Roy Reuther (UAW), Theodore Brown (Brotherhood of Sleeping Car Porters), William Jason (National Alliance of Postal Employees), Oscar Lee (National Council of Churches of Christ), Theodore Leskes (American Jewish Committee), Will Maslow (American Jewish Congress), William Oliver (UAW), Paul Sifton (UAW), and Roy Wilkins (NAACP).

115. The Minutes of Steering Committee Meeting, February 10, 1953, also suggest that they planned to rename the Leadership Conference to better convey its new permanent nature, but this does not appear to have been addressed again at any subsequent meeting.

116. Ibid.

117. Ibid.

## CHAPTER 3

1. The formation of this committee led to the Manuscript Division of the Library of Congress's accession of the LCCR Records, but the official history was never written.

2. Norma O. Leonard to Yvonne Price, April 17, 1974, Part I, Box 122, Folder 13, LCCR Records.

3. See, e.g., Keith M. Finley, *Delaying the Dream: Southern Senators and the Fight against Civil Rights, 1938–1965* (Baton Rouge: Louisiana State University Press, 2008); Ruth Bloch Rubin, *Building the Bloc: Intraparty Organization in the U.S. Congress* (Cambridge: Cambridge University Press, 2017), 145–156, 230–249; Eric Schickler, *Racial Realignment: The Transformation of American Liberalism, 1932–1965* (Princeton, NJ: Princeton University Press, 2016), chapter 8; and James L. Sundquist, *Politics and Policy: The Eisenhower, Kennedy, and Johnson Years* (Washington, DC: Brookings Institution, 1968), chapter 6. A notable exception is Steven F. Lawson, *Black Ballots: Voting Rights in the South, 1944–1969* (New York: Columbia University Press, 1976), which does offer some insight into the LCCR's participation in debates over inclusion of a jury trial amendment in the Civil Rights Act of 1957 (pp. 188–192) and alludes to its organizational limitations in accounting for the limitations of pre-1965 voting rights legislation (p. 344).

4. Clay Risen, *The Bill of the Century: The Epic Battle for the Civil Rights Act of 1964* (New York: Bloomsbury, 2014), 94; Yvonne Ryan, *Roy Wilkins: The Quiet Revolutionary and the NAACP* (Lexington: University Press of Kentucky, 2013), 59.

5. The number of member organizations fluctuated within a range of forty-eight to fifty-two during this period. A handful of the original fifty-two groups disaffiliated, either on their own accord (e.g., the National Council of Jewish Women) or at the behest of the Executive Committee (e.g., the Scottish Rite Masons), and a few others joined. Other fluctuations were due to exogenous developments, such as organizational mergers (e.g., of the AFL and CIO) and disbanding (e.g., of the American Council on Human Rights).

6. John A. Morsell to Richard B. Hertz, May 21, 1959, Part III, Box A205, Folder 4, NAACP Records.

7. See, e.g., Aronson's April 13, 1953, letter to George Meany, Part I, Box 123, Folder 4, LCCR Records, and his February 8, 1956, letter to Boris Shishkin, Box 4, Folder 32, AFL-CIO CRD Records.

8. The quote is from Wilkins's assistant John A. Morsell's March 28, 1961, letter to David A. Gillette, a political science student seeking information about the LCCR for a research paper, Part III, Box A206, Folder 1, NAACP Records. See also Aronson's March 9, 1962, letter to Mathew Ahmann, Part I, Box 1, Folder 4, LCCR Records.

9. John A. Morsell to Page S. Wilson, November 18, 1959, Part III, Box A205, Folder 4, NAACP Records.

10. Aronson called this group "a Washington Committee" in one response to a request for information about the LCCR, but this name is not used in any other communications that I have seen. See Aronson's letter to Walter F. Brown, July 24, 1957, Part I, Box 122, Folder 19, LCCR Records.

11. John J. Gunther to Clarence Mitchell, January 16, 1957, Part IX, Box 117, Folder 2, NAACP Records. On the FCNL's decision not to join the LCCR, see Wilmer A. Cooper's letter to Arnold Aronson, November 14, 1957, Part I, Box 122, Folder 19, LCCR Records, and Edward F. Snyder's letter to Marvin Caplan, February 3, 1964, Part I, Box 2, Folder 2, LCCR Records. The FCNL did eventually join the Leadership Conference in 1969; see Charles Harker to Marvin Caplan, April 2, 1969, Part I, Box 62, Folder 10, LCCR Records.

12. Rachel Kraus describes a similar autonomy for the lobbying arms of many religious denominational organizations; see her "Laity, Institution, Theology, or Politics? Protestant, Catholic, and Jewish Washington Offices' Agenda Setting," *Sociology of Religion* 68 (2007), 67–81.

13. Morsell's March 28, 1961, letter to Gillette.

14. Minutes of Steering Committee Meeting, April 21, 1953, Part 1, Series 5, Box 12, Folder 1, ADA Records.

15. Will Maslow to Walter White, January 19, 1954, Part II, Box A353, Folder 1, NAACP Records. The April 21, 1953, meeting was the last one prior to Maslow's letter, and the next one was on December 1, 1954. In the interim, Maslow's reports on civil rights to his home organization (the American Jewish Congress) suggest, without reference to the Leadership Conference, ongoing disagreement among pro–civil rights groups about their willingness to compromise on pending FEPC legislation (Minutes of the Joint Administrative and Executive Committee Meetings, January 24, 1954, and Minutes of the Administrative Committee Meeting, November 27, 1954, both in Box 4, Folder 10, AJCon Records).

16. While there was no official document stating as much, the point was made in response to inquiries about LCCR membership; see, e.g., Arnold Aronson to Wilmer A. Cooper, May 15, 1957, Part I, Box 122, Folder 19, LCCR Records.

17. Arnold Aronson to James A. Dombrowski, June 28, 1956, and Arnold Aronson to Savilla Willis Simons, May 10, 1956, both in Part I, Box 52, Folder 2, LCCR Records.

18. John A. Morsell to Richard B. Hertz, May 21, 1959, Part III, Box A205, Folder 4, NAACP Records; Aronson letter to Ahmann, March 9, 1962.

19. See, e.g., Frances T. Kahn's letters to Mae R. Gellman and Ruth Shields and to Arnold Aronson, April 26, 1956, and Florence A. Rogers to Edward J. Burton, April 27, 1956; all are in Part I, Box 52, Folder 2, LCCR Records.

20. Arnold Aronson to Edward J. Burton, May 4, 1956, Part I, Box 14, Folder 1, LCCR Records.

21. John Morsell to Juanita Jackson Mitchell, May 7, 1956, Part III, Box A205, Folder 2, NAACP Records.

22. The *New York Times* reported that "Fifty organizations . . . allied as the Leadership Conference on Civil Rights, urged a Senate Judiciary subcommittee to discard the Johnson Bill and approve the broader Douglas-Celler civil rights measure" and that "Joseph L. Rauh, Jr. . . . was the main witness for the civic, church, labor, professional and fraternal groups" (John D. Morris, "50 Groups Demand Broad Civil Rights Bill," *New York Times*, April 9, 1959, 22). A copy of Rauh's statement is in Part IX, Box 129, Folder 3, NAACP Records.

23. Joseph L. Rauh Jr. to Arnold Aronson, April 20, 1959, Part I, Box 157, Folder 15, LCCR Records. Emphasis in original. A copy of the March 2, 1959, press release is in Box 25, Folder 3, Rauh Papers.

24. Arnold Aronson to Joseph L. Rauh Jr, April 27, 1959, Part I, Box 157, Folder 15, LCCR Records.

25. These developments are summarized in many studies of the American Jewish organizational sector. A particularly thorough contemporaneous account appears in Selma G. Hirsh, "Jewish Community Relations," *American Jewish Yearbook* 54 (1953), 162–177; somewhat more recently, see, e.g., Howard M. Sachar, *A History of the Jews in America* (New York: Vintage, 1993), 677–679, and Jack Wertheimer, "Jewish Organizational Life in the United States since 1945," *American Jewish Year Book* 95 (1995), 22–25. AJC and ADL eventually rejoined NCRAC, which is now known as the Jewish Council for Public Affairs.

26. Arnold Aronson to participating organizations, May 7, 1952, Part I, Box 123, Folder 2, LCCR Records.

27. Mike Masaoka to Arnold Aronson, June 3, 1952, Part I, Box 123, Folder 2, LCCR Records. While Masaoka's papers do not shed light on the JACL's consideration of the LCCR's draft platform plank, they do offer ample evidence of the McCarran-Walter Act's extraordinary significance to the JACL and Masaoka himself, as well as of the mobilized opposition to it by many of the LCCR's other member organizations.

28. See, e.g., minutes of the February 25, 1952, meeting of the ADA Executive Committee, Box 16, Folder 3, Rauh Papers. Jewish groups were particularly well mobilized against the McCarran-Walter Act, as evidenced by Masaoka's daily activity log; see Box 12, Masaoka Papers. Minutes of various American Jewish Congress meetings likewise suggest that opposing McCarran-Walter, both before and after its passage, was a high priority for at least that organization; see Boxes 4–6, AJCon Records. The NAACP

also opposed the legislation in part because of its greater restriction on immigration from the West Indies; see the NAACP Washington Bureau newsletter, May 28, 1952, and Walter White's Testimony on Immigration and Naturalization before the President's Commission on Immigration and Naturalization, September 30, 1952. Transcripts of both documents are in Denton L. Watson, ed., *The Papers of Clarence Mitchell Jr.*, vol. 4, *1951–1954* (Athens: Ohio University Press, 2010), 634–637 and 641–645, respectively.

29. Part I, Box 123, Folder 3, LCCR Records. A plank supporting ratification of the UN's 1948 Genocide Convention was similarly abandoned. A copy of the final version of the LCCR's proposed civil rights plank, published as a glossy, letter-size brochure on June 21, 1952, is in Box 85, Folder 14, AJC Records.

30. Form letter from Walter White, January 8, 1952, Part II, Box A352, Folder 1, NAACP Records.

31. Sol Rabkin to Walter White, January 23, 1952, Part II, Box A352, Folder 1, NAACP Records.

32. Edwin J. Lukas to Walter White, January 22, 1952, Box 94, Folder 7, AJC Records.

33. Roy Wilkins to Sol Rabkin, January 29, 1952, Part II, Box A352, Folder 1, NAACP Records. An identical letter to Lukas is in Box 94, Folder 7, AJC Records.

34. Roy Wilkins to Edwin J. Lukas, March 3, 1952, Box 85, Folder 14, AJC Records.

35. Aronson to Ahmann, *op. cit.*

36. Ibid.

37. Adele S. Trobe to L.G.E. Edmondson, July 6, 1967, Box 166, Folder 1, NCJW Records. NCJW continued to work informally with the Leadership Conference—indeed, Olya Margolin, its longstanding Washington representative, continued to participate in Mitchell's committee of core lobbyists—and ultimately rejoined the coalition in December 1963; see Mrs. Joseph Willen to Roy Wilkins, December 13, 1963, and Violet Gunther to Mrs. Joseph Willen, December 19, 1963, Part I, Box 71, Folder 10, LCCR Records.

38. This challenges political scientists' suggestion that interest group coalitions necessarily adopt an expansive purview in response to member organization demands; see, e.g., Dara Z. Strolovitch, *Affirmative Advocacy: Race, Class, and Gender in Interest Group Politics* (Chicago: University of Chicago Press, 2007), chapter 6, and Laura R. Woliver, *Push Back, Move Forward: The National Council of Women's Organizations and Coalition Advocacy* (Philadelphia: Temple University Press, 2018), 132.

39. Memorandum, n.d. (late February 1955), Series V, Box 12, Folder 2, ADA Records.

40. The plank was drafted in late May and circulated to member organizations with a request for "comments . . . including any changes you may wish to suggest" on June 6, just over a week before the Executive Committee's June 14, 1956, meeting. A copy of the draft plank, dated May 29, 1956, and a June 6, 1956, notice of the upcoming Executive Committee meeting are in Box 85, Folder 14, AJC Records. A copy of Aronson's memo to member organizations is in Part I, Box 14, Folder 1, LCCR Records.

41. "Leadership Conf. Ex. Committee," June 14, 1956, Part I, Box 1, Folder 14, LCCR Records.

42. See, e.g., "Draft of Proposed Plank on Civil Rights to Be Submitted to Republican and Democratic National Conventions," June 21, 1956, Part 1, Series 5, Box 11, Folder 3 ADA Records; LCCR Press Release, "Strong Civil Rights Plank Urged by 30

Organizations," August 4, 1956, Part III, Box A205, Folder 2, NAACP Records; and the undated glossy pamphlet with the final draft of the proposed plank that was sent to convention delegates, a copy of which is in Part IX, Box 117, Folder 1, NAACP Records.

43. Arnold Aronson to Cooperating Organizations, August 5, 1960, Part III, Box A205, Folder 6, NAACP Records. In the memo he also credited "the rising independence movement in Africa, a growing awareness of the adverse effect of discrimination on our foreign relations, the lunch counter sit-ins and the strategic distribution of the Negro vote."

44. I have found memoranda and telegrams informing Executive Committee members of upcoming meetings for twenty-nine of the thirty-four Executive Committee meetings held between 1953 and 1962. In most cases, notices were sent at least a week prior to the meeting and in no instance was less than five days' notice given.

45. A second voting rights law, the Civil Rights Act of 1960, was enacted three years later, but it was so limited as to be practically disavowed by civil rights advocates. Thurgood Marshall famously declared that the 1960 legislation was "not worth the paper it's written on." Morsell similarly called it a "meager enactment" in response to a student's inquiry about interest groups' role in its achievement; see his letter to Sidney W. Cook, January 20, 1961, Part III, Box A206, Folder 1, NAACP Records.

46. Morsell's March 28, 1961, letter to Gillette.

47. See, e.g., John Weir Anderson, *Eisenhower, Brownell, and the Congress: The Tangled Origins of the Civil Rights Bill of 1956–1957* (Tuscaloosa: University of Alabama Press, 1964); Steven F. Lawson, *Black Ballots*, chapters 6–7; and Howard E. Shuman, "Senate Rules and the Civil Rights Bill: A Case Study," *American Political Science Review* 51 (1957): 955–975.

48. Will Maslow and Joseph B. Robison, "Civil Rights Legislation and the Fight for Equality, 1862–1952," *University of Chicago Law Review* 20 (1953), 389. As noted earlier, Maslow was member of the LCCR's Executive Committee. There is some evidence that Maslow and Robison's article was influential to the LCCR's work; see, e.g., Arnold Aronson to John Gunther, February 15, 1955, Part 1, Series 5, Box 12, Folder 2, ADA Records.

49. LCCR platform plank proposal, June 21, 1952; emphases added.

50. Arnold Aronson to John Gunther, November 24, 1954, Part 1, Series 5, Box 12, Folder 1, ADA Records.

51. Per ADA Legislative Representative John Gunther's report, "the Executive Committee . . . met on December 1 and . . . voted unanimously to urge that a fight be made on Rule XXII. The groups then proceeded to discuss ways and means for making this fight as productive as possible," including possibly bringing "a hundred or so" organizational leaders to Washington in January should their allies in the Senate agree to make the push for rules reform; see Gunther's letter to Julius C. C. Edelstein, December 7, 1954, Series V, Box 12, Folder 2, ADA Records. Summarizing the campaign's failure, Wilkins wrote, "the matter of the change in rules in the Senate was not brought up at the opening of the 84th Congress because only Senator Herbert H. Lehman was willing to launch the move. The Democratic leadership was hostile and the liberals were extremely reluctant to join with Senator Lehman. The Republicans did nothing" (Roy Wilkins to Executive Committee, January 27, 1955, Box 74, Folder 5, NCJW Records). See also David Lawrence, "Senate Civil Rights Bloc Gives Up on Rules Change," *Washington Post*, January 5, 1955; Kevin W. Boyle, *The UAW and the Heyday of American Liberalism, 1945–1968* (Ithaca, NY: Cornell University Press, 1998), 112.

52. "Humphrey Offers Civil Rights Bills," *New York Times*, February 2, 1955, 14. As the *Times* article indicates, Senator Hubert Humphrey (D-MN) introduced the bills with eighteen other senators, including nine Democrats, eight Republicans, and one independent, as cosponsors.

53. Roy Wilkins to Executive Committee, January 27, 1955.

54. The February 2, 1955, meeting is among the best documented of all those held during the period covered in this book. The discussion of it here relies on three independent accounts of its proceedings: The official summary prepared by Arnold Aronson, Part II, Box A353, Folder 10, NAACP Records; handwritten notes taken during the meeting by Olya Margolin, the National Council of Jewish Women's Washington representative, Box 74, Folder 7, NCJW Records; and a postmeeting report by Nathaniel Goodrich, who attended on behalf of the American Jewish Committee, in his February 2, 1955, memorandum to Ted Leskes, Box 85, Folder 14, AJC Records.

55. "Statement adopted at a meeting of the Executive Committee of the Leadership Conference on Civil Rights," February 2, 1955, Senate Legislative Correspondence, Box 117, Civil Rights—HHH Bills Folder, Hubert H. Humphrey Papers.

56. Goodrich to Ted Leskes, February 2, 1955.

57. Ibid. Goodrich added that this need was not felt universally and noted that he had pointed to the AJC's prioritization of civil rights on its lobbying agenda as evidence that organizations remained fully committed to the cause.

58. Quotes are from Arnold Aronson, summary of February 2 meeting, Part II, Box A353, Folder 10, NAACP Records. Margolin's notes on the meeting suggest that there was substantial disagreement over both the idea of holding a conference at all and its timing relative to other awareness-raising initiatives.

59. Aronson's summary of the meeting.

60. Arnold Aronson to members of the Executive Committee, February 18, 1955, Box 85, Folder 14, AJC Records.

61. Memorandum, n.d. (late February 1955), Part 1, Series 5, Box 12, Folder 2, ADA Records. As noted earlier, the home rule and statehood issues had been included in the LCCR's proposed civil rights plank for the Republican and Democratic platforms in 1952.

62. Ibid.

63. Sanford Bolz to Executive Committee, n.d. (late February 1955), Part 1, Series 5, Box 12, Folder 2, ADA Records.

64. Ibid., emphasis in original.

65. This account of the discussion relies on both Aronson's handwritten notes in Part I, Box 1, Folder 1, LCCR Records, and his official summary of the March 3 meeting in Part I, Box 14, Folder 1, LCCR Records.

66. Summary of Executive Committee Meeting, March 3, 1955.

67. A marked-up draft from mid-April is in Part I, Box 1, Folder 1, LCCR Records. Wilkins reported at an Executive Committee meeting on July 19, 1955, that the final product would be ready for circulation "in the not too distant future" (Executive Committee meeting minutes, Part I, Box 1, Folder 14, LCCR Records).

68. At the heart of the controversy was a sense that the draft pamphlet was not well tailored to its intended popular audience and a concern that the AJC's hard-earned reputation for producing high-quality advocacy publications would be tarnished by its association with this project. See, generally, Box 86, Folder 4, AJC Records. The final

document in the folder, a December 15, 1955, letter from Theodore Leskes to Arnold Aronson, indicates that the pamphlet had been produced and copies shipped for distribution earlier that month. A copy of the published pamphlet, "Congress Must ACT on Civil Rights," bearing a December 1955 publication date, is in Part 1, Series 5, Box 12, Folder 2, ADA Records.

69. Minutes of the July 19, 1955, LCCR Executive Committee meeting.

70. *Congressional Record*, 84th Cong., 1st Sess. (1955), 6573–6574.

71. As Maslow and Robison tell it, Powell amendments grew out of a recommendation by President Truman's Committee on Civil Rights that "Congress condition all federal grants-in-aid and other forms of federal assistance on the absence of religious or racial discrimination." They further note that such initiatives "split liberal groups" as early as 1949, when "a friend of civil rights" in the Senate led opposition to an antisegregation amendment to a public housing bill (Maslow and Robison, *Civil Rights Legislation*, 389–391). Antisegregation amendments were controversial even among civil rights organizations. While the NAACP committed itself to opposing any federal funding grant for segregated facilities at its 1949 annual convention, the National Council of Negro Women opposed an antisegregation amendment to a public housing bill that same year. See Charles V. Hamilton, *Adam Clayton Powell: The Political Biography of an American Dilemma* (New York: Aethenium, 1991), 225–226.

72. Dwight D. Eisenhower, "The President's News Conference," June 8, 1955, American Presidency Project, http://www.presidency.ucsb.edu/ws/index.php?pid=10253.

73. A copy of the statement, issued and released on June 10, 1955, is in Box 85, Folder 14, AJC Records.

74. John J. Gunther to Roy Wilkins, June 13, 1955, Part I, Box 1, Folder 1, LCCR Records.

75. The NAACP nevertheless continued lobbying for a Powell amendment on H.R. 7000; see telegram from Clarence Mitchell to twenty members of Congress, June 30, 1955, Part IX, Box 126, Folder 5, NAACP Records.

76. Paul Sifton to Roy L. Reuther and William H. Oliver, July 6, 1955, Box 23, Folder 22, Roy L. Reuther Papers.

77. Summary of Executive Committee meeting, July 19, 1955.

78. Ibid.; emphases in original.

79. Ibid.

80. Arnold Aronson to all cooperating organizations, November 21, 1955, Part 1, Series 5, Box 12, Folder 2, ADA Records.

81. Señora (Violet) Gunther to Señor (John) Gunther, December 20, 1955, Part 1, Series 5, Box 7, Folder 4, ADA Records.

82. A copy of the event program is in Part IX, Box 116, Folder 8, NAACP Records.

83. Bert Seidman to Boris Shishkin, March 8, 1956, Box 4, Folder 3, AFL-CIO CRD Records.

84. Arnold Aronson to Executive Committee, March 12, 1956, Part I, Box 14, Folder 1, LCCR Records.

85. Anderson, *Eisenhower*, 14.

86. James Roosevelt to Olya Margolin, April 4, 1956, Box 60, Folder 5, NCJW Records. A detailed account of the meeting is in John J. Gunther's memorandum to the files, April 9, 1956, Part 1, Series 5, Box 8, Folder 2, ADA Records.

87. See, e.g., Paul Sifton to Roy L. Reuther, May 7, 1956, Box 24, Folder 7, Roy L. Reuther Papers; Inverna L. Jones to Clarence Mitchell, June 1, 1956, Part IX, Box 127, Folder 2, NAACP Records; John J. Gunther memorandum to the files, June 4, 1956, Part 1, Series 5, Box 8, Folder 2, ADA Records; John J. Gunther to Arnold Aronson, June 7, 1956, Part 1, Series 5, Box 12, Folder 3, ADA Records.

88. Arnold Aronson to Edwin J. Lukas, June 5, 1956, Box 85, Folder 14, AJC Records.

89. LCCR press release, June 13, 1956, Part IX, Box 117, Folder 1, NAACP Records.

90. The only other reference I have found to the LCCR's poll of representatives is a July 1956 form letter from Clarence Mitchell on NAACP stationery asking House members who had not indicated that they signed the discharge petition to confirm that they indeed had not for purposes of accuracy in his office's end-of-session reporting (Part IX, Box 127, Folder 3, NAACP Records).

91. "Ex. Committee" notes, June 14, 1956, Part I, Box 14, Folder 1, LCCR Records.

92. Arnold Aronson to all cooperating agencies, July 10, 1956, Part IX, Box 117, Folder 1, NAACP Records.

93. Box 23, Folder 24, Roy L. Reuther Papers.

94. See, e.g., John J. Gunther to Edward D. Hollander, July 10, 1956, Part 1, Series 5, Box 8, Folder 2, ADA Records.

95. Ibid.

96. Copies of the press release are in Part IX, Box 117, Folder 1, NAACP Records; Part 1, Series 5, Box 8, Folder 3, ADA Records; and Box 24, Folder 6, Roy L. Reuther Papers.

97. Sifton's chronology, Box 23, Folder 24, Roy L. Reuther Papers.

98. See, e.g., Anderson, *Eisenhower*, 103–105; Lawson, *Black Ballots*, 160.

99. Sifton's chronology, Box 23, Folder 24, Roy L. Reuther Papers.

100. Paul Sifton to Walter P. Reuther, August 1, 1956, Box 24, Folder 6, Roy L. Reuther Papers.

101. John J. Gunther to Arnold Aronson, April 25, 1957, Part 1, Series 5, Box 8, Folder 3, ADA Records.

102. Arnold Aronson to Executive Committee Members, January 24, 1957, Part 1, Series 5, Box 12, Folder 3, ADA Records.

103. Arnold Aronson to participating organizations, February 1, 1957, Part IX, Box 117, Folder 2, NAACP Records; emphasis in original.

104. See, e.g., Arnold Aronson to Edwin J. Lukas, January 31, 1957, Box 85, Folder 14, AJC Records.

105. A copy of Wilkins's testimony and a list of the twenty-two endorsing organizations are in Part IX, Box 127, Folder 5, NAACP Records. The LCCR's and other organizations' statements are printed in Committee on the Judiciary, *Civil Rights: Hearings before Subcommittee No. 5 of the Committee on the Judiciary, House of Representatives, Eighty-fifth Congress, First Session, on H.R. 140 etc. Miscellaneous Bills regarding the Civil Rights of Persons within the Jurisdiction of the United States* (Washington, DC: U.S. Government Printing Office, 1957).

106. A copy of Wilkins's testimony, which includes a list of the twenty-five endorsing organizations, is in Box 60, Folder 5, NCJW Records.

107. Lorna Marple to Clarence Mitchell, March 7, 1957, Part IX, Box 117, Folder 2, NAACP Records.

108. Mae B. Hendricks to Lorna Marple, March 11, 1957, Part IX, Box 117, Folder 2, NAACP Records.

109. Committee on the Judiciary, *Civil Rights*, 653.

110. Arnold Aronson to Coordinating Organizations, May 7, 1957, Part 1, Series 5, Box 8, Folder 4, ADA Records.

111. John J. Gunther to Arnold Aronson, May 22, 1957, Part 1, Series 5, Box 8, Folder 4, ADA Records.

112. Roy Wilkins to Participating Organizations, June 4, 1957, Part 1, Series 5, Box 8, Folder 4, ADA Records; emphasis in original.

113. John J. Gunther to Arnold Aronson, June 14, 1957, Part 1, Series 5, Box 8, Folder 4, ADA Records.

114. Roy Wilkins to participating organizations, July 10, 1957, Part IX, Box 117, Folder 2, NAACP Records; emphasis in original.

115. John Morsell to Roy Wilkins, July 9, 1957, Part III, Box A205, Folder 3, NAACP Records. Outside lobbying includes activities aimed at mobilizing public opinion and media pressure in support of interest groups' policy goals.

116. Clarence Mitchell to Roy Wilkins, July 13, 1957, Part IX, Box 117, Folder 2, NAACP Records.

117. See, e.g., William H. Oliver to Ed Lucas [Lukas] [*sic*], July 23, 1957, Box 85, Folder 14, AJC Records; Stella Eberlin to Helen Raebeck, July 23, 1957, Box 60, Folder 2, NCJW Records; Arnold Aronson to Emanuel Muravchik, August 15, 1957, Part I, Box 52, Folder 4, LCCR Records.

118. Arnold Aronson to cooperating organizations, July 16, 1957, Part 1, Series 5, Box 9, Folder 1, ADA Records.

119. Copies of the August 7 and August 23, 1957, releases are, respectively, in Part IX, Box 117, Folder 2, NAACP Records, and Box 26, Folder 2, Rauh Papers.

120. Copies of the September 1, 1957, LCCR press release and full statement are in Part IX, Box 117, Folder 2, NAACP Records.

121. Arnold Aronson to all cooperating organizations, August 28, 1957, Part IX, Box 117, Folder 2, NAACP Records.

122. LCCR Press release, September 1, 1957.

123. Edward D. Hollander to John J. Gunther, October 25, 1957, Part 1, Series 5, Box 9, Folder 1, ADA Records.

124. Will Hathaway and David S. Meyer, "Competition and Cooperation in Social Movement Coalitions: Lobbying for Peace in the 1980s," *Berkeley Journal of Sociology* 38 (1993–1994), 172, 175.

125. As discussed in Chapter 1, this is the consensus of previous research.

## CHAPTER 4

1. Mike Masaoka, "Report of Washington JACL Representative, 1962–1964 Biennium, to the 18th Biennial National Convention of Japanese American Citizens League," June 29, 1964, Box 65, Folders 19–20, Masaoka Papers.

2. Masaoka's daily activity log shows he attended both the 1950 Emergency Civil Rights Mobilization and the 1952 Leadership Conference and was active in LCCR meetings and lobbying for the Civil Rights Acts of 1957 and 1960 prior to joining the Executive Committee; see Boxes 12–16, Masaoka Papers.

3. Arnold Aronson to Mathew Ahmann, March 9, 1962, Part I, Box 1, Folder 4, LCCR Records.

4. Robert D. Loevy, *To End All Segregation: The Politics of the Passage of the Civil Rights Act of 1964* (Lanham, MD: University Press of America, 1990), 58.

5. Martin Luther King Jr., "Bold Designs for a New South," *Nation*, March 30, 1963, 259–262.

6. Boris Shishkin to William F. Schnitzler, November 28, 1962, Box 4, Folder 33, AFL-CIO CRD Records.

7. Letters from Tilford E. Dudley to John A. Morsell and Roy Wilkins, December 8, 1962, Part III, Box A206, Folder 3, NAACP Records.

8. Tilford E. Dudley to constituent organizations, December 6, 1962, Part III, Box A206, Folder 3, NAACP Records, and Tilford E. Dudley to constituent organizations, December 14 and 20, 1962, Part 1, Series 5, Box 12, Folder 4, ADA Records.

9. In Dudley's account, even this minor achievement had seemed unlikely from the nose counts reported at the briefing meeting at the start of LCCR's January 6–8 conference; see his letter to David Dubinsky, January 9, 1963, and "Report of the Washington Office, December 1962–January 1963," January 15, 1963, both in Part III, Box A206, Folder 4, NAACP Records.

10. Dudley, "Report of the Washington Office." Debate in the Senate continued through the first week of February and ultimately yielded a loss for would-be reformers. For a more detailed account of the failure to achieve significant rules reform at the start of the Eighty-eighth Congress, see "Criticism of Congress Provokes Few Changes," in *CQ Almanac 1963*, 19th ed., 369–376 (Washington, DC: CQ, 1964).

11. To the extent that Kennedy did promote civil rights prior to mid-1963, he tended to do so through unilateral executive action; see, e.g., Kenneth T. Andrews and Sarah Gaby, "Local Protest and Federal Policy: The Impact of the Civil Rights Movement on the Civil Rights Act of 1964," *Sociological Forum* 30 (2015): 509–527; and Harold C. Fleming, "The Federal Executive and Civil Rights, 1961–1965," *Daedalus* 94 (1965): 921–948.

12. John F. Kennedy, "Annual Message to the Congress on the State of the Union," January 14, 1963, American Presidency Project, https://www.presidency.ucsb.edu/node/237129. As Berman notes, Kennedy's 1963 address offered less than Eisenhower's in 1959, which at least committed his administration to submitting civil rights legislative proposals "early in the session" (Daniel M. Berman, *A Bill Becomes Law: Congress Enacts Civil Rights Legislation*, 2nd ed. [New York: Macmillan, 1966], 7–8).

13. The message also highlighted administrative action that had been taken to promote fair employment practices and access to public accommodations but did not call for legislation on these issues (John F. Kennedy, "Special Message to the Congress on Civil Rights," February 28, 1963, American Presidency Project, https://www.presidency.ucsb.edu/documents/special-message-the-congress-civil-rights).

14. For example, the *New York Times* anticipated that the message would "deal with a plan to provide 'public defenders' for persons standing trial in Federal Courts and with measures to speed court handling of suits filed with the Justice Department alleging violations of voting rights" ("Civil Rights Message Today," *New York Times*, February 27, 1963). Coverage after the message was released described it as being "of unexpected sweep" (Anthony Lewis, "Program Is Broad," *New York Times*, March 1, 1963).

15. Quoted in "Kennedy's Civil Rights Program Hit by Rockefeller as Deficient," *New York Times*, March 6, 1963.

16. Quoted in Anthony Lewis, "Celler Charges Rights Politics to Rockefeller," *New York Times*, March 11, 1963.

17. A copy of the press release is in Part IX, Box 132, Folder 1, NAACP Records.

18. A June 6, 1963, letter from J. Francis Pohlhaus to Roy Wilkins suggests that the most recent meeting to that date was the one on March 28 (Part IX, Box 119, Folder 3, NAACP Records).

19. A draft of the proposed statement, dated March 22, 1963, is in Box 90, Folder 11, Walter P. Reuther Papers.

20. William H. Oliver to Walter P. Reuther, April 12, 1963, Box 90, Folder 11, Walter P. Reuther Papers.

21. Ibid.

22. Joseph L. Rauh Jr., "The Role of the Leadership Conference on Civil Rights in the Civil Rights Struggle of 1963–1964." Rauh drafted this essay shortly after the Civil Rights Act's passage, but it was not published until its inclusion in Robert D. Loevy, ed., *The Civil Rights Act of 1964: The Passage of the Law That Ended Racial Segregation* (Albany, NY: SUNY Press, 1997).

23. Hubert H. Humphrey et al. to John F. Kennedy, May 15, 1963, Box 218, Humphrey Papers.

24. J. Francis Pohlhaus to David Cohen, May 15, 1963, Par IX, Box 131, Folder 4, NAACP Records.

25. See, e.g., Cabell Phillips, "Civil Rights Fight Is Put to Kennedy," *New York Times*, May 25, 1963.

26. Joseph L. Rauh Jr. to Walter P. Reuther, May 28, 1963, Box 24, Folder 7, Rauh Papers.

27. Andrew J. Biemiller to Hubert H. Humphrey, June 7, 1963, Part IX, Box 132, Folder 1, NAACP Records; Boris Shishkin to George Meany, June 6, 1963, Box 31, Folder 17, Meany Papers.

28. John F. Kennedy, "Radio and Television Report to the American People on Civil Rights," June 11, 1963, American Presidency Project, https://www.presidency.ucsb.edu/documents/radio-and-television-report-the-american-people-civil-rights.

29. The quote is from an update on civil rights legislative developments in a memo from Isaiah Minkoff to the heads of the National Community Relations Advisory Council's member agencies, July 12, 1963, Box 77, Folder 14, NCRAC Records.

30. Including those already named, twenty LCCR member organizations were represented at the White House meeting on June 22. Meeting attendees are listed (without organizational affiliations) in Kennedy's appointment book for June 1963, available on the John F. Kennedy Presidential Library and Museum website at https://jfklibrary.libguides.com/ld.php?content_id=26059768.

31. Boris Shishkin, "Main Civil Rights Developments since Mid-May," memorandum to George Meany, July 19, 1963, Box 31, Folder 18, Meany Papers.

32. For example, see Marvin Caplan, *Farther Along: A Civil Rights Memoir* (Baton Rouge: Louisiana State University Press, 1999), 192; Clay Risen, *The Bill of the Century: The Epic Battle for the Civil Rights Act of 1964* (New York: Bloomsbury, 2014), 94–95, and Denton L. Watson, *Lion in the Lobby: Clarence Mitchell, Jr.'s Struggle for the Passage of Civil Rights Laws* (New York: William Morrow, 1990), 531. Wilkins's own autobiography recalls that "Walter Reuther of the United Automobile Workers wanted to set up a 'Coalition of Conscience' to run the lobbying. I wanted the Leadership Conference to

handle the job," but he offers no insight into the resolution of this disagreement (Roy Wilkins, *Standing Fast: The Autobiography of Roy Wilkins* (New York: Da Capo, 1982), 291. While Shishkin did not connect Wilkins's proposal to Reuther's plans and was not at the Statler Hotel meeting, his report does note that he subsequently "heard some cries of alarm in the Negro community ... that Walter Reuther ... was trying to grab control of the civil rights leadership" (Shishkin, "Main Civil Rights Developments").

33. On these developments, see William P. Jones, "The Unknown Origins of the March on Washington: Civil Rights Politics and the Black Working Class," *Labor* 7 (2010): 33–52.

34. Shishkin, "Main Civil Rights Developments."

35. This summary is based on several contemporaneous accounts by participants and observers of the July 2 meeting, including Shishkin, "Main Civil Rights Developments," David Cohen to John F. Roche, July 3, 1963, Part 1, Series 5, Box 10, Folder 5, ADA Records; Isaiah M. Minkoff to member agency executives, July 12, 1963, Box 77, Folder 14, NCRAC Records; J. Eugene Marans, "Negro Unity and the GOP," *Advance*, July 25, 1963, in Series V, Box 10, Folder 5, ADA Records; and Peter Khiss, "7 Negro Groups Unite on Civil Rights Activities," *New York Times*, July 3, 1963.

36. Cohen to Roche, July 3, 1963.

37. "Enlarged Leadership Conference" is the phrase used in Shishkin, "Main Civil Rights Developments."

38. On the financing, see Wilkins's June 25, 1963, memo to Mr. McClain, authorizing a $5,000 payment to the LCCR, which was to be "matched by the United Automobile Workers," in Part III, Box A206, Folder 4, NAACP Records; and Reuther's June 24, 1963, letter to UAW secretary-treasurer Emil Mezey, authorizing a $5,000 payment to the LCCR "to support the efforts of strengthening this group as a coordinating mechanism in the overall civil rights struggles," in Box 493, Folder 31, Walter P. Reuther Papers. Reuther mentioned that the Washington office opening was underway in a July 8, 1963, letter to Martin Luther King Jr., Box 523, Folder 1, Walter P. Reuther Papers.

39. Caplan's own account of his hiring appears in his memoir, Caplan, *Farther Along*, 181–200. In a letter written shortly after passage of the Civil Rights Act, Caplan stated that there were two secretaries, as well as "several dozen volunteers, housewives and students, who helped with mailing and filing" (Marvin Caplan to Pauline Dubkin, August 24, 1964, Part I, Box 3, Folder 3, LCCR Records).

40. LCCR press release, July 25, 1963, Part I, Box 34, Folder 3, LCCR Records. The sign-in sheet from the July 17 meeting is in Part I, Box 34, Folder 1, LCCR Records.

41. The first Washington representatives meeting was held on July 17, 1963, and the last on July 1, 1964, the day before President Lyndon Johnson signed the Civil Rights Act into law. Meetings were skipped when superseded by other significant events (e.g., August 7, 1963, which fell during a three-day legislative strategy conference convened by the NAACP; August 28, 1963, the day of the March on Washington; and April 1, 1964, when the LCCR held a special meeting for heads of member organizations) and when merited by the legislative calendar.

42. Attendance figures are gleaned from the meetings' sign-in sheets, all but one of which are in Part I, Box 34, LCCR Records. The sign-in sheet for the May 6, 1964, meeting is in Part IX, Box 119, Folder 6, NAACP Records. Recollections by two meeting participants suggest that the sign-in sheets underestimate meeting attendance

(Richard G. Hirsch, interview by author, January 19, 2017; Jane O'Grady, interview by author, March 15, 2019).

43. Examples include the National Civil Liberties Clearing House, another coalition whose membership overlapped substantially with the LCCR's and whose director attended Leadership Conference events as an observer to protect the Clearing House's tax-exempt status, and the Friends Committee on National Legislation, which declined to join the Leadership Conference despite frequent collaboration with it as a matter of Quaker principle (Edward F. Snyder to Marvin Caplan, February 3, 1964, Part I, Box 2, Folder 2, LCCR Records).

44. O'Grady interview, March 15, 2019. Caplan similarly emphasized the information sharing and coordinated resource mobilization functions to the head of a prospective member organization: "We hold weekly strategy meetings at which representatives of the cooperating groups exchange information and plan how best to pool their resources" (Marvin Caplan to Kurt Reichert, August 23, 1963, Part I, Box 1, Folder 5, LCCR Records).

45. O'Grady interview, March 15, 2019.

46. Marvin Caplan to Walter R. Hundley, November 5, 1965, Part I, Box 52, Folder 9, LCCR Records.

47. Caplan noted that the Executive Committee was responsible for evaluating new member organization applications in response to a journalism student's query about the LCCR's operations during the Civil Rights Act campaign (Caplan to Dubkin, August 24, 1964). However, I could find no record of any Executive Committee meetings after March 28, 1963.

48. Arnold Aronson to Julia Thompson, December 22, 1963, Part I, Box 1, Folder 8, LCCR Records.

49. See, e.g., Caplan to Hundley, November 5, 1965; Marvin Caplan to Rev. F. C. James, September 25, 1965, Part I, Box 3, Folder 7, LCCR Records.

50. O'Grady interview, March 15, 2019. SNCC was a notable exception to the rule, as discussed later in this chapter and in Chapter 5.

51. Adele S. Trobe to L. G. E. Edmondson, July 6, 1967, Box 166, Folder 1, NCJW Records. See also Hannah Stein to Arnold Aronson, August 14, 1963, and Mrs. Joseph Willen to Arnold Aronson, December 13, 1963, both in Part I, Box 71, Folder 10, LCCR Records.

52. Form letters from Arnold Aronson to various national media professionals, December 5, 1963, are in Part I, Box 1, Folder 8, LCCR Records.

53. Caplan to Dubkin, August 24, 1964.

54. Copies of 37 of the 44 *MEMO*s issued during the campaign for the Civil Rights Act of 1964 are in Part I, Box 38, Folders 1–2, LCCR Records. I found copies of the remaining seven issues in Box 165, NCJW Records, and Part 1, Series 5, Box 11, Folder 2, ADA Records.

55. For example, see Leanne Golden to [ACLU] affiliates, August 12, 1963, Part I, Box 44, Folder 3, LCCR Records; JACL Washington Office to chapter presidents et al., October 3, 1963, Part I, Box 64, Folder 2, LCCR Records; Leon Shull to [ADA] chapter chairmen and National Board members, November 13, 1963, Part 1, Series 5, Box 13, Folder 8, ADA Records; Memorandum to NCCW board members et al., December 29, 1963, Part I, Box 71, Folder 7, LCCR Records.

56. Caplan to Simmons, December 23, 1963.

57. Darren Halpin and Carsten Daugbjerg, "Identity as Constraint and Resource in Interest Group Evolution: A Case of Radical Organizational Change," *British Journal of Politics and International Relations* 17 (2015): 31–48.

58. Joseph L. Rauh Jr. and Frank Pohlhaus, "Memorandum concerning Administration's Civil Rights Bill as Background for Meeting," July 2, 1963, Part 1, Series 5, Box 13, Folder 8, ADA Records.

59. For a blow-by-blow account of its enactment, see, among others, Berman, *A Bill Becomes a Law*; David B. Filvaroff and Raymond E. Wolfinger, "The Origins and Enactment of the Civil Rights Act of 1964," in *Legacies of the 1964 Civil Rights Act*, ed. Bernard Grofman (Charlottesville: University of Virginia Press, 2000), 9–32; Robert D. Loevy, *To End All Segregation*; Todd S. Purdum, *An Idea Whose Time Has Come: Two Presidents, Two Parties, and the Battle for the Civil Rights Act of 1964* (New York: Henry Holt, 2014); Clay Risen, *The Bill of the Century: The Epic Battle for the Civil Rights Act* (New York: Bloomsbury, 2014); and Charles Whalen and Barbara Whalen, *The Longest Debate: A Legislative History of the 1964 Civil Rights Act* (Cabin John, MD: Seven Locks Press, 1985).

60. Ken Kollman *Outside Lobbying: Public Opinion and Interest Group Strategies* (Princeton, NJ: Princeton University Press, 1998), 109.

61. Kollman, *Outside Lobbying*, 110.

62. Attachment to memorandum from Edward D. Hollander to chapter chairmen and National Board members, Box 477, Folder 10, Roosevelt Papers. Emphasis in original.

63. Typically this charge is levied with little evidence. Filvaroff and Wolfinger, for example, state only that Celler was "egged on by interest groups" ("Origins and Enactment," 18) and several others quote Kennedy's outraged rhetorical question upon learning of Celler's stunt, implying but not actually demonstrating that the Leadership Conference had a hand in this development: "Can Clarence Mitchell and the Leadership group deliver three Republicans on the Rules Committee and sixty Republicans on the House floor?" (For example, Anthony S. Chen, *The Fifth Freedom: Jobs, Politics, and Civil Rights in the United States, 1941–1972* [Princeton, NJ: Princeton University Press, 2009], 186; Mark Stern, *Calculating Visions: Kennedy, Johnson, and Civil Rights* (New Brunswick, NJ: Rutgers University Press, 1992), 108; and Whalen and Whalen, *Longest Debate*, 39.

64. Both memoranda are dated June 24, 1963, and are in Series V, Box 10, Folder 4, ADA Records. The next few paragraphs draw heavily on both documents.

65. Labor organizations were especially committed to FEPC as a legislative priority and AFL-CIO lobbyists took pains to impress this on Kennedy at every opportunity; see, e.g., Shishkin's July 19, 1963, memorandum to Meany, *op. cit.*, "Statement by the AFL-CIO Executive Council on Civil Rights," May 14, 1963, and Andrew J. Biemiller to Hubert H. Humphrey, June 7, 1963, both in Part I, Box 109, Folder 10, LCCR Records.

66. Cohen to Rauh, June 24, 1963.

67. Ibid.

68. Ibid.

69. Ibid.

70. Rauh and Pohlhaus, "Memorandum concerning Administration's Civil Rights Bill."

71. Arnold Aronson to cooperating organizations (*MEMO* no. 1), July 25, 1963, Part I, Box 34, LCCR Records. Emphases in original; elided passages summarize corresponding deficiencies in the administration bill.

72. See, e.g., Uri Miller, John F. Cronin, and J. Irwin Miller to members of the House Judiciary Committee, September 24, 1963, Part IX, Box 131, Folder 5, NAACP Records; Arnold Aronson to cooperating organizations (*MEMO* no. 9), October 7, 1963, Part I, Box 38, Folder 1, LCCR Records; and Arnold Aronson to cooperating organizations (*MEMO* no. 12), November 4, 1963, Part I, Box 38, Folder 1, LCCR Records.

73. Rauh and Pohlhaus, "Memorandum concerning Administration's Civil Rights Bill." In summarizing the rationale for this priority, Aronson to cooperating organizations (*MEMO* no. 1) notes merely that "the Administration bill lends itself to the possibility of exempting smaller businesses."

74. Rauh and Pohlhaus, "Memorandum concerning Administration's Civil Rights Bill."

75. The quote is from Olya Margolin's undated handwritten notes on an early Washington representatives meeting, Box 166, Folder 7, NCJW Records.

76. Draft minutes of the July 31, 1963, meeting, Part I, Box 34, Folder 2, LCCR Records.

77. John F. Kennedy, "Special Message to Congress on Civil Rights and Job Opportunities," June 19, 1963, American Presidency Project, http://www.presidency.ucsb.edu/node/236711.

78. Calendar Wednesday is a House of Representatives procedure that allows standing committees to bring up for limited-debate consideration any bill that has been reported on or before the previous day.

79. Strategy meeting minutes, July 24, 1963, Part I, Box 34, Folder 3, LCCR Records.

80. R. W. Taylor to Arnold Aronson et al., July 25, 1963, Part I, Box 34, Folder 3, LCCR Records.

81. July 31, 1963, draft meeting minutes.

82. According to the July 31 meeting minutes, a White House aide who attended the meeting as an observer noted that the LCCR's Washington office "should be the central clearing house [for background information] on each individual member."

83. Ibid.

84. Arnold Aronson to cooperating organizations (*MEMO* no. 2), August 5, 1963, Part I, Box 38, Folder 1, LCCR Records.

85. "Rights Proponents Open Parley Today," *New York Times*, August 5, 1963; "Wilkins Exhorts G.O.P. on Rights," *New York Times*, August 6, 1963.

86. A copy of the memorandum is in Part 1, Series 5, Box 13, Folder 8, ADA Records.

87. Dave Cohen's numerous memoranda to Aronson (and occasionally others) are especially illustrative; copies are in Part 1, Series 5, Box 10, Folder 5, and Box 11, Folder 1, ADA Records. See also, e.g., John D. Unruh Jr. to Arnold Aronson, August 23, 1963, Part I, Box 1, Folder 5, LCCR Records; and Olya Margolin to Arnold Aronson, August 13, 1963, Box 165, Folder 2, NCJW Records.

88. On the DSG and its role in civil rights legislation, see Ruth Bloch Rubin, *Building the Bloc: Intraparty Organization in the U.S. Congress* (New York: Cambridge University Press, 2017), 238–251.

89. Bill Phillips, "Confidential Summary of DSG Civil Rights Activity," August 30, 1963, Part I, Box 43, Folder 3, DSG Records.

90. Arnold Aronson to Cooperating Organizations (*MEMO* no. 5), August 30, 1963, Part I, Box 38, Folder 1, LCCR Records.

91. Arnold Aronson to cooperating organizations (*MEMO* no. 6), September 13, 1963, Part I, Box 38, Folder 1, LCCR Records. Emphases in original.

92. The quote is in Arnold Aronson to cooperating organizations (*MEMO* no. 8), September 27, 1963, Part I, Box 38, Folder 1, LCCR Records. An analysis of the subcommittee changes is in a memorandum from J. Francis Pohlhaus to Roy Wilkins, October 8, 1963, Part IX, Box 131, Folder 5, NAACP Records.

93. *MEMO* no. 8; see also *MEMO* no. 9 and Joseph L. Rauh Jr. to the editor of the *New York Times*, October 8, 1963, Part 1, Series 5, Box 11, Folder 1, ADA Records.

94. Arnold Aronson to Emanuel Celler, October 1, 1963, Part I, Box 1, Folder 6, LCCR Records.

95. *MEMO* no. 9.

96. David Cohen to Joseph L. Rauh Jr., October 8, 1963, Part V, Box 11, Folder 1, ADA Records.

97. Arnold Aronson to cooperating organizations (*MEMO* no. 10), October 14, 1963, Part I, Box 38, Folder 1, LCCR Records.

98. Robert F. Kennedy, "Statement by Attorney General Robert F. Kennedy on H.R. 7152 before the House Judiciary Committee," October 15, 1963, Department of Justice, https://www.justice.gov/sites/default/files/ag/legacy/2011/01/20/10-15-1963.pdf.

99. See, e.g., Purdum, *An Idea*, 135; Risen, *Bill of the Century*, 122; Stern, *Calculating Visions*, 109.

100. Telegram from Arnold Aronson, October 17, 1963; a copy of the text is attached to *MEMO* no. 11 from Arnold Aronson to cooperating organizations, October 18, 1963, Part I, Box 38, Folder 1, LCCR Records.

101. *MEMO* no. 11. Emphases in original.

102. Lyndon B. Johnson, "Address before a Joint Session of the Congress," November 27, 1963, American Presidency Project, https://www.presidency.ucsb.edu/documents/address-before-joint-session-the-congress-0.

103. See, e.g., E. W. Kenworthy, "Civil Rights: Bill Is Heading to Tougher Senate Battleground," *New York Times*, February 9, 1964; Loevy, *To End All Segregation*, chapter 6; Purdum, *An Idea*, 187–189; Risen, *Bill of the Century*, 157–158.

104. David Cohen to Violet M. Gunther and Joseph L. Rauh, November 8, 1963, Part 1, Series 5, Box 11, Folder 1, ADA Records.

105. Arnold Aronson to cooperating organizations (*MEMO* no. 13), November 11, 1963, Part I, Box 37, Folder 1, LCCR Records. Emphases in original.

106. Arnold Aronson to cooperating organizations (*MEMO* no. 21), January 20, 1964, Part I, Box 37, Folder 2, LCCR Records.

107. Arnold Aronson to cooperating organizations (*MEMO* no. 22), January 27, 1964, Part I, Box 37, Folder 2, LCCR Records. Emphasis in original.

108. *MEMO* no. 24 credits Representative James A. Haley of Florida with the "vultures" aspersion, which Aronson subsequently embraced in the *MEMO*'s main headline ("Gallery 'Vultures' Help House Pass an Effective Bill") (Arnold Aronson to cooperating organizations [*MEMO* no. 24], February 11, 1964, Part I, Box 37, Folder 2, LCCR Records).

109. *MEMO* no. 24.

110. Ibid.

111. This phrase was first used in a *New York Times* report and subsequently quoted in the *MEMO* (Kenworthy, "Civil Rights"; *MEMO* no. 24).

112. O'Grady arrived in Washington in the fall of 1963 and began attending LCCR meetings in December; by her own account, she was "new to the entire operation . . . new to Washington . . . new to the unions, and . . . new to the civil rights agenda" (O'Grady interview, March 15, 2019). Roach had moved to Washington about a year earlier to become the NCCW's social action and legislative secretary (Nicholas A. Patricca, *Peggy Roach: One Woman's Journey, a Nation's Progress* (Chicago: Loyola University, Ann Ida Gannon, BVM, Center for Women and Leadership, 2015).

113. O'Grady interview, March 15, 2019.

114. Kenworthy, "Civil Rights."

115. Rauh and Pohlhaus, "Memorandum concerning Administration's Civil Rights Bill."

116. O'Grady interview, March 15, 2019.

117. Arnold Aronson to cooperating organizations (*MEMO* no. 25), February 17, 1964, Part 1, Series 5, Box 11, Folder 2, ADA Records. Emphasis in original.

118. Violet Gunther to Richard G. Hirsch, February 27, 1964, Part I, Box 2, Folder 2, LCCR Records.

119. Memorandum on Senate Gallery Audiences from Violet Gunther to all participants in the Leadership Conference on Civil Rights, March 13, 1964, Box 165, Folder 3, NCJW Records.

120. O'Grady, interview, March 15, 2019.

121. Quotes and information about Margolin's work on this come from her April 14, 1964, letter to women's organization liaisons and an April 20, 1964, memorandum to Violet Gunther, both in Box 165, Folder 4, NCJW Records.

122. Telegram from Roy Wilkins, March 20, 1964, Part I, Box 2, Folder 3, LCCR Records.

123. The meeting's sign-in sheet lists representatives from fifty-four organizations, including the thirteen and eight referred to here (Part I, Box 34, Folder 30, LCCR Records). A report in the *MEMO* stated that "about 80 persons, representing 62 organizations" were there (Arnold Aronson to cooperating organizations [*MEMO* no. 32], April 6, 1964, Part I, Box 38, Folder 2, LCCR Records).

124. Arnold Aronson to cooperating organizations (*MEMO* no. 33), April 13, 1964, Part I, Box 38, Folder 2, LCCR Records.

125. An extensive paper trail attests to the variety of delegation-related activities carried out by the LCCR's Washington office staff; see especially Part IX, Box 119, Folders 4–6, NAACP Records.

126. Arnold Aronson to cooperating organizations (*MEMO* no. 38), May 18, 1964, Part I, Box 38, Folder 2, LCCR Records. Emphases in original.

127. Arnold Aronson to cooperating organizations (*MEMO* no. 39), May 25, 1964, Part I, Box 38, Folder 2. LCCR Records.

128. *MEMO* no. 32.

129. Arnold Aronson to cooperating organizations (*MEMO* no. 33), April 14, 1964, Part I, Box 38, Folder 2, LCCR Records.

130. Arnold Aronson to cooperating organizations (*MEMO* no. 41), June 10, 1964, Part I, Box 38, Folder 2, LCCR Records.

131. Caplan to Dubkin, August 24, 1964.

132. O'Grady interview, March 15, 2019. This resonates with Will Hathaway and David S. Meyer's suggestion that "the solidary benefits of training, mentoring, profes-

sional association, support for personal initiative, opportunity for career advancement, and friendship make [lobbying] coalitions attractive for the people who attend the frequent meetings" and, in turn, facilitate coalitions' survival in the face of less-conducive environmental conditions; see their "Competition and Cooperation in Social Movement Coalitions: Lobbying for Peace in the 1980s," *Berkeley Journal of Sociology* 38 (1993–1994), 178.

## CHAPTER 5

1. "A permanent ad hoc body" was the phrase Roy Wilkins's assistant used to describe the early Leadership Conference to the new public affairs chairman of one of its member organization (John A. Morsell to Richard B. Hertz, May 21, 1959, Part III, Box A205, Folder 4, NAACP Records).

2. Information in this paragraph was gleaned from the Leadership Conference website, http://www.civilrights.org.

3. Marvin Caplan to Robert E. Jones, July 2, 1964, Part I, Box 3, Folder 2, LCCR Records.

4. Arnold Aronson to S. Garry Oniki, July 7, 1964, Part I, Box 3, Folder 2, LCCR Records.

5. Arnold Aronson to cooperating organizations, July 6, 1964 (*MEMO* no. 44), Part I, Box 38, Folder 2, LCCR Records. On the history of the Mills Building, including its 1964 demolition, see Marvin Caplan, "The Mills Building's Corner on History," *Washington Post*, March 13, 1986, and John DeFerrari, "General Anson Mills and His Office Building on Pennsylvania Avenue," Streets of Washington blog, July 9, 2018, http://www.streetsofwashington.com/2018/07/general-anson-mills-and-his-office.html.

6. Marvin Caplan to Harry M. Reynolds, June 30, 1964, Part I, Box 3, Folder 1, LCCR Records.

7. *MEMO* no. 44.

8. Marvin Caplan to Rev. Elizabeth Miller, July 17, 1964, Part I, Box 3, Folder 2, LCCR Records.

9. Copies of these letters, dated July 8, 1964, are in Part I, Box 3, Folder 2, LCCR Records. Emphasis added.

10. Arnold Aronson to cooperating organizations, August 5, 1960, Part III, Box A205, Folder 6, NAACP Records.

11. While I could find no record of LCCR efforts to influence the Democratic platform, Wilkins did testify before the Republican Platform Committee and there was a hasty effort to have LCCR members endorse his statement. The telegram sent to member organizations noted that "our concentration on the civil rights bill made it impossible to follow our customary practice" and stated that Wilkins's testimony would ask the parties to include four civil rights positions in their platforms: endorsement of the Civil Rights Act of 1964, support for congressional rules reform, support for protections for civil rights workers, and broadened economic opportunity (Part I, Box 108, Folder 5, LCCR Records).

12. The new office address, 132 Third Street S.E., was announced in an August 19, 1964, memorandum from Arnold Aronson to cooperating organizations (*MEMO* no. 46), Part I, Box 38, Folder 2, LCCR Records. An August 10, 1964, letter from Caplan's secretary Geraldine P. Boykin to Mrs. G. E. Vaupel suggests that the second office had opened at least a couple of weeks prior to the *MEMO* announcement (Part

I, Box 3, Folder 3, LCCR Records). The LCCR relocated again, to the Union of Hebrew American Congregation's Religion Action Center of Reform Judaism building at 2027 Massachusetts Ave. N.W., about six months later (Arnold Aronson to cooperating organizations, March 2, 1965, Box 165, Folder 6, NCJW Records). Caplan discusses his retirement in his memoir, *Farther Along: A Civil Rights Memoir* (Baton Rouge: Louisiana State University Press, 1999), 245–247.

13. Arnold Aronson to cooperating organizations (*MEMO* no. 45), August 13, 1964, Part I, Box 38, Folder 2, LCCR Records.

14. The most famous of the six cases that set off the legislative firestorm is *Reynolds v. Sims*, 377 U.S. 533 (1964). The others are *Davis v. Mann*, 377 U.S. 678 (1964); *Lucas v. Forty-fourth General Assembly of Colorado*, 377 U.S. 713 (1964); *Maryland Committee for Fair Representation v. Tawes*, 377 U.S. 656 (1964); *Roman v. Sincock* 377 U.S. 695 (1964); and *WMCA, Inc. v. Lomenzo*, 377 U.S. 633 (1964).

15. *MEMO* no. 46.

16. A copy of the undated memo to Washington representatives announcing the August 31, 1964, meeting is in Box 165, Folder 5, NCJW Records. The discussion agenda Clarence Mitchell set for the meeting is in Part IX, Box 119, Folder 7, NAACP Records.

17. A copy of the September 3, 1964, statement and list of endorsing organizations is in Box 166, Folder 4, NCJW Records.

18. Jack [Pemberton] to Arnold Aronson, July 20, 1964, Part IX, Box 119, Folder 7, NAACP Records. The draft *MEMO* is attached to his letter.

19. See, e.g., Olya Margolin to Marvin Caplan, September 2, 1964, Box 165, Folder 5, NCJW Records.

20. *MEMO* no. 46. Emphasis in original.

21. Margolin's September 2 memorandum to Caplan indicates that the Washington representatives agreed to collect copies of LCCR members' relevant position statements. The NCJW resolution she enclosed with the memo was a general statement that had been adopted fifteen years earlier and was not tailored to the particular nuances of the reapportionment issue in 1964. I have found no other follow-up on the August 31 meeting, however, and the issue was crossed off a draft agenda for the November 24, 1964, meeting (in Part IX, Box 119, Folder 7, NAACP Records) at which Washington representatives discussed plans for the 89th Congress.

22. Sandy Bolz to John Slawson, June 15, 1965, Box 1, Folder 29, AJC Records; Arnold Aronson to cooperating organizations (*MEMO* no. 66), June 24, 1965, Part I, Box 38, Folder 3, LCCR Records. The National Committee for Fair Representation's leadership of the reapportionment lobbying campaign had the LCCR's blessing; see form letter from Arnold Aronson, April 8, 1965, Box 165, Folder 6, NCJW Records.

23. Arnold Aronson to cooperating organizations, August 19, 1965 (*MEMO* no. 72), Part I, Box 38, Folder 3, LCCR Records.

24. Copies of all the 1965 *MEMO*s are in Part I, Box 38, Folder 3, LCCR Records. For purposes of this content analysis, issues were considered to have been addressed in the *MEMO* when there is a substantive discussion of legislative developments, Leadership Conference activity (whether completed, planned, or ongoing), or specific action prompts for member groups and other supporters. Mere mentions were not counted.

25. Copies of all but one of the 1966 *MEMO*s are in Part I, Box 38, Folder 4, LCCR Records. A copy of *MEMO* no. 89, dated July 15, 1966, is in Part IX, Box 135, Folder 3, NAACP Records.

26. Arnold Aronson to cooperating organizations, January 21, 1966 (*MEMO* no. 80), Part I, Box 38, Folder 4, LCCR Records.

27. These are the "other" issues covered in *MEMO* nos. 94–96 and designated in the last column of Table 5.2.

28. Arnold Aronson to cooperating organizations, October 11, 1966, Part I, Box 38, Folder 3, LCCR Records.

29. For this and subsequent figures, I tracked membership growth by simply counting the "participating organizations" listed on the back of the LCCR's letterhead stationery each year. Anecdotal records indicate both that updated stationery orders were placed as organizations joined the Leadership Conference and that its leaders would refer media and public officials (among others) to the stationery listing for information about the coalition's size and diversity, as well as its specific membership.

30. Arnold Aronson to members of the Finance Committee, n.d., Part I, Box 27, Folder 6, LCCR Records.

31. See, e.g., Arnold Aronson to cooperating organizations (*MEMO* no. 78), November 24, 1965, Part I, Box 38, Folder 3, LCCR Records.

32. Form letter from Margaret Mealey to 136 Catholic women's colleges' alumnae directors, September 6, 1963, Part I, Box 71, Folder 7, LCCR Records.

33. Several documents pertaining to the dissolution of the National Women's Committee for Civil Rights are in Part IX, Box 120, Folder 1, NAACP Records. See also Helen Laville, "'Women of Conscience' or 'Women of Conviction'? The National Women's Committee on Civil Rights," *Journal of American Studies* 43 (2009): 277–295.

34. Betty Friedan to Arnold Aronson, December 13, 1966. Aronson's December 19, 1964 reply indicated that the application would be considered and a decision rendered "in due course." Both letters are in Part I, Box 74, Folder 3, LCCR Records.

35. A. Philip Randolph to Clarence Mitchell, August 9, 1965, Part IX, Box 134, Folder 4, NAACP Records. A copy of the letter was appended to Marvin Caplan's subsequent memorandum to Washington representatives announcing a special meeting to consider Randolph's suggestion in Part I, Box 35, Folder 23, LCCR Records.

36. The creation of the Committee on Compliance and Enforcement was announced in *MEMO* no. 86: Arnold Aronson to cooperating organizations, May 11, 1966, Part I, Box 34, Folder 4, LCCR Records.

37. Sandy Bolz to Edwin J. Lukas, September 22, 1965, Box 1, Folder 29, AJC Records.

38. Roy H. Millenson to Arnold Aronson, December 11, 1964, Part IX, Box 120, Folder 1, NAACP Records.

39. Mildred C. Boone to Arnold Aronson, February 21, 1966, Part I, Box 82, Folder 17, LCCR Records. While some of the LCCR's members maintained well-resourced Washington offices with paid lobbyists, in the case of this and a number of other member organizations, Washington representatives were poorly compensated or unpaid liaisons.

40. Boris Shishkin to George Meany, July 19, 1963, Box 31, Folder 18, Meany Papers.

41. Semiform fundraising letters were sent over Arnold Aronson's signature in November 1963, March 1964, and May 1964; see, e.g., letters to Edward S. Miller, David Dubinsky, and James B. Carey in Part II, Box 76, Folders 1, 6, and 8 (respectively), LCCR Records. These letters contain some information about the LCCR's expenses

during the Civil Rights Act campaign, including the $750-per-week figure to operate the Washington office. Roy Wilkins also conducted some targeted outreach for funding from African American organizations; see his letters to various organizational leaders in Part III, Box A206, Folder 5, NAACP Records.

42. "Statement of Contributions," July 31, 1964, Part III, Box A206, Folder 5, NAACP Records. While this statement does not itemize contributions smaller than $500, a table of annual contributions from member organizations from 1963 through 1969 in Part I, Box 27, Folder 5 LCCR Records lends insight into the full range of contribution sizes.

43. Arnold Aronson to Oliver C. Eastman, August 19, 1964, Part I, Box 3, Folder 3, LCCR Records.

44. Arnold Aronson to cooperating organizations (*MEMO* no. 56), March 24, 1965, Part I, Box 38, Folder 3, LCCR Records.

45. Arnold Aronson to cooperating organizations (*MEMO* no. 80), January 25, 1966, Part I, Box 38, Folder 4, LCCR Records. Emphasis in original. As it turned out (as Table 5.2 suggests), *MEMO* circulation was far from weekly in 1966, perhaps reflecting an effort to curb operating expenses.

46. One such appeal is in Arnold Aronson to Edward S. Miller, December 27, 1965, Part II, Box 76, Folder 1, LCCR Records. Emphasis in original.

47. For example, Arnold Aronson to Edward S. Miller, May 25, 1966, Part II, Box 76, Folder 1, LCCR Records.

48. For example, Arnold Aronson to Edward S. Miller, December 23, 1966, Part II, Box 76, Folder 1, LCCR Records.

49. For example, Arnold Aronson to Arthur E. Walmsley, February 9, 1966, Part I, Box 4, Folder 1, LCCR Records. Emphasis added.

50. Table of contributions from member organizations, 1963–1969.

51. As Barkan intimates, *moderate* and *militant* are generic terms used to distinguish social movement organizations according to their ideological and tactical inclinations (Steven E. Barkan, "Interorganizational Conflict in the Southern Civil Rights Movement," *Sociological Inquiry* 56 [1986]: 190–209). In the context of the civil rights movement, moderate groups were often labeled "integrationist," while "militant" groups were labeled "radical" or grouped together under the rubric of the movement's "black power" wing.

52. See, e.g., Manning Marable, *Race, Reform, and Rebellion: The Second Reconstruction in Black America, 1945–1990* (Jackson: University Press of Mississippi, 1991), 82–85.

53. Doug McAdam, *Political Process and the Development of Black Insurgency 1930–1970* (Chicago: University of Chicago Press, 1982), 182–183.

54. John Lewis to Walter P. Reuther, March 17, 1965, Box 578, Folder 2, Walter P. Reuther Papers.

55. The preceding paragraph synthesizes (and to some extent stylizes) a vast literature on the mid-to-late-1960s development of the civil rights movement. In addition to Barkan, "Interorganizational Conflict," see Marable, *Race*, and McAdam, *Political Process*, which offer insight into the divisions and development of the civil rights movement generally. For insight into the rise of black power as a prominent ideology within the movement, see Aram Goudsouzian, *Down to the Crossroads: Civil Rights, Black Power, and the Meredith March against Fear* (New York: Farrar, Straus and Giroux, 2014), and the essays in Peniel E. Joseph, ed., *The Black Power Movement: Rethinking the Civil Rights—Black Power Era* (London: Routledge, 2006).

56. On SNCC's growing militancy, see Clayborne Carson, *In Struggle: SNCC and the Black Awakening of the 1960s* (Cambridge, MA: Harvard University Press, 1981), and Wesley Hogan, *Many Minds, One Heart: SNCC's Dream for a New America* (Chapel Hill: University of North Carolina Press, 2009).

57. See, for example, Caplan's notes and draft minutes of the July 24 and 31, 1963, Washington representatives meetings in Part I, Box 34, Folders 2–3, LCCR Records. Though he does not address the implications for SNCC's role within the LCCR, Frank Tuerkheimer, one of SNCC's two principal lobbyists in 1963–1964, later recounted how the organization's embedded community work led to its favoring H.R. 7702 over the administration bill ("Bob Kastenmeier and 1960s Civil Rights Legislation: Leadership through Commitment and Foresight," *Wisconsin Law Review* [2005]: 947–956).

58. The LCCR's strict focus on lobbying, as opposed to protest activity, was appreciated well by Washington representatives. Rabbi Richard G. Hirsch, who served as Washington representative for the Union of American Hebrew Congregations within the Leadership Conference and participated as a member of the clergy in the Selma-to-Montgomery marches alongside Dr. King recalled, "I remember regular [Leadership Conference] meetings, as distinct from the march in Selma, Alabama. . . . As distinct from that [march], the Leadership Conference concentrated almost exclusively on legislation. The legislative process, that was its function" (Richard G. Hirsch, interview by author, January 19, 2017).

59. A copy of the AFL-CIO Executive Council's August 13, 1963, statement on the March on Washington is in Part I, Box 109, Folder 11, LCCR Records. For a discussion of its decision to issue this statement, see Alan Draper, *Conflict of Interests: Organized Labor and the Civil Rights Movement in the South, 1954–1968* (Ithaca, NY: Cornell University Press, 1994), 3–5.

60. Marvin Caplan to Fielding Simmons, December 24, 1963, Part I, Box 1, Folder 3, LCCR Records. Minutes from the July 24 and 31 meetings both contain brief reports on March on Washington plans by Walter Fauntroy, Washington representative for the Southern Christian Leadership Conference, which are in Part I, Box 34, Folders 2–3, LCCR Records.

61. Arnold Aronson to Robert M. Stein, November 15, 1963, Part I, Box 1, Folder 7, LCCR Records.

62. Arnold Aronson to Mrs. Lester J. Senechalle, vice president of United Church Women of Greater Chicago, April 28, 1964, Part I, Box 2, Folder 5, LCCR Records.

63. Arnold Aronson to cooperating organizations, June 24, 1964, Part I, Box 38, Folder 2, LCCR Records.

64. *MEMO* no. 45.

65. Rauh's experience with the MFDP challenge is recounted at length in Michael E. Parrish, *Citizen Rauh: An American Liberal's Life in Law and Politics* (Ann Arbor: University of Michigan Press, 2011), 164–174. Clarence Mitchell's biographer wrote that "Rauh was a study of conflicting loyalties" in this episode (Denton L. Watson, *Lion in the Lobby: Clarence Mitchell, Jr.'s Struggle for the Passage of Civil Rights Laws* [New York: Morrow, 1990], 630).

66. In addition to Parrish, *Citizen Rauh*, and Watson, *Lion*, see, e.g., Carson, *In Struggle*, 123–129; Hogan, *Many Minds*, 187–195; and Lisa Anderson Todd, *For a Voice and a Vote: My Journey with the Mississippi Freedom Democratic Party* (Lexington: University Press of Kentucky, 2014).

67. William H. Oliver to Walter P. Reuther, December 16, 1964, Box 493, Folder 32, Walter P. Reuther Papers. Oliver's handwritten notes, in the same box and folder, indicate that the "meeting [was] in shambles" by the time Mitchell's ruling was upheld.

68. "Agenda for Leadership Conference Meeting," December 30, 1964, Part I, Box 34, Folder 47, LCCR Records.

69. William Oliver to Roy L. Reuther and William Dodds, December 30, 1964, Box 493, Folder 32, Walter P. Reuther Papers.

70. A copy of both the February 27 memorandum and the MFDP's February 21, 1965, position statement are in Box 165, Folder 6, NCJW Records.

71. Martin Luther King Jr. to members of the Leadership Conference on Civil Rights and all participating groups in the American Civil Rights Movement, n.d., Part IX, Box 119, Folder 8, LCCR Records.

72. Memorandum from Marvin Caplan, September 9, 1965, Part I, Box 35, Folder 25, LCCR Records.

73. The sign-in sheet for this meeting is in Part I, Box 35, Folder 25, LCCR Records.

74. Watson, *Lion*, 636. He names Mitchell himself, as well as Rauh and Andy Biemiller, the AFL-CIO's legislative director who was a regular and prominent participant at the Washington representatives meetings. Rauh's and Biemiller's names do not appear on the sign-in sheet, but Mitchell's does (though not in his own hand).

75. Handwritten notes, Box 165, Folder 7, NCJW Records. Adoption of the statement was announced and a copy of the statement and list of endorsing organizations enclosed in Arnold Aronson to cooperating organizations (*MEMO* no. 74), September 15, 1965, Part I, Box 38, Folder 3, LCCR Records.

76. Memorandum from Clifford L. Alexander Jr. for the president, January 7, 1966, Box 3, HU2, WHCF.

77. Marion S. Barry Jr. to participants in the Leadership Conference, n.d. Part IX, Box 120, Folder 4, NAACP Records. See also Daniel S. Lucks, *From Selma to Saigon: The Civil Rights Movement and the Vietnam War* (Lexington: University Press of Kentucky, 2014), chapter 4.

78. Joseph L. Rauh Jr. to Eugene J. Lipman, December 20, 1965, Box 82, Folder 6, Rauh Papers. The ad hoc committee was established at a December 3, 1965, meeting of the Washington representatives (Marvin Caplan to Ben Sissel, December 7, 1965, Part I, Box 3, Folder 8, LCCR Records).

79. A copy of the relevant excerpts from Higgs's testimony are in Part I, Box 35, Folder 33, LCCR Records. His full testimony is available in the official record of the hearings, *Hearings before the Subcommittee on Executive Reorganization of the Committee on Government Operations, United States Senate, 89th Congress, Second Session, on S. Res. 220 to Disapprove Reorganization Plan No. 1 of 1966* (Washington, DC: U.S. Government Printing Office, 1966), 125–134.

80. Roy Wilkins to John Lewis, April 7, 1966, Part I, Box 35, Folder 33, LCCR Records.

81. Julius W. Hobson to Marvin Caplan, January 10, 1966, Part I, Box 38, Folder 6, LCCR Records.

82. Roy Wilkins to Julius W. Hobson, January 28 and March 22, 1966, Part IX, Box 120, Folder 5, NAACP Records; Julius W. Hobson to Roy Wilkins, February 16, 1966, Part I, Box 38, Folder 6, LCCR Records.

83. Draft memorandum to Washington representatives, n.d., Part IX, Box 120, Folder 5, NAACP Records.

84. ACT pamphlet, quoted in draft memorandum to Washington representatives, n.d.

85. Text quoted, with emphasis added, from the telegram from Roy Wilkins to Olya Margolin, December 30, 1966, Box 165, Folder 9, NCJW Records.

86. Roy Wilkins to cooperating organizations, n.d., Box 166, Folder 1, NCJW Records. Rauh likewise anticipated that it would be the LCCR's "most important meeting in a long time" in a letter canceling his participation at another event that evening; see his letter to Harry H. Wachtel, January 9, 1967, Box 82, Folder 7, Rauh Papers.

87. Quotes and other information in the next few paragraphs are drawn from a copy of the adopted by-laws that was sent to member organizations after the January 11 meeting. As noted in the cover letter, changes to the premeeting draft are underlined in the adopted version (Roy Wilkins to Mrs. Joseph Willen, January 26, 1967, Box 166, Folder 1, NCJW Records).

88. *Sex* was not in the original draft of the by-laws but was added prior to adoption at the January 11 meeting.

89. Per the by-laws, the annual meeting of the National Board would be held every January, with additional meetings called as necessary by the coalition chairman or "upon the request of one-fifth of the [National Board] members."

90. Wilkins clarified that "Washington representatives to the Conference will continue to meet as heretofore and they will be designated as the Legislative Committee" shortly after the by-laws' ratification; see his January 26, 1967, letter to Willen.

91. Stokely Carmichael to Roy Wilkins, March 8, 1967, Part IX, Box 120, Folder 6, NAACP Records.

92. For another example, see the discussion of how enactment of a series of significant environmental protection laws in the early 1970s benefited the Natural Resources Defense Council by helping to concretize its agenda and by creating launchpads for new projects that enhanced its reputation in McGee Young, *Developing Interests: Organizational Change and the Politics of Advocacy* (Lawrence: University Press of Kansas, 2010), 126–132.

## CONCLUSION

1. Marvin Caplan to Florence A. Holmes, November 1, 1963, Part I, Box 1, Folder 7, LCCR Records.

2. As discussed in Chapter 1, recent political science scholarship on interest group coalitions has converged on both a signaling-based approach to conceptualizing coalitions' role in the policy process and a consensus that diversity enhances interest group coalitions' signaling capabilities. See, for example, Wiebke Marie Junk, "When Diversity Works: The Effects of Coalition Composition on the Success of Lobbying Coalitions," *American Journal of Political Science* 63, no. 3 (July 2019): 660–674; Geoffrey Miles Lorenz, "Prioritized Interests: Diverse Lobbying Coalitions and Congressional Committee Agenda-Setting," *Journal of Politics* 82, no. 1 (January 2020): 225–240; David Nelson and Susan Webb Yackee, "Lobbying Coalitions and Government Policy Change: An Analysis of Federal Agency Rulemaking," *Journal of Politics* 74, no. 2 (April 2012): 339–353; and Robin Phinney, *Strange Bedfellows: Interest Group Coalitions,*

*Diverse Partners, and Influence in American Social Policy* (New York: Cambridge University Press, 2017).

3. "Increasingly conflicting" is from Walter White to Messrs. Carter, Marshall, Moon, and Wilkins, January 27, 1949, Part II, Box A183, Folder 6, NAACP Records.

4. The quote is from a January 2, 1956, LCCR press release, Part I, Box 14, Folder 1, LCCR Records. While the precise phrasing varies, similar descriptions of the LCCR's composition appear in communications to public officials and public-facing statements throughout the 1950s and 1960s.

5. See, for example, Will Hathaway and David S. Meyer, "Competition and Cooperation in Social Movement Coalitions: Lobbying for Peace in the 1980s," *Berkeley Journal of Sociology* 38 (1993–1994): 157–183; Junk, "When Diversity Works."

6. Wiebke Marie Junk, "Synergies in Lobbying? Conceptualising and Measuring Lobbying Coalitions to Study Interest Group Strategies, Access, and Influence," *Interest Groups and Advocacy* 9, no. 1 (March 2020): 21–37.

7. Darren R. Halpin, *The Organization of Political Interest Groups: Designing Advocacy* (London: Routledge, 2014), 33.

8. Junk, "Synergies," 27.

9. Ibid.

10. This tension is not unique to interest group coalitions; as Hathaway and Meyer note, it is a long-standing insight of sociological resource mobilization scholarship that "there is often a conflict between the purposive or political goals of an organization and its organizational needs" (Hathaway and Meyer, "Competition and Cooperation," 159).

11. For lobbying coalitions specifically, see Hathaway and Meyer, "Competition and Cooperation." On social movement coalitions generally, see Suzanne Staggenborg, "Coalition Work in the Pro-Choice Movement: Organizational and Environmental Opportunities and Obstacles," *Social Problems* 33, no. 5 (June 1986): 374–390.

12. Hathaway and Meyer, "Competition and Cooperation," 164.

13. The term *preference attainment* was introduced in Andreas Dür, "Measuring Interest Group Influence in the EU: A Note on Methodology," *European Union Politics* 9, no. 4 (December 2008): 559–576. In a recent review, Matia Vannoni writes that "preference attainment has become the mainstream approach to account for interest group influence" ("Studying Preference Attainment Using Spatial Models," *European Political Science* 16, no. 3 [September 2017], 370). While the language of "preference attainment" has been adopted primarily by researchers studying the influence of lobbying in European politics in the last decade, the approach behind it is both more widespread and predates the coinage of the term.

14. In this respect, the LCCR's experience resonates well with the late-twentieth-century arms control coalitions Hathaway and Meyer study. As they note in the case of the Monday Lobby Group (MLG), "Early legislative victories generated momentum and boosted morale among the MLG lobbyists. These victories may have seemed marginal and indecisive in terms of the larger goal of ending the arms race . . . but there were significant accomplishments in the 'gray areas' of establishing relationships with Congressional and media elites, and in preventing further erosion . . . of existing arms control agreements" (Hathaway and Meyer, "Cooperation and Competition," 171).

15. Kenneth T. Andrews and Bob Edwards, "Advocacy Organizations in the U.S. Political Process," *Annual Review of Sociology* 30 (2004), 491–492.

16. These mechanisms are elucidated in, e.g., Kenneth T. Andrews and Sarah Gaby, "Local Protest and Federal Policy: The Impact of the Civil Rights Movement on the Civil Rights Act of 1964," *Sociological Forum* 30, no. S1 (June 2015): 509–527; Taeku Lee, *Mobilizing Public Opinion: Black Insurgency and Racial Attitudes in the Civil Rights Era* (Chicago: University of Chicago Press, 2002); and Joseph E. Luders, *The Civil Rights Movement and the Logic of Social Change* (Cambridge: Cambridge University Press, 2010).

17. Kay Lehman Schlozman, "Representing Women in Washington: Sisterhood and Pressure Politics," in *Women, Politics, and Change*, ed. Louise A. Tilly and Patricia Gurin (New York: Russel Sage Foundation, 1990), 342.

18. Bayard Rustin, "From Protest to Politics: The Future of the Civil Rights Movement," *Commentary* (February 1965): 25.

19. See, e.g., Bilal Dabir Sekou, "The Limits of Black Politics in the Post-Civil Rights Era," *Sociological Forum* 35, no. 1 (September 2020): 954–973; Robert C. Smith, "Black Power and the Transformation from Protest to Politics," *Political Science Quarterly* 96, no. 3 (Autumn 1981): 431–443; and Katherine Tate, *From Protest to Politics: The New Black Voters in American Elections* (Cambridge, MA: Harvard University Press, 1994).

20. Michael D. Minta, "Diversity and Minority Interest Group Advocacy in Congress," *Political Research Quarterly* 73, no. 1 (March 2020), 208; emphasis added.

21. E.g., Janet M. Box-Steffensmeier, Dino P. Christenson, and Alison W. Craig, "Cue-Taking in Congress: Interest Group Signals from Dear Colleague Letters," *American Journal of Political Science* 63, no. 1 (January 2019): 163–180; and Richard L. Hall and Alan V. Deardorff, "Lobbying as Legislative Subsidy," *American Political Science Review* 100, no. 1 (February 2006): 69–84.

22. The former includes Megan Ming Francis, *Civil Rights and the Making of the Modern American State* (New York: Cambridge University Press, 2014). The latter includes Christopher Baylor, *First to the Party: The Group Origins of Party Transformation* (Philadelphia: University of Pennsylvania Press, 2018); and Eric Schickler, *Racial Realignment: The Transformation of American Liberalism, 1932–1965* (Princeton, NJ: Princeton University Press, 2016).

23. As a number of studies suggest they do: Wiebke Marie Junk, "Co-operation as Currency: How Active Coalitions Affect Lobbying Success," *Journal of European Public Policy* 27, no. 1 (2020): 873–892; Phinney, *Strange Bedfellows*; and Dara Z. Strolovitch, *Affirmative Advocacy: Race, Class, and Gender in Interest Group Politics* (Chicago: University of Chicago Press, 2007).

# References

Ainsworth, Scott. 1993. "Regulating Lobbyists and Interest Group Influence." *Journal of Politics* 55, no. 1 (February): 41–56.
Anderson, John Weir. 1964. *Eisenhower, Brownell, and the Congress: The Tangled Origins of the Civil Rights Bill of 1956–1957*. Tuscaloosa: University of Alabama Press.
Andrews, Kenneth T., and Bob Edwards. 2004. "Advocacy Organizations in the U.S. Political Process." *Annual Review of Sociology* 30:479–506.
Andrews, Kenneth T., and Sarah Gaby. 2015. "Local Protest and Federal Policy: The Impact of the Civil Rights Movement on the Civil Rights Act of 1964." *Sociological Forum* 30, no. S1 (June): 509–527.
Austen-Smith, David, and John Wright. 1992. "Competitive Lobbying for a Legislator's Vote." *Social Choice and Welfare* 9:229–257.
Bangarth, Stephanie. 2008. *Voices Raised in Protest: Defending North American Citizens of Japanese Ancestry, 1942–49*. Vancouver, BC: University of British Columbia Press.
Barkan, Steven E. 1986. "Interorganizational Conflict in the Southern Civil Rights Movement." *Sociological Inquiry* 56, no. 2 (April): 109–209.
Bates, Beth Tompkins. 1997. "A New Crowd Challenges the Agenda of the Old Guard in the NAACP, 1933–1941." *American Historical Review* 102, no. 2 (April): 340–377.
Baumgartner, Frank R., Jeffrey M. Berry, Marie Hojnacki, David C. Kimball, and Beth L. Leech. 2009. *Lobbying and Policy Change: Who Wins, Who Loses, and Why*. Chicago: University of Chicago Press.
Baylor, Christopher. 2018. *First to the Party: The Group Origins of Party Transformation*. Philadelphia: University of Pennsylvania Press.
Berman, Daniel M. 1966. *A Bill Becomes a Law: Congress Enacts Civil Rights Legislation*. 2nd ed. New York: Macmillan.
Beyers, Jan, and Iskander de Bruycker. 2018. "Lobbying Makes (Strange) Bedfellows: Explaining the Formation and Composition of Lobbying Coalitions in EU Politics." *Political Studies* 66, no. 4 (November): 959–984.

Bloch Rubin, Ruth. 2017. *Building the Bloc: Intraparty Organization in the U.S. Congress.* Cambridge: Cambridge University Press.

Box-Steffensmeier, Janet M., and Dino P. Christenson. 2015. "Comparing Membership Interest Group Networks across Space and Time, Size, Issue and Industry." *Network Science* 3, no. 1: 78–97.

Box-Steffensmeier, Janet M., Dino P. Christenson, and Alison W. Craig. 2019. "Cue-Taking in Congress: Interest Group Signals from Dear Colleague Letters." *American Journal of Political Science* 63, no. 1 (January): 163–180.

Boyle, Kevin. 1995. *The UAW and the Heyday of American Liberalism 1945–1968.* Ithaca, NY: Cornell University Press.

Brock, Clifton. 1962. *Americans for Democratic Action: Its Role in National Politics.* Washington, DC: Public Affairs.

Browne, William P. 1990. "Organized Interests and Their Issue Niches: A Search for Pluralism in the Policy Domain." *Journal of Politics* 52, no. 2 (May): 477–509.

Burrows, Vanessa, and Barbara Burney. 2019. "Creating Equal Health Opportunity: How the Medical Civil Rights Movement and the Johnson Administration Desegregated U.S. Hospitals." *Journal of American History* 105, no. 4 (March): 885–911.

Byker, Loree, and Ardith Maney. 1995. "Consumer Groups and Coalition Politics on Capitol Hill." In *Interest Group Politics*, 4th ed. Edited by Allan J. Cigler and Burdett A. Loomis, 259–280. Washington, DC: CQ.

Caplan, Marvin. 1999. *Farther Along: A Civil Rights Memoir.* Baton Rouge: Louisiana State University Press.

Carson, Clayborne. 1981. *In Struggle: SNCC and the Black Awakening of the 1960s.* Cambridge, MA: Harvard University Press.

Chanes, Jerome A. 2004. "Who Does What? Jewish Advocacy and Jewish 'Interest.'" In *Jews and American Politics.* Edited by Sandy Maisel and Ira N. Forman, 99–119. Lanham, MD: Rowman and Littlefield.

Chen, Anthony S. 2009. *The Fifth Freedom: Jobs, Politics, and Civil Rights in the United States, 1941–1972.* Princeton, NJ: Princeton University Press.

Chong, Dennis. 1991. *Collective Action and the Civil Rights Movement.* Chicago: University of Chicago Press.

Clemens, Elisabeth. 1997. *The People's Lobby: Organizational Innovation and the Rise of Interest Group Politics in the United States.* Chicago: University of Chicago Press.

"Criticism of Congress Provokes Few Changes." 1964. In *CQ Almanac 1963*, 19th ed., 369–376. Washington, DC: CQ.

Dalfiume, Richard M. 1968. "The 'Forgotten Years' of the Negro Revolution." *Journal of American History* 55, no. 1 (June): 90–106.

Draper, Alan. 1994. *Conflict of Interests: Organized Labor and the Civil Rights Movement in the South, 1954–1968.* Ithaca, NY: Cornell University Press.

Drutman, Lee. 2015. *The Business of America Is Lobbying: How Corporations Became Politicized and Politics Became More Corporate.* New York: Oxford University Press.

Dudziak, Mary L. 2000. *Cold War Civil Rights: Race and the Image of American Democracy.* Princeton, NJ: Princeton University Press.

Dür, Andreas. 2008. "Measuring Interest Group Influence in the EU: A Note on Methodology." *European Union Politics* 9, no. 4 (December): 559–576.

Filvaroff, David B., and Raymond E. Wolfinger. 2000. "The Origins and Enactment of the Civil Rights Act of 1964." In *Legacies of the 1964 Civil Rights Act*. Edited by Bernard Grofman, 9–32. Charlottesville: University of Virginia Press.

Findlay, James F. Jr. 1993. *Church People in the Struggle: The National Council of Churches and the Black Freedom Movement, 1950–1970*. Oxford: Oxford University Press.

Finley, Keith M. 2008. *Delaying the Dream: Southern Senators and the Fight against Civil Rights, 1938–1965*. Baton Rouge: Louisiana State University Press.

Fleming, Harold C. 1965. "The Federal Executive and Civil Rights, 1961–1965." *Daedalus* 94, no. 4 (Fall): 921–948.

Foner, Philip S. 1974. *Organized Labor and the Black Worker, 1619–1973*. New York: International.

Francis, Megan Ming. 2014. *Civil Rights and the Making of the Modern American State*. New York: Cambridge University Press.

———. 2018. "The Strange Fruit of American Political Development." *Politics, Groups, and Identities* 6, no. 1: 128–137.

Frymer, Paul. 1999. *Uneasy Alliances: Race and Party Competition in America*. Princeton, NJ: Princeton University Press.

———. 2008. *Black and Blue: African Americans, the Labor Movement, and the Decline of the Democratic Party*. Princeton, NJ: Princeton University Press.

Gamble, Vanessa Northington. 1995. *Making a Place for Ourselves: The Black Hospital Movement, 1920–1945*. New York: Oxford University Press.

Gergel, Richard. 2019. *Unexampled Courage: The Blinding of Sgt. Isaac Woodard and the Awakening of President Harry S. Truman and Judge J. Waties Waring*. New York: Sarah Crichton.

Gilens, Martin, and Benjamin I. Page. 2014. "Testing Theories of American Politics: Elites, Interest Groups, and Average Citizens." *Perspectives on Politics* 12, no. 3 (September): 564–581.

Goldfield, Michael. 1993. "Race and the CIO: The Possibilities for Racial Egalitarianism during the 1930s and 1940s." *International Labor and Working-Class History* 44 (Fall): 1–32.

Goudsouzian, Aram. 2014. *Down to the Crossroads: Civil Rights, Black Power, and the Meredith March against Fear*. New York: Farrar, Straus and Giroux.

Graham, Hugh Davis. 1990. *The Civil Rights Era: Origins and Development of National Policy, 1960–1972*. New York: Oxford University Press.

Greenberg, Cheryl Lynn. 2010. *Troubling the Waters: Black-Jewish Relations in the American Century*. Princeton, NJ: Princeton University Press.

Grossmann, Matt. 2012. *The Not-So-Special Interests: Interest Groups, Public Representation, and American Governance*. Stanford, CA: Stanford University Press.

Grossmann, Matt, and Casey B. K. Dominguez. 2009. "Party Coalitions and Interest Group Networks." *American Politics Research* 37, no. 5 (September): 767–800.

Hall, Donald R. 1969. *Cooperative Lobbying—the Power of Pressure*. Tucson: University of Arizona Press.

Hall, Jacquelyn Dowd. 1979. *Revolt against Chivalry: Jesse Daniel Ames and the Women's Campaign against Lynching*. New York: Columbia University Press.

Hall, Richard L., and Alan V. Deardorff. 2006. "Lobbying as Legislative Subsidy." *American Political Science Review* 100, no. 1 (February): 69–84.

Halpin, Darren R. 2014. *The Organizational Politics of Political Interest Groups: Designing Advocacy*. London: Routledge.

Halpin, Darrin R., and Carsten Daugbjerg. 2015. "Identity as Constraint and Resource in Interest Group Evolution: A Case of Radical Organizational Change." *British Journal of Politics and International Relations* 17, no. 1 (February): 31–48.

Hamilton, Charles V. 1991. *Adam Clayton Powell: The Political Biography of an American Dilemma*. New York: Atheneum.

Hanegraaf, Marcel, and Andrea Pritoni. 2019. "United in Fear: Interest Group Coalition Formation as a Weapon of the Weak?" *European Union Politics* 20, no. 2 (June): 198–218.

Harris, Robert L. Jr. 2005. "Lobbying Congress for Civil Rights: The American Council on Human Rights, 1948–1963." In *African American Fraternities and Sororities: The Legacy and the Vision*. Edited by Tamara L. Brown, Gregory S. Parks, and Clarenda M. Phillips, 211–230. Lexington: University Press of Kentucky.

Hathaway, Will, and David S. Meyer. 1993–1994. "Cooperation and Competition in Social Movement Coalitions: Lobbying for Peace in the 1980s." *Berkeley Journal of Sociology* 38:157–183.

Heaney, Michael T. 2006. "Brokering Health Policy: Coalitions, Parties, and Interest Group Influence." *Journal of Health Politics, Policy, and Law* 31, no. 5 (October): 887–944.

Heaney, Michael T., and Philip Leifeld. 2018. "Contributions by Interest Groups to Lobbying Coalitions." *Journal of Politics* 80, no. 2 (April): 494–509.

Heaney, Michael T., and Geoffrey M. Lorenz. 2013. "Coalition Portfolios and Interest Group Influence over the Policy Process." *Interest Groups and Advocacy* 2, no. 3 (October): 251–277.

Hirsch, Selma G. 1953. "Jewish Community Relations." *American Jewish Year Book* 54:162–177.

Hogan, Wesley. 2009. *Many Minds, One Heart: SNCC's Dream for a New America*. Chapel Hill: University of North Carolina Press.

Hojnacki, Marie. 1997. "Interest Groups' Decisions to Join Alliances or Work Alone." *American Journal of Political Science* 41, no. 1 (January): 61–87.

———. 1998. "Organized Interests' Advocacy Behavior in Alliances." *Political Research Quarterly* 51, no. 4 (December): 437–459.

Holloway, Vanessa. 2018. *Black Rights in the Reconstruction Era*. Lanham, MD: Hamilton.

Holyoke, Thomas T. 2009. "Interest Group Competition and Coalition Formation." *American Journal of Political Science* 53, no. 2 (April): 260–275.

Hosokawa, Bill. 1982. *JACL in Quest of Justice*. New York: Morrow.

Hula, Kevin W. 1999. *Lobbying Together: Interest Group Coalitions in Legislative Politics*. Washington, DC: Georgetown University Press.

Johnson, Karen Joy. 2015. "Another Long Civil Rights Movement: How Catholic Interracialists Used the Resources of Their Faith to Tear Down Racial Hierarchies." *American Catholic Studies* 126, no. 4 (Winter): 1–27.

Johnson, Richard. 2020. *The End of the Second Reconstruction*. Cambridge, UK: Polity.

Jones, William P. 2010. "The Unknown Origins of the March on Washington: Civil Rights Politics and the Black Working Class." *Labor* 7, no. 3 (Fall): 33–52.

Joseph, Peniel E., ed. 2006. *The Black Power Movement: Rethinking the Civil Rights—Black Power Era*. London: Routledge.

Juhnke, William E. 1989. "President Truman's Committee on Civil Rights: The Interaction of Politics, Protest, and Presidential Advisory Commission." *Presidential Studies Quarterly* 19, no. 3 (Summer): 593–610.

Junk, Wiebke Marie. 2019. "When Diversity Works: The Effects of Coalition Composition on the Success of Lobbying Coalitions." *American Journal of Political Science* 63, no. 3 (July): 660–674.

———. 2020. "Co-operation as Currency: How Active Coalitions Affect Lobbying Success." *Journal of European Public Policy* 27, no. 6:873–892.

———. 2020. "Synergies in Lobbying? Conceptualising and Measuring Lobbying Coalitions to Study Interest Group Strategies, Access, and Influence." *Interest Groups and Advocacy* 9, no. 1 (March): 21–37.

Junk, Wiebke Marie, and Anne Rasmussen. 2019. "Framing by the Flock: Collective Issue Definition and Advocacy Success." *Comparative Political Studies* 52, no. 4 (March): 483–513.

Kersten, Andrew Edmund. 2000. *Race, Jobs, and the War: The FEPC in the Midwest, 1941–46*. Urbana: University of Illinois Press.

Kesselman, Louis C. 1948. *The Social Politics of FEPC: A Study in Reform Pressure Movements*. Chapel Hill: University of North Carolina Press.

King, Desmond, and Robert C. Lieberman. 2016. "The American State." In *The Oxford Handbook of American Political Development*. Edited by Richard Valelly, Suzanne Mettler, and Robert C. Lieberman, 231–258. Oxford: Oxford University Press.

Klinkner, Philip A. 1999. *The Unsteady March: The Rise and Decline of Racial Equality in America*. Chicago: University of Chicago Press.

Koehler, Sebastian. 2019. *Lobbying, Political Uncertainty and Policy Outcomes*. Cham, Switz.: Palgrave Macmillan.

Kollman, Ken. 1998. *Outside Lobbying: Public Opinion and Interest Group Strategies*. Princeton, NJ: Princeton University Press.

Kraus, Rachel. 2007. "Laity, Institution, Theology, or Politics? Protestant, Catholic, and Jewish Washington Offices' Agenda Setting." *Sociology of Religion* 68, no. 1 (Spring): 67–81.

Laville, Helen. 2009. "'Women of Conscience' or 'Women of Conviction'? The National Women's Committee on Civil Rights." *Journal of American Studies* 43, no. 2 (August): 277–295.

Lawson, Steven F. 1976. *Black Ballots: Voting Rights in the South, 1944–1969*. New York: Columbia University Press.

Layton, Azza Salama. 2000. *International Politics and Civil Rights Policies in the United States, 1941–1960*. Cambridge: Cambridge University Press.

Lee, Taeku. 2002. *Mobilizing Public Opinion: Black Insurgency and Racial Attitudes in the Civil Rights Era*. Chicago: University of Chicago Press.

Loevy, Robert D. 1990. *To End All Segregation: The Politics of the Passage of the Civil Rights Act of 1964*. Lanham, MD: University Press of America.

———, ed. 1997. *The Civil Rights Act of 1964: The Passage of the Law That Ended Racial Segregation*. Albany, NY: SUNY Press.

Lorenz, Geoffrey Miles. 2020. "Prioritized Interests: Diverse Lobbying Coalitions and Congressional Committee Agenda-Setting." *Journal of Politics* 82, no. 1 (January): 225–240.

Lucks, Daniel S. 2014. *From Selma to Saigon: The Civil Rights Movement and the Vietnam War.* Lexington: University Press of Kentucky.

Luders, Joseph E. 2010. *The Civil Rights Movement and the Logic of Social Change.* Cambridge: Cambridge University Press.

Mahoney, Christine. 2007. "Networking vs. Allying: The Decision of Interest Groups to Join Coalitions in the US and the EU." *Journal of European Public Policy* 14, no. 3: 366–383.

Mahoney, Christine, and Frank L. Baumgartner. 2015. "Partners in Advocacy: Lobbyists and Government Officials in Washington." *Journal of Politics* 77, no. 1 (January): 202–215.

Marable, Manning. 1991. *Race, Reform, and Rebellion: The Second Reconstruction in Black America, 1945–1990.* Jackson: University Press of Mississippi.

Maslow, Will, and Joseph B. Robison. 1953. "Civil Rights Legislation and the Fight for Equality, 1862–1952." *University of Chicago Law Review* 20, no. 3 (Spring): 363–413.

Matthews, Donald R. 1960. *U.S. Senators and Their World.* Chapel Hill: University of North Carolina Press.

McAdam, Doug. 1982. *Political Process and the Development of Black Insurgency 1930–1970.* Chicago: University of Chicago Press.

McAdam, Doug, Sidney Tarrow, and Charles Tilly. 2001. *Dynamics of Contention.* Cambridge: Cambridge University Press.

McGreevy, John T. 2016. *Parish Boundaries: The Catholic Encounter with Race in the Twentieth-Century Urban North.* Chicago: University of Chicago Press.

Meier, August, and John H. Bracey Jr. 1993. "The NAACP as Reform Movement, 1909–1965: 'To Reach the Conscience of America.'" *Journal of Southern History* 59, no. 1 (February): 3–30.

Minta, Michael D. 2020. "Diversity and Minority Group Advocacy in Congress." *Political Research Quarterly* 73, no. 1 (March): 208–220.

Moreno, Paul D. 2008. *Black Americans and Organized Labor: A New History.* Baton Rouge: Louisiana State University Press.

Murray, Paul T. 2014. "From the Sidelines to the Frontlines: Mathew Ahmann Leads American Catholics into the Civil Rights Movement." *Journal of the Illinois State Historical Society* 107, no. 1 (Spring): 77–115.

Myrdal, Gunnar. 1944. *An American Dilemma: The Negro Problem and American Democracy.* New York: Harper.

Nelson, David, and Susan Webb Yackee. 2012. "Lobbying Coalitions and Government Policy Change: An Analysis of Federal Agency Rulemaking." *Journal of Politics* 74, no. 2 (April): 339–353.

Newmark, Adam J., and Anthony J. Nownes. 2019. "Lobbying Conflict, Competition, and Working in Coalitions." *Social Science Quarterly* 100, no. 4 (June): 1284–1296.

Parker, Christopher S. 2009. *Fighting for Democracy: Black Veterans and the Struggle against White Supremacy in the Postwar South.* Princeton, NJ: Princeton University Press.

Parrish, Michael E. 2011. *Citizen Rauh: An American Liberal's Life in Law and Politics.* Ann Arbor: University of Michigan Press.

Patricca, Nicholas A. 2015. *Peggy Roach: One Woman's Journey, a Nation's Progress.* Chicago: Loyola University, Ann Ida Gannon, BVM, Center for Women and Leadership.

Payne, Charles M. 1996. *I've Got the Light of Freedom: The Organizing Tradition and the Mississippi Freedom Struggle*. Berkeley: University of California Press.

Phinney, Robin. 2017. *Strange Bedfellows: Interest Group Coalitions, Diverse Partners, and Influence in American Social Policy*. New York: Cambridge University Press.

Purdum, Todd S. 2014. *An Idea Whose Time Has Come: Two Presidents, Two Parties, and the Battle for the Civil Rights Act of 1964*. New York: Henry Holt.

Reynolds, P. Preston. 2000. "Dr. Louis T. Wright and the NAACP: Pioneers in Hospital Racial Integration." *American Journal of Public Health* 90, no. 6 (June): 883–892.

Risen, Clay. 2014. *The Bill of the Century: The Epic Battle for the Civil Rights Act*. New York: Bloomsbury.

Robison, Joseph B. 1951. "Organizations Promoting Civil Rights and Liberties." *Annals of the American Academy of Political and Social Science* 275, no. 1 (May): 18–26.

Roediger, David R. 1991. *The Wages of Whiteness: Race and the Making of the American Working Class*. London: Verso.

Rustin, Bayard. 1965. "From Protest to Politics: The Future of the Civil Rights Movement." *Commentary* (February): 25–31.

Ryan, Yvonne. 2013. *Roy Wilkins: The Quiet Revolutionary and the NAACP*. Lexington: University Press of Kentucky.

Sachar, Howard M. 1993. *A History of the Jews in America*. New York: Vintage.

Saldin, Robert P. 2010. *War, the American State, and Politics since 1898*. New York: Cambridge University Press, 2010.

Scanlon, Jennifer. 2016. *Until There Is Justice: The Life of Anna Arnold Hedgeman*. New York: Oxford University Press.

Schattschneider, E. E. 1960. *The Semisovereign People: A Realist's View of Democracy in America*. New York: Holt, Rinehart and Winston.

Schickler, Eric. 2016. *Racial Realignment: The Transformation of American Liberalism, 1932–1965*. Princeton, NJ: Princeton University Press.

Schlozman, Kay Lehman. 1990. "Representing Women in Washington: Sisterhood and Pressure Politics." In *Women, Politics, and Change*. Edited by Louise A. Tilly and Patricia Gurin, 339–382. New York: Russell Sage Foundation.

———. 2010. "Who Sings in the Heavenly Chorus?: The Shape of the Organized Interest System." In *The Oxford Handbook of American Political Parties and Interest Groups*. Edited by L. Sandy Maisel and Jeffrey M. Berry. Oxford: Oxford University Press.

Schlozman, Kay Lehman, and John T. Tierney. 1983. "More of the Same: Washington Pressure Group Activity in a Decade of Change." *Journal of Politics* 45, no. 2 (May): 351–377.

———. 1986. *Organized Interests and American Democracy*. Boston: Harper Collins.

Schnakenberg, Keith E. 2017. "Informational Lobbying and Legislative Voting." *American Journal of Political Science* 61, no. 1 (January): 129–145.

Schultz, Kevin M. 2008. "The FEPC and the Legacy of the Labor-Based Civil Rights Movement of the 1940s." *Labor History* 49, no. 1: 71–92.

Schuman, Howard E. 1957. "Senate Rules and the Civil Rights Bill: A Case Study." *American Political Science Review* 51, no. 4 (December): 955–975.

Sekou, Bilal Dabir. 2020. "The Limits of Black Politics in the Post-Civil Rights Era." *Sociological Forum* 35, no. S1 (September): 954–973.

Sitkoff, Harvard. 1971. "Harry Truman and the Election of 1948: The Coming of Age of Civil Rights in American Politics." *Journal of Southern History* 37, no. 4 (November): 597–616.

Skrentny, David. 1998. "The Effect of the Cold War on African-American Civil Rights: America and the World Audience, 1945–1968." *Theory and Society* 27, no. 2 (April): 237–285.

Smith, Robert C. 1981. "Black Power and the Transformation from Protest to Politics." *Political Science Quarterly* 96, no. 3 (Autumn): 431–443.

Sorurbakhsh, Laila. 2016. "Interest Group Coalitions and Lobbying Environments: Toward a New Theoretical Perspective." *Interest Groups and Advocacy* 5, no. 3 (October): 200–223.

Spickard, Paul R. 1983. "The Nisei Assume Power: The Japanese Citizens League, 1941–1942." *Pacific Historical Review* 52, no. 2 (May): 147–174.

Staggenborg, Suzanne. 1986. "Coalition Work in the Pro-Choice Movement: Organizational and Environmental Opportunities and Obstacles." *Social Problems* 33, no. 5 (June): 374–390.

Stern, Mark. 1992. *Calculating Visions: Kennedy, Johnson, and Civil Rights*. New Brunswick, NJ: Rutgers University Press.

Strolovitch, Dara Z. 2007. *Affirmative Advocacy: Race, Class, and Gender in Interest Group Politics*. Chicago: Chicago University Press.

Sundquist, James L. 1968. *Politics and Policy: The Eisenhower, Kennedy, and Johnson Years*. Washington, DC: Brookings Institution.

Svonkin, Stuart. 1997. *Jews against Prejudice: American Jews and the Fight for Civil Liberties*. New York: Columbia University Press.

Tate, Katherine. 1994. *From Protest to Politics: The New Black Voters in American Elections*. Cambridge, MA: Harvard University Press.

Thurston, Chloe N. 2018. *At the Boundaries of Homeownership: Credit, Discrimination, and the American State*. New York: Cambridge University Press.

Todd, Lisa Anderson. 2014. *For a Voice and a Vote: My Journey with the Mississippi Freedom Democratic Party*. Lexington: University Press of Kentucky.

Tuerkheimer, Frank. 2005. "Bob Kastenmeier and 1960s Civil Rights Legislation: Leadership through Commitment and Foresight." *Wisconsin Law Review*, no. 4: 947–956.

Tuuri, Rebecca. 2018. *Strategic Sisterhood: The National Council of Negro Women in the Black Freedom Struggle*. Chapel Hill: University of North Carolina Press.

Valelly, Richard M. 2004. *The Two Reconstructions: The Struggle for Black Enfranchisement*. Chicago: University of Chicago Press.

Vannoni, Matia. 2017. "Studying Preference Attainment Using Spatial Models." *European Political Science* 16, no. 3 (September): 369–382.

Walker, Samuel. 1990. *In Defense of American Liberties: A History of the ACLU*. Carbondale: Southern Illinois University Press.

Ware, Gilbert. 1964. "Lobbying as a Means of Protest: The NAACP as an Agent of Equality." *Journal of Negro Education* 33, no. 2 (Spring): 103–110.

Watson, Denton L. 1990. *Lion in the Lobby: Clarence Mitchell, Jr.'s Struggle for Passage of Civil Rights Laws*. New York: Morrow.

———, ed. 2010. *The Papers of Clarence Mitchell, Jr.* Vol. 4, *1951–1954*. Athens: Ohio University Press.

Wertheimer, Jack. 1995. "Jewish Organizational Life in the United States since 1945." *American Jewish Year Book* 95:3–98.
Whalen, Charles, and Barbara Whalen. 1985. *The Longest Debate: A Legislative History of the 1964 Civil Rights Act*. Cabin John, MD: Seven Locks.
White, Deborah Gray. 1999. *Too Heavy a Load: Black Women in Defense of Themselves, 1894–1994*. New York: W. W. Norton.
White, Steven. 2016. "Civil Rights, World War II, and U.S. Public Opinion." *Studies in American Political Development* 30, no. 1 (April): 38–61.
Wilkins, Roy. 1982. *Standing Fast: The Autobiography of Roy Wilkins*. New York: Da Capo.
Woliver, Laura R. 2018. *Push Back, Move Forward: The National Council of Women's Organizations and Coalition Advocacy*. Philadelphia: Temple University Press.
Woodward, C. Vann. 1955. *The Strange Career of Jim Crow*. New York: Oxford University Press.
Wu, Ellen D. 2014. *The Color of Success: Asian Americans and the Origins of the Model Minority*. Princeton, NJ: Princeton University Press.
Young, McGee. 2010. *Developing Interests: Organizational Change and the Politics of Advocacy*. Lawrence: University Press of Kansas.
Zieger, Robert H. 1995. *The CIO, 1935–1955*. Chapel Hill: University of North Carolina Press.

# Index

Page references in *italics* refer to illustrations.

ad-hoc structure: and the 1967 by-laws, 125–126, 128; advantages of, 103–104; in civil rights lobbying, 1955-1957, 54–68; in coalition building, 39; implications for civil rights lobbying, 52–54; implications for coordination capacity, 16, 68–70; in interest group coalitions, 134, 135; of LCCR, pre-1963, 41–42, 43–54, 69; in lobbying for the FEPC, 30–31; transformation of, 102, 103, 129. *See also* structure, organizational

advocacy, public interest/advocacy sector: coalitional lobbying strategies in, 10; in conflict with coalition viability, 134–135; coordination among, and the NECRM, 35; diversity in, 13, 18–19; institutional, in the life cycle of social movements, 137–138; in lobbying for H.R. 7152, 90; lobbying in, 1–2; post-Civil Rights Act expansion of, 129; in the rise of interest group coalitions, 26–27, 28–29

affiliation/disaffiliation: with the NCAPT, 30; organizational change in, 17–18; organizational structure and practices in, 47–48, 52, 69, 80–81, 134–135; post-Civil Rights Act increase in, 110; in preserving autonomy, 49–50; of SNCC, 129

African American organizations, 23–24, 25–26, 27–28. *See also* CORE; NAACP; NCNW; SCLC; SNCC

agenda, lobbying: 1967 by-laws in setting, 127–128; collaboration in setting of, 44, 46, 140; coordination capacity in defining, 14–15; on H.R. 7152, 83–92; organizational structure in setting, 5, 52–53, 58, 64, 68–69, 131–132, 140; post-Civil Rights Act of 1964, 103–110, 113–116, 135; "tag alongs" in setting, 148n29

Ahmann, Mathew, 47

amendments: to the Constitution, on post-Civil Rights Act legislative agenda, 107; to H.R. 7152, 83–92, 93; jury trial amendment to H.R. 6127, 67–68

ACLU (American Civil Liberties Union), 28, 153n47

American Council on Human Rights, 25

AFL (American Federation of Labor), 27–28, 33

AFL-CIO, 63–64, 66–67, 76, 77, 78, 119–120. *See also* CIO

AJC (American Jewish Committee), 34–35, 49–51

AJCon (American Jewish Congress), 28

American political development, 136–140

ADA (Americans for Democratic Action), 28–29, 35–36, 84–85

AVC (American Veterans Committee), 66–67, 111, 113

Anderson, John Weir, 61–62
Andrews, Kenneth, 135
ADL (Anti-Defamation League of B'nai B'rith), 26, 49–51, 66–67
antilynching, 3–4, 37–38
anti-poll tax legislation, 30–31, 33, 37–38
anti-Semitism, 26
A. Philip Randolph Institute, 114
arms-control lobbying coalitions, 69, 182n14
Aronson, Arnold: and ad hoc structure of LCCR, 43, 47–51, 52; on consensus, 80; in creation of LCCR, 37; in the early network of civil rights professionals, 24; on finances, 116; in lobbying for H.R. 6127, 64–65; on lobbying for H.R. 7152, 90; membership classification scheme of, 110–114; in NCPFEPC, 31; in post-Civil Rights Act LCCR continuation, 104, 110–114, 119–120; Presidential Medal of Freedom ceremony for, 1
ACT (Associated Community Teams), 125, 126–127
attorney general, U.S., 54–55, 67, 68–69, 75–76, 84–85, 86–87, 91, 92. *See also* Justice Department
authority: of the attorney general in Part III, 54–55, 67, 68–69, 75–76, 84–85, 86–87, 91, 92; in coordination capacity, 15, 17–18; of governmental institutions, in lawmaking, 3–4; informal structure in, 47–50; of the National Board in the 1967 by-laws, 127–128, 135
autonomy of member groups, 5, 17–18, 47–51, 69, 80, 126, 128–129
awareness raising, 46, 56, 61, 99

Baumgartner, Frank, 12
Baylor, Christopher, 27–28
Bernheim, Al, 32
Bethune, Mary McLeod, 25
Biemiller, Andrew J. ("Andy"), 76, 88–89
Bill of Rights Day rallies, 61
bipartisanship, 56, 75–76, 91–92
Birmingham, Alabama, 75–76
"black power," 118–119
Bolz, Sanford H. ("Sandy"), 57–58
Bracey, John H., 25–26
*Brown v. Board of Education,* 55–56
Burney, Barbara, 4
Burrows, Vanessa, 4
by-laws, LCCR, 102, 125–128, 129–130

Caplan, Marvin, 68–69, 104–106, 131–132
Catholic Interracial Conference, 29

Catholic organizations and church groups, 29, 111
Celler, Emanuel, 74, 83–84, 85, 88–89, 90
Chaney, James, 120–121
change: demographic, 23; organizational, 16–18, 31, 71–72, 78–82, 101, 110–118, 140 (*see also* structure, organizational)
Chen, Anthony, 24
Church Representation, Committee on, 96–97
citizen-lobbyists/lobbying, 4–5, 34, 98–99, 105
civil disobedience, 77–78, 119–120
civil injunctive suits in civil rights cases (Part III), 54–55, 75–76, 86–87
civil rights: defining, post-Civil Rights Act, 114–115, 126–127; demonstrating breadth of support for, 12, 34, 46, 59–60, 61, 91–92, 98–99; pessimism on, 72–73
Civil Rights Act of 1957, 54–55, 61–62, 64–69. *See also* H.R. 6127
Civil Rights Act of 1960, 68–69
Civil Rights Act of 1964, 6, 71–72, 82–92, 93, 96, 100. *See also* H.R. 7152; post-Civil Rights Act period
Civil Rights Commission, 54–55, 68, 74, 82–83
civil rights movement: in the 1963 civil rights agenda and legislation, 76–78; coalition partner groups in, 26–27; coordination of lobbying in, 1–2; lobbyists in, 3–4; pessimism of, on legislation, 72–73; post-Civil Rights Act, 102–103, 118–125, 136–139
civil rights state, 3–5, 136–137, 139, 146n9
Clifford, Clark, 33
Clinton, William J., 1
Coalition for Arms Control, 69
Cohen, David ("Dave"), 78, 84–85, 86
Cold War, 23
collaboration: in the 1967 by-laws, 128; changing civil rights movement in, 118–119; diversity in, 132–133; informal structure in, 44–46, 49–50, 53–54, 55, 59, 63, 66–68, 134–135, 140; of interest groups in U.S. politics, 9–10, 13, 15–16, 18; in LCCR's formation, 6, 21–23, 25–26, 27–30, 31–33, 37, 39–40; in lobbying for H.R. 7152, 93; mechanisms of, 18–20, 22; in policy development, 139; in unity, 8–9, 131–132; women's organizations in, 113–114
committees, congressional, 62, 83–92, 137–138
Communism/Communist organizations, 30, 32, 34–35
Compliance and Enforcement, LCCR Committee on, 115, 128

conflict, moderate/militant, 118–120
CIO (Congress of Industrial Organizations), 27–28, 32–33. *See also* AFL-CIO
CORE (Congress of Racial Equality), 25, 119–120
consensus: in the 1967 by-laws, 128; in agenda-setting, 140; autonomy of member groups in need for, 5; in coordination capacity, 17–18, 131–132; in creation of the LCCR, 37–38; in interest group coalitions, 9–10, 11–13, 14–15, 17–18; in lobbying for H.R. 7152, 86–87, 91–92; organizational structure in, 47–48, 50, 57–58, 60, 61, 80–81, 131–132, 133–134; post-Civil Rights Act, 106–107, 115–116, 121, 123–124; in prospects for civil rights legislation, 76; in unity, 87
context, historical: in significance of the LCCR, 19–20; wartime, in rise of civil rights causes, 22
context, policy-making: in organizational capacity, 6–7; in organizational change and coordination capacity, 17–18; post-Civil Rights Act, 102–103, 120; postwar, in the rise of civil rights coalitions, 23; in postwar cooperation, 39; in success, 133–134
continuation, post-Civil Rights Act of 1964: 1967 by-laws in, 102, 125–128; changes in the civil rights movement in, 102–103, 118–125; lobbying agenda in, 103–110, 113–116, 135; organizational change and growth in, 110–118
contributions, financial and in-kind, 37–38, 39, 46, 52, 116–118, 127, 135. *See also* donations
Conway, Jack, 88–89
cooperation, interorganizational, 22–23, 26, 36, 39, 47–48, 68, 74, 76–77
coordination: of lobbying, 1–3, 8–9, 13–19, 39, 71–72; in unity, 2–3, 21–22, 35, 71–72, 79–82, 83, 131, 132–135
coordination capacity: 1967 by-laws in, 129–130; authority in, 15, 17–18; consensus in, 17–19, 131–132; diversity in, 12–14; in lessons for interest group coalitions, 135; in lobbying on H.R. 7152, 71–72, 83, 93, 96, 100; organizational structure in, 6–7, 9, 14–18, 42–43, 54, 55, 68–70, 79–80; post-Civil Rights Act, 105, 113–114, 129–130
creativity in lobbying on H.R. 7152, 83, 93–94, 99

Daugbjerg, Carsten, 16–17, 82
debate and voting phase of the Civil Rights Act of 1964, 83, 92–94, 97–99

decision-making: in the 1967 by-laws, 127, 129; cooperative lobbying in, 9–10; coordination capacity in, 14–15, 18; lessons for coalitions on, 135, 136; organizational change in, 80–81; organizational structure in, 47, 54, 69
DSG (Democratic Study Group) civil rights steering committee, 89–90, 93–94
demonstrations, mass. *See* protest activity
desegregation. *See* segregation/desegregation
development, organizational, 1–2, 19–20, 34, 42–43, 68–69, 102–103, 125–130. *See also* change: organizational; structure, organizational
Dirksen, Everett, 106–107
disaffiliation. *See* affiliation/disaffiliation
diversity/homogeneity: in interest group coalitions, 5–6, 9–14, 17–19, 23–24, 31; in LCCR, 42, 54, 68–70, 71–72, 100, 129, 132–133, 140, 148–149n33
donations, 37–38, 39, 46, 52, 116–118, 127, 135. *See also* contributions, financial and in-kind
Douglas, Paul, 63–64, 67–68
Dudley, Tilford E. ("Ted"), 73

economic stability, 114
Edwards, Bob, 136
effectiveness: ad-hoc structure in, 41–42, 66–67; coalition diversity in, 11–13; coordination capacity in, 14, 129; of interest group coalitions, diversity in, 9–10; post-Civil Rights Act, 105, 114–116, 123–124, 129
Eisenhower, Dwight D., 59, 61–64
Emancipation Proclamation centennial, 73–74
employment, 23, 27–28, 30–31, 37–38, 75, 113–114. *See also* FEPC
endorsements, 16–17, 47, 54–55, 60, 62, 64–65, 68
enforcement of civil rights: authority of the attorney general in, in Part III, 54–55, 67, 68–69, 75–76, 84–85, 86–87, 91, 92; of the Civil Rights Act of 1964, 104–106, 107–109, 115
Executive Committee, 43–50, 45, 46, 75, 105, 128

Fair Labor Standards Act, 114
Farmer, James, 123
Federal Council of Churches, 29
feminist movement, 113–114
FEPC (Fair Employment Practices Committee): in formation of the LCCR, 23–24, 26, 28, 29–31, 33, 34–39; in H.R. 7152 lobbying, 84–85, 86, 88–89, 92. *See also* NCPFEPC

filibuster, Senate, 32–33, 35–36, 37–38, 57–58, 73, 96–97, 98–100, 126
financing of LCCR: contributions in, 39, 44, 46, 52, 116–118, 127, 135; in organizational change, 78–79; in post-Civil Rights Act continuation, 102–103, 116–118, 127, 129, 177–178n41
form, organizational. *See* structure, organizational
formality/informality, organizational: in 1967 by-laws, 125–128, 129; ad hoc nature in, 41–51; in civil rights lobbying, 1955-1957, 52–68; in coordination capacity, 42–43, 54, 55, 68–70, 71–72; persistence of, through lobbying for H.R. 7152, 101
Forman, James, 123
formation of LCCR: coalition partners in, 24–29; collaboration in, 6, 21–23, 25–26, 27–30, 31–33, 37, 39–40; FEPC in, 23–24, 26, 28, 29–31, 33, 34–39; NECRM in, 22–23, 34–39; WWII civil rights coalitions in, 23–24
Francis, Megan Ming, 3–4
fraternities, Black, 25
Freedom Summer, 120–121
FCNL (Friends Committee on National Legislation), 43–44
Frymer, Paul, 27–28

Geyer, Lee, 30
goals, policy: conflicting, 134–135; coordination capacity in resources for, 14, 16; coordination in prioritization of, 21; in creation of the LCCR, 36, 39–40; issue salience mediating with diversity, 148–149n33; lobbying coalitions in achieving, 1–3, 8–10; *MEMO* in communicating, 81, 82; organizational structure in lobbying for, 56, 60, 69–70, 72; post-Civil Rights Act, 102–103, 105, 113–114
Goodman, Andrew, 120–121
Goodrich, Nathaniel, 57
grassroots members: coordination capacity in mobilizing, 2–3, 14, 15–16, 131; in creation of the LCCR, 37–38; diversity of, 42; informal structure in lobbying by, 54, 58; in lobbying for H.R. 7152, 71–72, 79–80, 82, 84, 86, 89–91, 92
Great Depression, 25–26
Greenberg, Cheryl Lynn, 26
Grossmann, Matt, 1–2
growth, organizational, 18, 110–114. *See also* change: organizational
Gunther, John, 35–36, 43–44, 59, 62, 64

Gunther, Violet Megrath, 78–79
Guyot, Lawrence, 123

Hall, Donald R., 9–10
Halpin, Darrin, 12–13, 16–17, 82, 134
Hanegraaff, Marcel, 9–10
Hathaway, Will, 134–135
Heaney, Michael, 9–10
hearings, congressional, 59–60, 64–66, 84–86, 88, 93–94
Hedgeman, Anna Arnold, 31
Henderson, Elmer, 24
heterogeneity. *See* diversity/homogeneity
Higgs, William L. ("Bill"), 121–122, 124–125
Hirsch, Richard G., 179n58
Hobson, Julius, 125
home rule for Washington, D.C., 52–53, 57, 107–110, 114–115
House Judiciary Committee, 62, 65–66, 83–92, 100–101
H.R. 627, 55, 62–65
H.R. 6127, 55, 64–68. *See also* Civil Rights Act of 1957
H.R. 7152: capacity for coordination in lobbying on, 71–72, 83, 93, 96, 100; debate and voting phase of, 92–100; lobbying to strengthen in the Judiciary Committee, 83–92; organizational structure in lobbying for, 100–101. *See also* Civil Rights Act of 1964; post-Civil Rights Act period
housing market regulation/fair housing, 4, 109–111, 164n71
human rights, 102, 124–125
Humphrey, Hubert, 33, 121

identities of interest groups, 16–18, 128
immigration, 50, 52–53, 160–161n28
implementation of civil rights policy, 3–4, 104–107, 128, 136
influence: ad hoc organizational style in, 41–42, 53, 69–70; of coalitions, 10–11; coalitions in, 132–133, 135–136, 139; diversity in, 5–6, 11–13; measuring, 136
informality, organizational. *See* formality/informality, organizational
information: coalition diversity in conveying, 11–12; coordination capacity in sharing of, 15–16; lobbyists providing to policymakers, 139; *MEMO* newsletters in sharing of, 82, 89, 98, 99; organizational structure in sharing of, 64, 79–80
interest groups: civil rights, in the postwar organizational landscape, 24–29; coalitions in force of, 8–20; identities of, 16–18, 128;

as legacy of social movements, 137–138; in lobbying on H.R. 7152, 98; mobilization of, in creation of the LCCR, 37–38; pro-civil rights, in the 1940s, 6. *See also under* interest group name
interest group coalitions: in the 1940s, 29–33; diversity in, 5–6, 9–14, 17–19, 23–24, 31; in federal civil rights policy, 139; in force of interest groups, 8–20; lessons from LCCR for, 132–136; post-war building of, 39–40; "tagging along" in structure of, 148n29; in U.S. politics and political science, 9–18; WWII in rise of, for civil rights, 23–24
internment of Japanese Americans, 26–27, 28, 152n35, 153n47
intersectionality, 10, 113–114
issues: new, post-Civil Rights Act, 113–116; salience of, 16, 18–19, 129, 134–136, 148–149n33

JACL (Japanese American Citizens League), 26–27, 28, 50, 71–72, 111, 113–114, 152n35, 153n47
Jewish advocacy organizations, 26, 27–28, 49–50, 111, 160–161n28
Johnson, Lyndon and administration, 63–64, 92–93, 100, 104–105, 109–110, 121–122
JCCR (Joint Committee on Civil Rights), 32–33
judiciary committee: House of Representatives, 62, 65–66, 83–92, 100–101; Senate, 96
Junk, Wiebke Marie, 10, 134, 150n8
Justice Department, 61–62. *See also* attorney general, U.S.

Kennedy, John F. and administration, 72, 73–74, 75–78, 92–93
Kennedy, Robert F., 76, 91–92
King, Martin Luther, Jr., 72–73, 77–78, 123–124
Kollman, Ken, 83

labor unions/organizations, 27–28, 76, 111. *See also* AFL; AFL-CIO; CIO; UAW
landscape, organizational, 21–22, 24–29
Lawson, Steven, 29–30
Leadership Conference Steering Committee, 37–39, 50
legislation: H.R. 627, 55, 62–65; H.R. 6127, 55, 64–68; LCCR in building support for, 4–5; LCCR in drafting, 109–110; mid-1960s policymaking environment in, 6–7; post-Civil Rights Act priorities on, 104–105; postwar, 28, 39; prospects for, in 1963, 72–78; structural informality in lobbying on, 54–68. *See also* Civil Rights Act of 1957; Civil Rights Act of 1964; H.R. 7152
Legislative Committee, LCCR, 128
Legislative Strategy Conference (NAACP-sponsored), 89–90
Leonard, Norma O., 41–42
Lewis, John, 118–119
lobbying: 1955-1957, 54–68; in American political development, 135–140; for the Civil Rights Act of 1964, 82–100; informal structure in, 52–54; negative popular conception of, 1–2; post-Civil Rights Act focus on, 179n58; in social movement periodization, 137–139
lobbyists, professional: in the 1967 by-laws, 128; coordination capacity in mobilizing, 14, 16; in lobbying on H.R. 7152, 84–85, 86, 89–90, 92, 93–94, 96–97, 98; in organizational changes, 71–72, 79–80; in post-Civil Rights Act continuation, 104
lobbyists committee, 43–44, 45, 67–68
Lukas, Edwin J. ("Ed"), 50–51
lynching, 3–4, 32, 37–38

March on Washington for Jobs and Freedom, 77–78, 119–120
March on Washington Movement, 23–24, 77–78
Margolin, Olya, 97, 124, 161n37
Maryland LCCR division controversy, 47–48
Masaoka, Mike, 26–27, 28, 50, 71–72
Maslow, Will, 24, 55–56
Matthews, Donald R., 9–10
McCarran-Walter Act (Immigration and Nationality Act of 1952), 50, 52–53, 160–161n28
medical civil rights movement, 4, 25
meetings: closed door, in lobbying for H.R. 7152, 96; emergency session, post-Civil Rights Act, 106; Executive Committee, 44, 46, 46; moderate/militant conflict in, 119–120; regularization of, 79–81, 100; of Washington Representatives, in post-Civil Rights Act continuation, 114–116
Meier, August, 25–26
member organizations: in the 1967 by-laws, 127, 128, 129–130; by advocacy sector, *112*; autonomy of, in organizational structure, 47–51, 128; base, 100, 102–103, 110–114; expansion of, 101; financial support from, 39, 117–118; growth and diversity of, post-Civil Rights Act, 110–114; informality in ability to get consent from, 52–53;

member organizations *(continued)*
    in lobbying for civil rights legislation, 63, 64–65; *MEMO* newsletter in coordination of, 81–82; in post-Civil Rights Act continuation, 106–107; representation of, in LCCR, 43–44, *45*, 46; in the twenty-first century, 102–103. *See also* name of organization
*MEMO* newsletters: in coordination, 81–82; on Freedom Summer disappearances, 120–121; in fundraising, 117; in lobbying on H.R. 7152, 86–87, 89, 90–92, 93–95, 96–97, 98–100; in post-Civil Rights Act continuation, 104–110; post-Civil Rights Act issue coverage in, 107–109, *109–110*
Meredith March against Fear, 118–119
Meyer, David, 134–135
Midwestern legislators, 85, 89–90, 96–97
militancy in the civil rights movement, 118–120
Millenson, Roy, 115
minimum wage, 107, 109–110, 113–115
Minkoff, Isaiah, 33
Minta, Michael, 137–138
MFDP (Mississippi Freedom Democratic Party) convention and congressional challenges, 105–106, 121–124
Mitchell, Clarence, 24, 38–39, 43–44, 64, 79–81, 91–92, 121–122, 124
mobilization: ad-hoc structure in, 50–51, 68–70; coordination capacity in, 2–3, 14–17, 18, 19, 100, 131; diversity in, 5–6, 12–14, 71–72; grassroots, 82, 84, 86, 89–90, 133–134; informal structure in, 55, 62, 64, 65–66, 68–70, 79–80; lessons for coalitions in, 133–135; in lobbying for H.R. 7152, 71–72, 79–80, 81–82, 83–84, 86, 89–90, 93, 96, 100–101; post-Civil Rights Act, 113–114; in representation of marginalized groups, 140; WWII-era, in formation of the LCCR, 22–24, 33, 34–35, 36–38
moderate/militant conflict, 118–120
Monday Lobby Group, 69, 182n14
Morsell, John, 43, 44, 47–48
Mountain State legislators, 85, 89–90, 96–97

NAACP (National Association for the Advancement of Colored People): antilynching campaign by, 3–4; in the formation of LCCR, 22–23, 34–39; in LCCR structure, 43–44; Legislative Strategy Conference sponsored by, 89–90; in lobbying for H.R. 6127, 66–67; opposition to the McCarran-Walter Act, 160–161n28; in post-Civil Rights Act conflict, 118–119; in the postwar organizational landscape, 22–23, 25–26, 31, 32–33, 34–39; in social movement periodization, 138–139
National Board of LCCR, 127–128
NCAPT (National Committee to Abolish the Poll Tax), 29–30
NCRAC (National Community Relations Advisory Council), 26, 49–50
NCPFEPC (National Council for a Permanent FEPC), 29–31, 35–36, 51. *See also* FEPC
NCPFEPC-NCRM, 35–36
NCC (National Council of Churches), 29
NCJW (National Council of Jewish Women), 52, 80–81
NCNW (National Council of Negro Women), 25
National Delegate Assembly for Civil Rights, 61–62
NECRM (National Emergency Civil Rights Mobilization), 22–23, 34–39
NECAMV (National Emergency Committee Against Mob Violence), 32–33
National Lawyers Guild, 30
National Negro Congress, 30
NOW (National Organization for Women), 113–114
National Urban League, 25, 151n22
National Women's Committee for Civil Rights, 113–114
Nelson, David, 11, 12–13
nongovernmental organizations, 136–140
nonviolence, principles of, 119

O'Grady, Jane, 8–9, 79–81, 95–96, 101
Oliver, William H. ("Bill"), 75, 121–122

Pemberton, Jack, 106–107
personal security bills, 107, 109–110
Phinney, Robin, 10, 11–12
platform planks for civil rights: in election of 1948, 28–29; in election of 1952, 22–23, 50–51, 52–53, 55–56; in election of 1956, 61, 62; in election of 1960, 105; in election of 1964, 105; in the NECRM and formation of the LCCR, 37–38; structural informality in member consensus/consent on, 50–51, 52–53
Pohlhaus, J. Francis ("Frank"), 86, 87, 96
policy positions: authority on, in the 1967 by-laws, 128; coalition diversity in signaling, 11; coalition leaders in developing, 2–3; coordination capacity in identification of, 14; informal structure in establishing, 47; member autonomy in acceptance of, 50–51

policy positions, support for: for 1955 civil rights legislation, 59–60; ad hoc structure in securing, 67–68; collaboration in building, 9; demonstrating breadth of, for civil rights, 12, 34, 46, 59–60, 61, 91–92, 98–99
politics: American, interest group coalitions in, 9–10; American, lobbying in, 136–140; black, periodization of, 137–138; interorganizational of NECRM and the LCCR, 34–39
poll taxes, 30–31
post-Civil Rights Act period: changing civil rights movement in, 118–125; coordination capacity in, 105, 113–114, 129–130; defining civil rights in, 114–115, 126–127; growth and structural change in, 110–118; LCCR by-laws in, 125–128; lobbying agenda in, 103–110; opportunities and challenges in, 102–103
postwar period: civil rights coalitions in, 29–33; organizational landscape in, 22–23, 24–29, 31, 32–33, 34–39
Powell, Adam Clayton, Jr., 59
Powell amendments, 59, 164n71
power, countervailing, 1–2
practices, organizational, 5–6, 18, 71–72, 79, 134–135. *See also* structure, organizational
preference attainment, 182n13
President's Committee on Civil Rights, 32
Price, Yvonne, 113–114
priorities, legislative: in amendments to H.R. 7152, 84–85, 88; in civil rights legislation of 1963, 75; commonalities in, in postwar coalition building, 39; diversity in, 13; lobbyists in pressing for, 137; Part III in, 68–69; post-Civil Rights Act, 104–105, 129; structural informality in identification of, 53, 54, 55, 57–58, 60
Pritoni, Andrea, 9–10
procedures, operating: by-laws of 1967, 125–128, 129–130; change in, in 1963, 18; codification of, 102–103; in coordination capacity, 16–18, 133–134; informality of, 42–43, 52–53, 64–65, 69; in lobbying for the Civil Rights Act of 1964, 72, 101; in mobilization of member groups, 9; organizational growing pains in, 114–115, 116. *See also* structure, organizational
process, legislative: agenda-shaping phase of, 83–92; coordination capacity in, 19; debate and voting phase of, 93–96, 100; diversity of coalition membership in, 42; in lobbying for the Civil Rights Act, 79–81, 83–92, 98; lobbyists in, 2, 3–5, 137, 138–139

process, policy, 5–6, 9, 10–11, 132–133, 136
protest activity, 1–2, 34–35, 61, 75–78, 119–120, 137–139
Protestant organizations and church groups, 29, 111
public accommodation provisions in H.R. 7152, 86–87, 89–90, 91, 92

quorum calls on H.R. 7152, 95–96, 99

Rabkin, Sol, 50–51
radicalism, 119, 140, 178n51
Randolph, A. Philip, 23–24, 27–28, 31, 35, 77–78, 114
Rauh, Joseph L., Jr., 48–49, 75, 79–81, 84–85, 86, 87, 96, 121–122. *See also* ADA (Americans for Democratic Action)
reapportionment issue, 105–107, 176n21
Reconstruction, original, 3
religious organizations, 29, 85, 89, 96–97, 98, 111
representation of interest groups, 10–12, 45, 66–67, 139
Republican civil rights bills of 1963, 74–75
resource mobilization: coalition diversity in, 5–6, 12–14; coordination capacity in, 2–3, 14–17, 18, 19; in lobbying for H.R. 7152, 71–72, 79–80, 81–82, 83, 93, 96, 100; organizational structure in, 19, 54, 55, 62, 64, 68–70. *See also* mobilization
Reuther, Walter, 77, 78–79, 121–122
rights, women's, 113–114
Risen, Clay, 41–42
Roach, Peggy, 95–96
Robison, Joseph B., 21–22, 24–29, 55–56
Rockefeller, Nelson, 74
roll call votes, 57, 63–64, 79–80, 94–95
Roosevelt, James, 61–62, 88–89, 138–139
Rules Committee, 62, 65–66, 73, 81, 88–89, 92–94
rules reform, congressional, 35–36, 37–38, 46, 50–51, 73–74, 107–109
Rustin, Bayard, 137–138
Ryan, Yvonne, 41–42

Schickler, Eric, 22, 27–28
Schlozman, Kay Lehman, 9–10, 137–138
Schultz, Kevin, 29–30
Schwerner, Mickey, 120–121
Second Reconstruction, 3, 136–137
segregation/desegregation: in 1952 party platforms, 55–56; in Civil Rights Act of 1966, 110–111; federal funding contingent on, 59, 164n71; in H.R. 7152, 84–85;

segregation/desegregation *(continued)*
   in Kennedy's civil rights agenda of 1963, 76; in post-Civil Rights Act tension, 119; of schools, 74, 75, 86–87, 110–111
segregationists, 2, 3, 59, 92–93, 137
Seidman, Bert, 61
Senate, U.S., 63–64, 67–68, 96–100
Senate Judiciary Committee, 96
"separate but equal" doctrine, 55–56
Shishkin, Boris, 24
Sifton, Paul, 63–64
signaling, legislative: coalition diversity in, 5–6, 9, 11–14, 132–133; coordination capacity in, 14, 16, 18–19; in lobbying on H.R. 7152, 85–86; organizational structure in, 42, 50–51, 53–54, 65, 69–70, 134; in WWII-era coalition building, 34–35, 39
Smith, Howard, 92–93
Soldier Voting Act, 23, 30
sororities, Black, 25
SCLC (Southern Christian Leadership Conference), 118–119
Southern Conference for Human Welfare, 25
Southern Regional Council, 25
specialization of interest groups, 16–18
staff: ad hoc structure in lack of, 43, 51, 52, 69; difficulty in maintaining, 31; in financial strain, 116; in lobbying for H.R. 7152, 81, 97–99, 100; and organizational change, 71–72, 78–79; post-Civil Rights Act, 102–104, 105–106; professional, 71–72, 78–79, 98–99, 100, 102–103
strategy: coalitions in, 9–10; coordination capacity in, 14–15; on FEPC in the 1940s, 32–33; informal structure in, 43–44, 46, 57–58; in lobbying for H.R. 7152, 85–86, 88, 89–90, 91–92, 93–99; in mobilization and creation of LCCR, 35–38; organizational structure in, 133–134. *See also* tactics
Strolovitch, Dara, 10
structure, organizational: 1967 by-laws in, 125–128; change in, 78–82; codification of, 102–103; in consensus, 47–48, 50, 57–58, 60, 61, 80–81, 131–132, 133–134; in coordination capacity, 6–7, 9, 14–19, 42–43, 54, 55, 68–70, 79–80, 133–134; and diversity in signaling coherence, 12–13; durability of, in coordination capacity, 16–17; in lobbying capacity, 5; in lobbying on H.R. 7152, 100–101; post-Civil Rights Act, 110–118, 125–128, 129–130. *See also* ad-hoc structure; change, organizational; procedures, operating
SNCC (Student Nonviolent Coordinating Committee), 87–88, 118–120, 124–125, 129
Svonkin, Stuart, 26

tactics, 9–10, 12, 77–78, 89–90, 120. *See also* strategy
"tagging along," 148n29
teller votes, 94–95
testimony, 48–49, 60, 64–65, 85–86, 91
Thurston, Chloe, 4
Tierney, John, 9–10
Tobias, Channing, 32–33
Truman, Harry S., 32
Tuck Bill (H.R. 11926), 106–107
twenty-first century Leadership Conference, 102
typology of membership organizations, 110–114

UDA (Union for Democratic Action), 28–29
UAW (United Automobile Workers), 25–26, 27–28, 66–67. *See also* labor unions/organizations
unity: coordination in, 2–3, 21–22, 35, 71–72, 79–82, 83, 131, 132–135; diversity in, 11, 13; in effectiveness, 11–12, 131–132; informal structure in, 47–48, 51, 68–69; issue focus in, 119–120; issue salience in, 134–135; LCCR in, 1; in lobbying for H.R. 7152, 87, 91–92; at the NECRM, 35; organizational structure in, 6, 71–72, 78–82, 101, 131–132; in signaling, 11–12, 133

veterans, Black, 23
Vietnam War opposition, 124–125
violence, anti-civil rights, 61, 75–76, 118–119
Voting Rights Act of 1965, 107–108, 114–115, 117, 123–124, 131–132
voting rights protection, 74, 76, 84–85, 86–87, 106

Washington Bureau (NAACP), 25–26, 138–139
Washington headquarters, LCCR, 71–72, 78–79, 86–87, 98–99, 100, 116, 131–132
Washington Human Rights Project, 124–125
Washington representatives: esprit de corps of, 101; formalization of meetings of, 43–44; in lobbying for H.R. 7152, 86–92, 95–98, 100; meetings of, in organizational change, 79–81, 82; in post-Civil Rights Act

continuation, 104–107, 113–116, 119–120, 121–122, 124–125, 128; in unity, 131–132
White, Walter, 32–33, 35–37, 43
Wilkins, Roy, 31, 34–36, 43, 58–59, 64–66, 76–79, 80–81, 177–178n41

women's organizations, 113–114
World War II, 6, 22, 23–24, 25–26

Yackee, Susan, 11, 12–13
Young, McGee, 16–17

Shamira Gelbman is Daniel F. Evans Associate Professor in the Social Sciences at Wabash College.

www.ingramcontent.com/pod-product-compliance
Lightning Source LLC
Chambersburg PA
CBHW032024230426
43671CB00005B/192